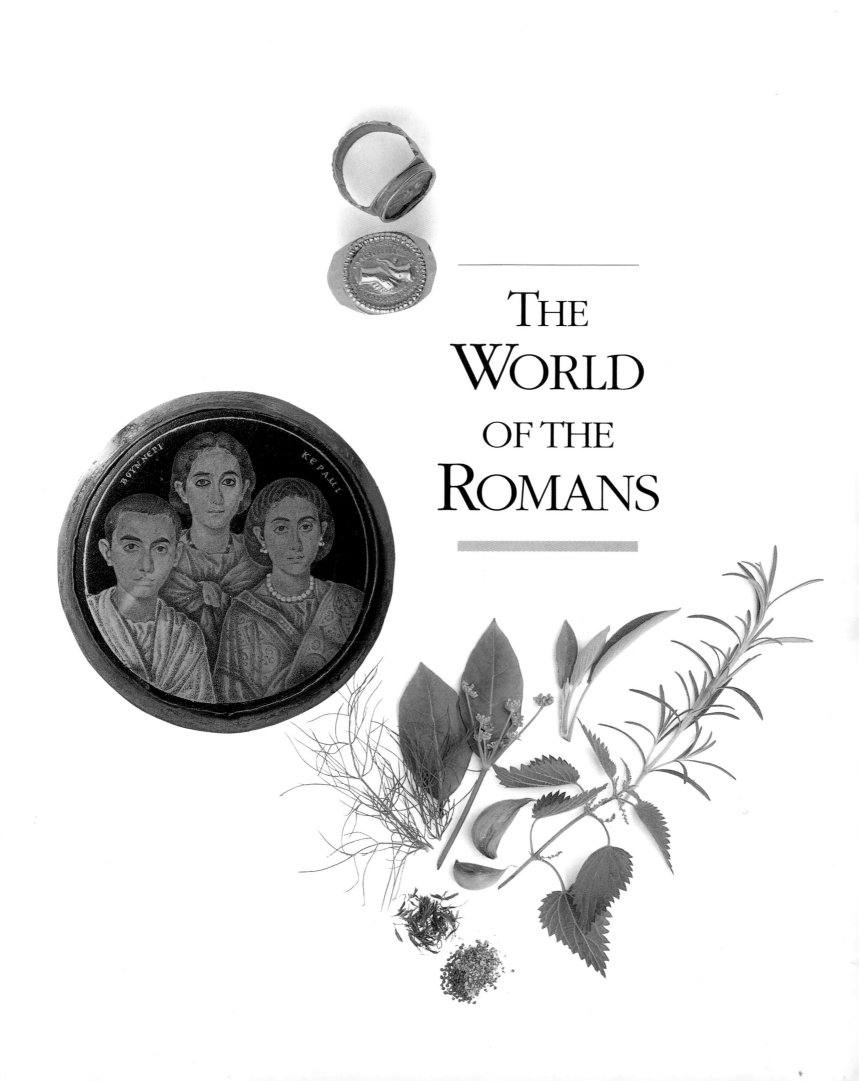

THE
WORLD
OF THE
ROMANS

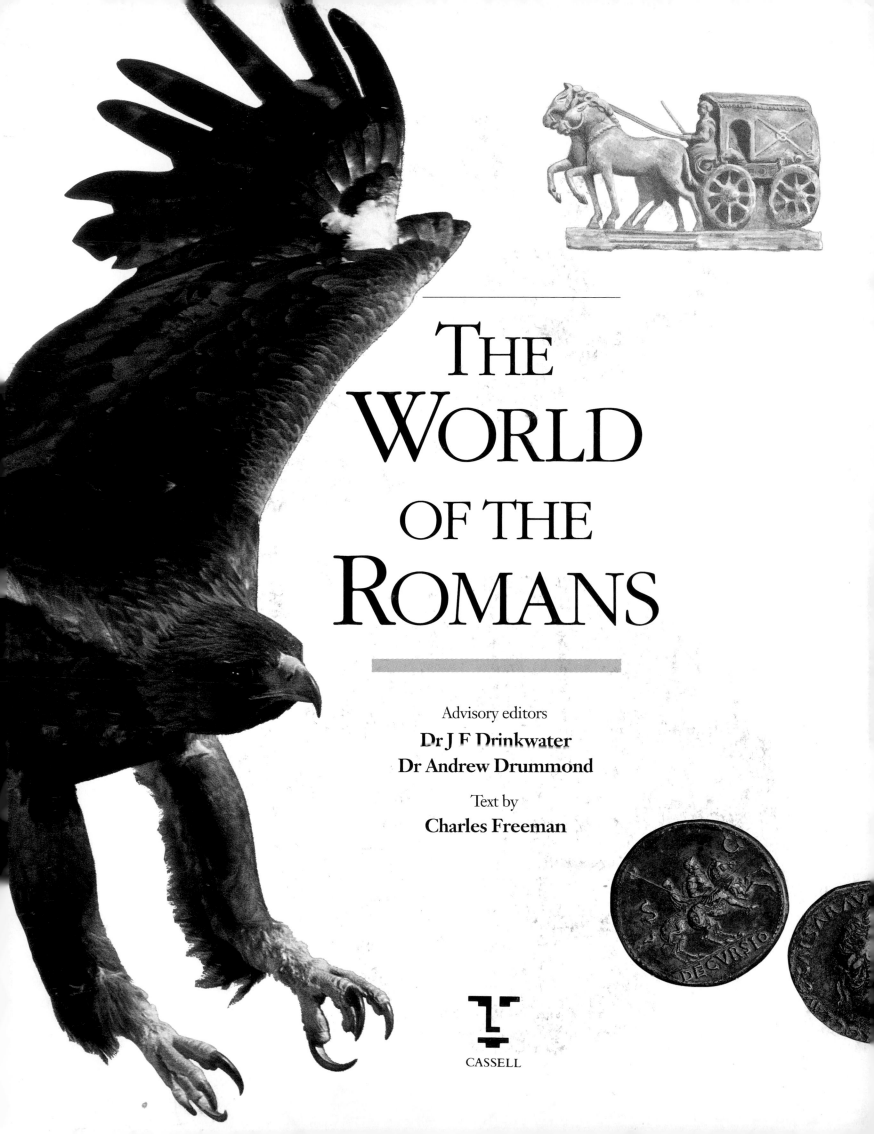

THE
WORLD
OF THE
ROMANS

Advisory editors

Dr J F Drinkwater
Dr Andrew Drummond

Text by

Charles Freeman

CASSELL

Project editor Peter Furtado

Art editor Ayala Kingsley

Volume editor
Elizabeth Toppin

Design Frankie Wood,
Martin Anderson

Picture management
Therese Maitland, Alison
Renney, Leanda Shrimpton

Picture research Linda Proud,
Charlotte Ward-Perkins

Cartographic manager
Olive Pearson

Cartographic editor
Pauline Morrow

Cartographer Richard Watts

Production Steve Elliott

Advisory Editors
Dr J F Drinkwater,
University of Nottingham, UK

Dr Andrew Drummond,
University of Nottingham, UK

Research Editor
Dr John Haywood,
Specialist on ancient seapower

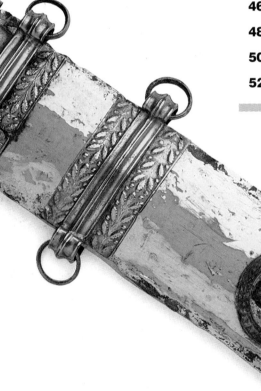

First published in the UK 1993
by Cassell, Villiers House
41/47 Strand
London WC2N 5JE

CIP applied for

Copyright © 1993 Andromeda
Oxford Ltd

AN ANDROMEDA BOOK

Devised and produced by
Andromeda Oxford Ltd
9-15 The Vineyard,
Abingdon Oxfordshire
OX14 3PX, England

ISBN 0-30434-325-0

Printed in Singapore by
CS Graphics

CONTENTS

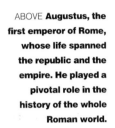

INTRODUCTION

At the height of its power, in the 2nd century AD, the Roman empire stretched as far north as Britain and Germany and as far east as the Euphrates river. The heirs of ancient civilizations, such as the Phoenicians, Egyptians and Greeks: wandering unsettled tribes, peoples of the desert – in total about one hundred million people – were subject to the rule of Rome.

Unlike many early empires, that of Rome was more than the temporary acquisition of a conqueror. The Roman empire lasted for centuries – in the east until the fall of Constantinople in 1453. The origins of Rome are uncertain, but in later centuries Romans created their own legend out of conflicting myths from Greek and Roman sources. A Trojan hero, Aeneas, fleeing from the sack of Troy, had come to Italy and there founded a line of kings. Two descendants, twin brothers Romulus and Remus, were abandoned on the banks of the Tiber, saved by a she-wolf and then rescued by shepherds. Later, Romulus, having killed his brother in a quarrel, founded a city on the site where he had been rescued.

The low hills around Rome held human settlements at least as far back as the 10th or 11th centuries BC. The area was a natural site for settlement: it was the first crossing place of the Tiber up-river from the sea, but was far enough inland to be safe from pirates. There were good communications south to the plains of Campania, while the hilltops offered protection against attack.

In the 7th and 6th centuries Rome came under the domination of kings from Etruria, the territory of the Etruscans to the north of the city. It was a prosperous time. By the late 7th century Rome was becoming a well-established city. A formal public square, surrounded by temples and sanctuaries, was laid out in what later became the Forum. The city, while maintaining its own Latin culture, was open to the influences of the cultures around it: Greek, from the Greek colonies of the Italian coast, and Etruscan. It was during this period that the Greek alphabet and the olive and vine – already used by the Etruscans – were passed on to Rome.

This was also a time of expansion over the plain of Latium. By 500 BC Rome was the most powerful city of the plains with its territory extending as far as the sea. Already the city was becoming oriented toward a cult of war. Its kings celebrated their victories with great triumphs – public parades through the city ending with a sacrifice to the gods – and games. A citizen army of up to 6,000 infantrymen, with 600 cavalry provided by its noble families, was raised for each campaign of conquest.

In 509 BC, according to tradition, there was a revolt and Tarquinius Superbus, the last of the Etruscan kings, was expelled. Later Romans regarded this as the turning point in their history – the moment when Rome had

LEFT **The ruins of a Greek temple at Segesta in modern Sicily. Many Roman towns were originally settled by Greeks and Roman history is interlaced throughout with the influence of Greek world.**

achieved its freedom and independence as a republic. Power now passed to the male heads of a small number of leading families. They were grouped together in the Senate, originally a body of the king's advisers but now the center of influence in the new state.

While the Senate took increasing responsibility for affairs of state, day-to-day decision-making was left in the hands of magistrates, elected for one year at a time. The new rulers of Rome were determined that power should never again be concentrated in the hands of one family or group. The two consuls were the most powerful magistrates: they had supreme power to decide the conduct of war and also dealt with cases under both criminal and civil law. So that neither could emerge as a dictator, each had the power to check the decisions of the other. In time, other magistrates were added: the *quaestors*, four of them after 421, were responsible for financial matters, the *aediles* for city administration, the *praetors* for judicial affairs and the censors for revising the citizen register.

Although elections took place in assemblies open to all citizens – freeborn adult males – the system was weighted so that the votes of richer men carried the most influence. As magistracies were unpaid posts only the rich could compete for them and, in effect, the powers of government rested with only a few aristocratic families. The oldest and most powerful of these were the patrician families who fought to maintain a monopoly of power. Resisting them was the mass of citizenry, the plebeians, and the battle between patricians and plebeians was the first great political struggle of the republic.

The plebeians consisted of both rich and poor: wealthy men fighting for a place in the center of government, as well as peasants and small landholders burdened by debt. To coordinate their struggle, they organized themselves in a new assembly for the people – the *Concilium Plebis*, or Popular Assembly – and they elected their own officers, the tribunes, to defend them against the patricians. Tribunes were declared sacrosanct and the murder of a tribune carried the death penalty.

It took 200 years of plebeian pressure before full equality was achieved. An important victory came in the 440s when the plebeians forced the publication of the Twelve Tables, the ancient laws of Rome. From then on, the penalties and procedures of Roman civil law were known to all citizens, not guarded by the patrician elite. Gradually the magistracies were opened to plebeians and the first plebeian consul was elected in 366. A final victory came in 287 BC when the decisions of the Popular Assembly were recognized as having the full force of law.

Despite their victory, few plebeians ever enjoyed any individual political power. Only the richer members had the status, influence and means to stand for the magistracies and so, by the 3rd century BC, Rome's government – though less exclusive than once it had been – was still aristocratic, with a small number of families competing for office. The Senate, composed officially of former magistrates, provided the leadership of the expanding city-state. The only effective challenge to its power could come from ambitious tribunes passing legislation through the Popular Assembly but many tribunes were using their posts as a stepping-stone to a magistracy and were unwilling to challenge the system. The Senate held the real power, particularly in times of crisis.

The crises were many. Although Rome had exploited its position on the Tiber to become the leading city of the Latin plain, it was always vulnerable. One of the early acts of the republic (493 BC) was to form a treaty with

LEFT **The Capitoline wolf, symbol of Roman beginnings. This bronze depiction of the legend of Romulus and Remus is possibly Etruscan, dating back to 500 BC. The twins were added much later but are probably a faithful reproduction of earlier ones.**

ABOVE **The *fasces* was a bundle of rods and axes, symbol of the magistrates' power and carried by their assistants. This symbol was one of the royal insignia that Romans borrowed from the Etruscans.**

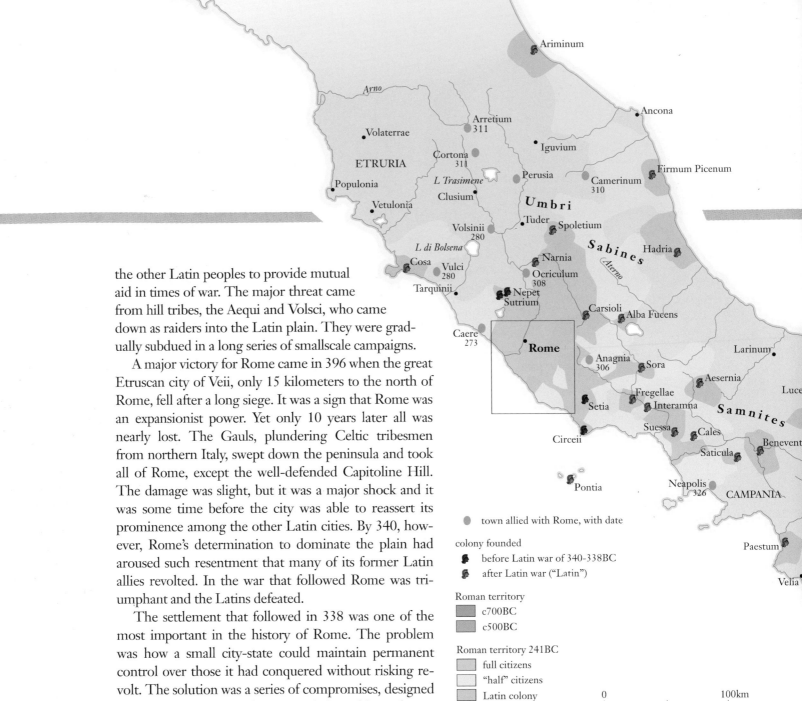

the other Latin peoples to provide mutual aid in times of war. The major threat came from hill tribes, the Aequi and Volsci, who came down as raiders into the Latin plain. They were gradually subdued in a long series of smallscale campaigns.

A major victory for Rome came in 396 when the great Etruscan city of Veii, only 15 kilometers to the north of Rome, fell after a long siege. It was a sign that Rome was an expansionist power. Yet only 10 years later all was nearly lost. The Gauls, plundering Celtic tribesmen from northern Italy, swept down the peninsula and took all of Rome, except the well-defended Capitoline Hill. The damage was slight, but it was a major shock and it was some time before the city was able to reassert its prominence among the other Latin cities. By 340, however, Rome's determination to dominate the plain had aroused such resentment that many of its former Latin allies revolted. In the war that followed Rome was triumphant and the Latins defeated.

The settlement that followed in 338 was one of the most important in the history of Rome. The problem was how a small city-state could maintain permanent control over those it had conquered without risking revolt. The solution was a series of compromises, designed to ensure that Rome, when it needed, could use the resources of dependent communities and peoples. The neighboring Latin towns were given full citizenship, probably with the right to vote in the assemblies. For others, largely those who did not share its culture or language, there was another solution, the *municipium*. The citizens of a municipium kept their local government, and could trade or intermarry with Roman citizens but, unlike full citizens, could not vote in the Roman assemblies. As the municipia were forced to provide troops for Rome this was not ideal, but the people of a municipium might proceed to full Roman citizenship in time. Some strategically important conquered land was settled with small Roman colonies of about 300 inhabitants, directly under Rome's control. There were also allies, cities or peoples which were, in theory, independent, but in practice were still expected to comply with the demands of

RIGHT **The love of the rural life contrasted with the pursuit of war and the domination of other peoples, but was a strong part of the Roman character, as this Pompeian wall painting indicates .**

Map legend:

- town allied with Rome, with date

colony founded
- before Latin war of 340-338BC
- after Latin war ("Latin")

Roman territory
- c700BC
- c500BC

Roman territory 241BC
- full citizens
- "half" citizens
- Latin colony
- allies

0   100km
0   80mi

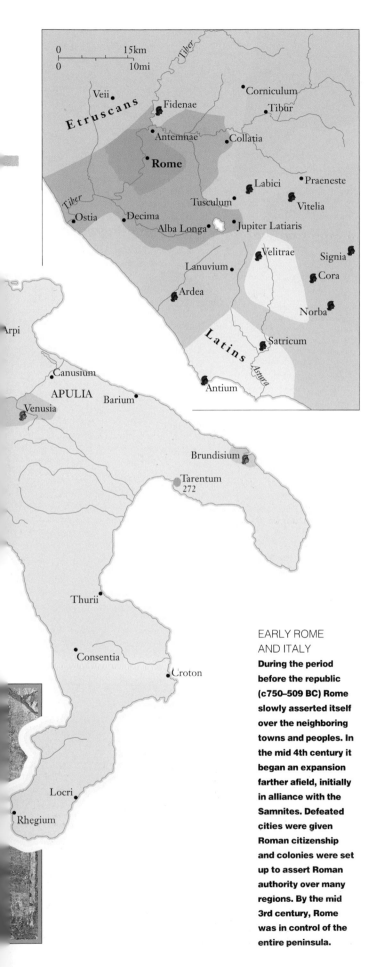

Rome, especially for manpower.

In the next 50 years Roman power expanded through the rest of the peninsula and there were few inhibitions about launching wars of conquest. War brought the chance of land and plunder and, for commanders, prestige and political success came to rest on achievement in war. The most intractable enemies of Rome at this time were the Samnites, a mountain people of the central southern highlands of Italy. Fighting lasted for nearly 40 years. In the end, the Samnites tried to form a coalition with the threatened peoples of central Italy including the Etruscans and, farther north, the Umbrians, but even this was in vain. By the 290s Roman influence extended across the whole of central Italy.

In the south the Greek coastline cities remained but were vulnerable to the growing power of Rome. With little unity among themselves and harassed by inland tribes, many had already come to terms with the Romans. Neapolis (modern Naples), the largest commercial center of central Italy, had formed an alliance with Rome as early as 326. One city – Tarentum, in the heel of Italy – was determined to resist and called on a Greek king, Pyrrhus, for help. In the battles that followed, Pyrrhus was gradually worn down by the Romans and finally abandoned the struggle. Tarentum was captured in 272 and the independence of Italy was over.

By 280 Rome controlled the Italian peninsula as far north as Pisae (modern Pisa) and Ariminum (modern Rimini). Gradually the influence of Rome permeated and transformed the non-Latin cultures of the peninsula. Rome had grown wealthy on the booty of war and a new phase of public building began in a city which now had close to 150,000 inhabitants. Thousands of slaves supported the economy, and Rome could also draw on the manpower of its allies for further wars of conquest. Rome was now in a position to challenge the other powers around the Mediterranean sea.

EARLY ROME AND ITALY

During the period before the republic (c750–509 BC) Rome slowly asserted itself over the neighboring towns and peoples. In the mid 4th century it began an expansion farther afield, initially in alliance with the Samnites. Defeated cities were given Roman citizenship and colonies were set up to assert Roman authority over many regions. By the mid 3rd century, Rome was in control of the entire peninsula.

Chapter 1

THE ROMAN REPUBLIC

By the year 270 BC Rome had firmly established its control over mainland Italy. Over the next 130 years it became the greatest political power of the Mediterranean, defeating Carthage in the west and the city-states and kingdoms of the Hellenistic east. Roman campaigns were often brutal, designed to humiliate their enemies. "One can often see in cities captured by the Romans, not only human beings who have been slaughtered, but even dogs sliced in two and the limbs of other animals cut off," recorded the Greek historian Polybius. When Epirus, on the western Greek coast, was captured in 168, the entire population of 150,000 was sold into slavery.

What were the motives for Roman expansion? First, military achievements were glorified in Rome. Decisions to go to war – often after a plea for help from an ally – were usually made with little hesitation. Few Romans could achieve renown without a successful military career; the desire for status provided incentive for war. Rome's armies were well-equipped, and its enemies often divided. With each successful war Rome's power increased; at the same time, it gained more people for its ever-stronger armies. The massive plunder gained in the east also fueled the desire for expansion.

Rome had not, however, always been superior: its first overseas wars with Carthage were epic struggles in which the city was tested to the limits. Carthage was a naval power while Rome, at the beginning of the struggle, was not; the Carthaginians also produced one of the greatest generals in history: Hannibal.

Even in ruins, the Temple of Saturn in Rome reflects the great splendor and mighty strength that was once the Roman republic.

Carthage, traditionally settled on the north coast of Africa in 814 BC, was the capital city of the Phoenicians, an ancient race of peoples. The word Punic comes from *Punica*, the Latin word for Phoenician.

The great port of Carthage overlooked the Mediterranean from a superb site on a peninsula on the north African coast. From here Carthage had built up a jealously guarded commercial and land empire with outposts as far east as Sicily. Rome had once respected Carthage's trading interests but, as the Italian peninsula fell under Rome's supremacy, a conflict between the two states became increasingly likely. A minor incident started the First Punic War (264–241 BC). Italian mercenaries clashed with a Carthaginian garrison in Sicily and called on Rome for help. Rome came to their rescue, and the dispute quickly escalated into war with Carthage, the Mediterranean's greatest naval power. For Rome to achieve a decisive victory it had to win at sea.

Roman determination helps to build a navy from scratch

At that time Rome had no navy and no tradition of seamanship. Roman determination and ingenuity, however, were soon shown at their best: the Romans not only built their own fleet but trained over 100,000 sailors. What followed was, according to the Greek historian Polybius, "the longest, most continuous and most severely contested war known to us in history". Rome finally won command of the sea and forced Carthage into surrender, claiming a fine and possession of Sicily.

Sicily was the chief gain of the war for Rome but within a few years Rome broke the peace treaty, seized Sardinia and forced the surrender of Corsica from the Carthaginians. Carthage now turned to build a new empire in Spain. Even this, however, brought renewed conflict with Rome; in 219 when the Carthaginian general, Hannibal, seized a town – Saguntum – which the Romans claimed as an ally, war broke out again.

In Hannibal, however, the Romans met their match. With the pick of Carthage's mercenary troops – including 6,000 cavalry and a small contingent of elephants – he undertook a grueling six-month march along the Spanish coastline, through Gaul, over the Alps and down into Italy itself. In northern Italy he was welcomed by Celtic tribes whom the Romans had recently defeated. By 217 he was in central Italy where he crushed a Roman army, trapping it against the marshland around Lake Trasimene.

Hannibal's plan was to break the links between Rome and its subject allies and so isolate the city. His intelligence reports told Hannibal that it was the peoples of southern Italy who were the most restive under Roman rule, so he bypassed Rome and marched south. In Apulia, in 216, one of the

Sicily, Sardinia and Corsica were the first provinces. The word *provincia* originally meant a magistrate's responsibilities. The word later came to be used for the actual territory administered.

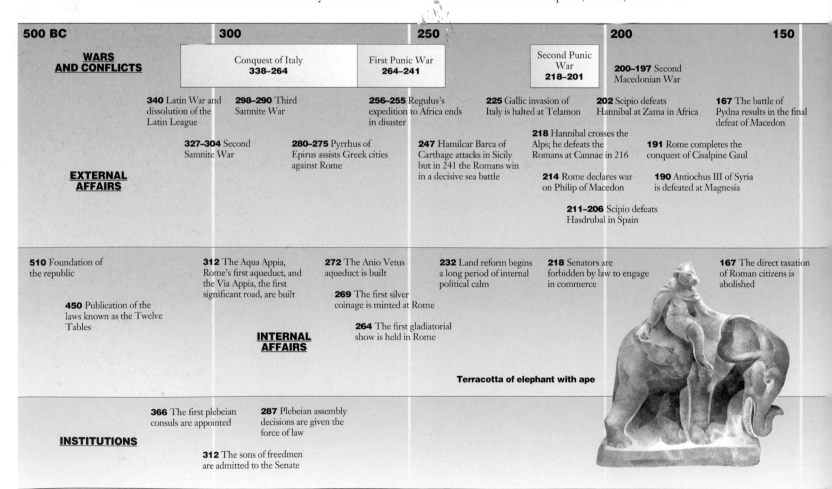

	500 BC		300		250		200		150
WARS AND CONFLICTS			Conquest of Italy 338–264		First Punic War 264–241		Second Punic War 218–201	200–197 Second Macedonian War	
		340 Latin War and dissolution of the Latin League	298–290 Third Samnite War		256–255 Regulus's expedition to Africa ends in disaster	225 Gallic invasion of Italy is halted at Telamon	202 Scipio defeats Hannibal at Zama in Africa	167 The battle of Pydna results in the final defeat of Macedon	
		327–304 Second Samnite War		280–275 Pyrrhus of Epirus assists Greek cities against Rome	247 Hamilcar Barca of Carthage attacks in Sicily but in 241 the Romans win in a decisive sea battle	218 Hannibal crosses the Alps; he defeats the Romans at Cannae in 216	191 Rome completes the conquest of Cisalpine Gaul	
EXTERNAL AFFAIRS						214 Rome declares war on Philip of Macedon	190 Antiochus III of Syria is defeated at Magnesia	
						211–206 Scipio defeats Hasdrubal in Spain		
	510 Foundation of the republic		312 The Aqua Appia, Rome's first aqueduct, and the Via Appia, the first significant road, are built	272 The Anio Vetus aqueduct is built	232 Land reform begins a long period of internal political calm	218 Senators are forbidden by law to engage in commerce	167 The direct taxation of Roman citizens is abolished	
		450 Publication of the laws known as the Twelve Tables		269 The first silver coinage is minted at Rome				
INTERNAL AFFAIRS				264 The first gladiatorial show is held in Rome				
		366 The first plebeian consuls are appointed	287 Plebeian assembly decisions are given the force of law					
INSTITUTIONS			312 The sons of freedmen are admitted to the Senate					

Terracotta of elephant with ape

strongest Roman armies ever raised was rushed down to meet him and Hannibal was attacked in an open plain at Cannae. The Carthaginian infantry fell back but, as the Romans moved forward, Hannibal ordered his cavalry to swing round on either side of them. The Romans were trapped and virtually all of them were annihilated. Major cities of the south – including Capua, the second city of Italy – rallied to Hannibal.

Rome now resorted to other tactics. Many of its old allies, particularly in central Italy, remained loyal and Hannibal could never feel totally secure in enemy territory. At first he had no port from which to receive reinforcements, and the Romans raised an army to send to Spain and stop Spanish resources being sent to help him. The Romans were unlikely to defeat Hannibal in open battle and the Senate followed the advice of Quintus Fabius Maximus to avoid any direct confrontation with Hannibal. The aim was to wear him down gradually.

For 12 years Hannibal persisted but the sheer number of Romans began to tell. Capua was recaptured in 211 and in 207 a Carthaginian relief army, led by Hasdrubal, Hannibal's brother-in-law, was defeated in northern Italy. Hannibal's position was precarious. However, the Romans still needed to win

the war and to do this they had to take the fight to the west. In 209 an outstanding young commander, Publius Scipio, took over the Roman armies in Spain. In a surprise attack he seized the main enemy base, Nova Cartagena, and then outfought the remaining Carthaginian armies. By 206 most of the Romans' enemies had been expelled from Spain. In 204 Scipio persuaded the Senate to allow him to lead an army to Africa. Hannibal was forced to return home to defend his native city. In 202 Scipio and Hannibal clashed in a battle at Zama. For the first time, Hannibal had met a Roman commander of his own caliber, and, in a

RIGHT **A dying Numidian horseman. It was with the help of cavalry sent by Massimissa, the king of Numidia, that Publius Scipio and his troops were finally able to defeat Hannibal.**

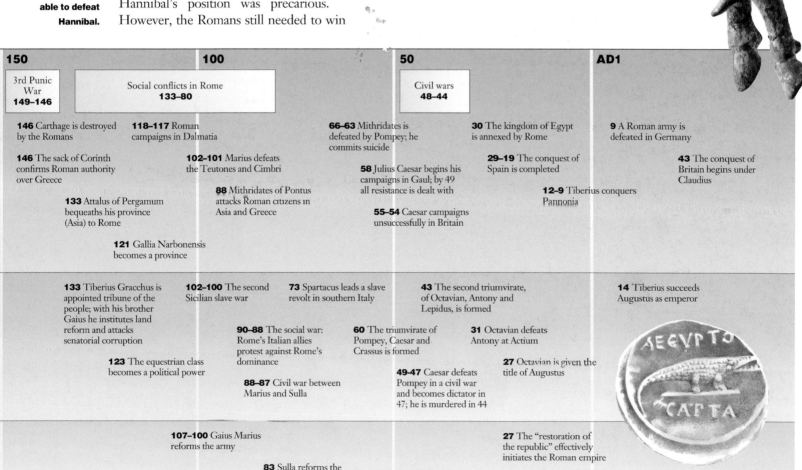

150		100			50		AD1	
3rd Punic War **149–146**	Social conflicts in Rome **133–80**				Civil wars **48–44**			
146 Carthage is destroyed by the Romans	**118–117** Roman campaigns in Dalmatia				**66–63** Mithridates is defeated by Pompey; he commits suicide		**30** The kingdom of Egypt is annexed by Rome	**9** A Roman army is defeated in Germany
146 The sack of Corinth confirms Roman authority over Greece		**102–101** Marius defeats the Teutones and Cimbri					**29–19** The conquest of Spain is completed	**43** The conquest of Britain begins under Claudius
			88 Mithridates of Pontus attacks Roman citizens in Asia and Greece		**58** Julius Caesar begins his campaigns in Gaul; by 49 all resistance is dealt with		**12–9** Tiberius conquers Pannonia	
133 Attalus of Pergamum bequeaths his province (Asia) to Rome					**55–54** Caesar campaigns unsuccessfully in Britain			
	121 Gallia Narbonensis becomes a province							
133 Tiberius Gracchus is appointed tribune of the people; with his brother Gaius he institutes land reform and attacks senatorial corruption	**102–100** The second Sicilian slave war		**73** Spartacus leads a slave revolt in southern Italy		**43** The second triumvirate, of Octavian, Antony and Lepidus, is formed		**14** Tiberius succeeds Augustus as emperor	
		90–88 The social war: Rome's Italian allies protest against Rome's dominance		**60** The triumvirate of Pompey, Caesar and Crassus is formed		**31** Octavian defeats Antony at Actium		
123 The equestrian class becomes a political power						**27** Octavian is given the title of Augustus		
		88–87 Civil war between Marius and Sulla		**49–47** Caesar defeats Pompey in a civil war and becomes dictator in 47; he is murdered in 44				
107–100 Gaius Marius reforms the army					**27** The "restoration of the republic" effectively initiates the Roman empire			
	83 Sulla reforms the judicial system							

"Egypt captured" – a denarius of 28 BC

Philip V (238–179 BC) initiated the First Macedonian War. He was later defeated, fined and made to give up his son as hostage. His son was returned when Philip allied himself with Rome.

great victory for the Romans, he was defeated.

The defeat of Carthage in the Second Punic War was a turning point in the history of the ancient world. Rome now dominated the western Mediterranean and subsequently consolidated its victory by creating two new provinces from Spain.

One of Carthage's allies in the Second Punic War had been Philip V, king of Macedon. Macedon was the surviving core of the vast empire built up by Alexander the Great in Greece and across western Asia. The empire had fragmented on Alexander's death and the lands bordering on the eastern Mediterranean were now a mixture of peoples existing uneasily alongside each other in city-states and kingdoms.

In the 190s, responding to calls from some of the smaller city-states who feared the resurgent power of Macedon, Rome became inextricably involved in the tangled politics of the area. In 168, at the battle of Pydna, Macedon was defeated by Rome and became a province in 146. The trading state of Rhodes was forced into a dependent alliance with Rome in 165. The cities of the Peloponnese struggled to maintain their independence but were crushed by Rome in 146. As an example to those who dared oppose Rome, the city of Corinth was sacked and its marble statues brought back in triumph to Italy.

Also in 146 the Romans completely destroyed Carthage. The city had offered no real threat to Rome since its defeat in the Second Punic War but in many Roman minds only a complete destruction of the city would prevent a future challenge. The city was razed to the ground and 50,000 of its surviving citizens were sold into slavery. Finally, in 133, the rich kingdom of Pergamum on the coast of Asia Minor was bequeathed to Rome by its last king, Attalus III, in the hope of keeping it intact. Instead, it became the Roman province of Asia.

Rivalry is fierce within the aristocracy of Rome

In Rome, the Senate was the center of government: 300 men drawn from the aristocrats of Rome and holding their seats for life. Qualification for the post of senator was service as a magistrate, in the first place usually as a *quaestor*, a post with mainly financial duties. Even this post could not be obtained without 10 years' military service. Elections to the post of magistrate were by the people's assembly, in which every citizen had a vote. In practice, elections were dominated by the

THE SECOND PUNIC WAR
Hannibal's invasion of Italy in 218 from the north before crossing the Alps took the Romans by surprise. Although unable to control the peninsula, he spent several years there before returning to north Africa to face defeat at Zama in 202.

RIGHT **A narrow gorge in France, like the one Hannibal used to cross the Alps. This crossing with his army of men and elephants was a daring move but cost the lives of between 5,000 and 10,000 men.**

Map key:
× battle, with date
→ Hannibal's routes
→ Scipio's routes
Carthaginian territory 218BC
Roman territory 218BC
territory lost to Rome 204BC

0   600 km
0   400 mi

leading families of Rome, relying on their power and prestige to win the leading magistracies for themselves. The consulship was the highest prize and it was rare for a complete outsider to achieve it, though there was a steady trickle of new families into the ranks of the nobility. Even so, there were always more candidates for magistracies than there were posts available and competition and infighting within the aristocracy was intense.

An aristocratic government was accepted by the people of Rome because its leaders had brought success in war, established internal stability and increased Rome's wealth. Until the middle of the 2nd century BC the Senate enjoyed enormous prestige. It had played a crucial role in the Punic Wars and then had successfully grappled with the politics of the Greek states. Even the tribunes, the 10 officers elected each year to represent the people, were drawn from the elite and normally introduced laws only after consultation with the Senate.

Eventually the power and prestige of the Senate was weakened by a land crisis. The senators and the equestrians – the wealthy outside the senate, prospered from the successful expansion of Rome's possessions overseas. They spent their new riches on high living or on the purchase of land. From the middle of the 2nd century, the aristocrats extended their estates throughout Italy, particularly on state land that might otherwise have been distributed to poor or landless citizens. A new pattern of larger farms, often owned by absentee landlords, began to develop. In contrast to the traditional subsistence farms, these had a commercial bias: grain was grown as a cash crop, sheep provided wool, milk and cheese. Rome and other growing towns of Italy provided a market.

The loss of their subsistence farms, however, brought unimaginable hardship to the new landless poor who had long been under pressure. Many had seen their holdings deteriorate while they were serving in the army overseas, but in the 1st century BC a further crisis arose. Land was confiscated and given to discharged soldiers, forcing about half the peasant families of Roman Italy – perhaps one and a half million people – from their land. By the end of the republic, Italy was in deep social crisis: rival aristocrats were fighting it out with armies partially recruited from the very people they had displaced from the land.

Half a million men served in these armies during the civil wars, but what happened to their families is not known. Displaced peasants flooded into Rome and other Italian towns; in Rome, poor families crammed into tenements that speculators had begun building in the 2nd century BC. Urban life, though, was no easier. Despite new opportunities in building and in craft industries due to the expansion of the towns, displaced peasants were often at a disadvantage compared with slaves, who formed most of the domestic work force.

One thing the new poor of Rome did have was the right, as citizens, to vote in the public assemblies, providing incentive for ambitious politicians to pay at least lip service to their needs. The position of *aedile* was particularly desirable: public games were the responsibility of the aediles whose popularity with the voting public could be greatly increased through a lavish expenditure on games and other entertainments.

In 133 Tiberius Gracchus, a tribune, proposed a modest program to tackle the problem of the poor. He suggested that landowners who had taken more than their due from the *ager publicus*, the state lands, should surrender the surplus which could then be distributed to the landless. Tiberius needed to be careful: the interests of the aristocracy would be adversely affected by any such measures. Unwisely, he pushed his reform

Land ownership, early in the republic, was spread so that almost all citizens owned at least a small plot. The practice of agriculture was said to have developed the hardy character of the typical Roman.

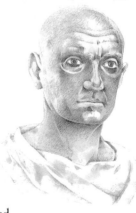

ABOVE **Hannibal (top) and Scipio. His defeat of Hannibal in Africa earned Scipio the name Africanus.**

LEFT **This decorative plate depicts a war elephant with ornamental draperies.**

through the Popular Assembly, rather than following the traditional route of testing it first in the Senate to gain the senators' approval.

When the Senate's opposition was aroused, Tiberius tried to have himself elected for a second term as tribune. No tribune had been reelected for at least 200 years, and this blatant breach of custom was the last straw for many. When the Senate was discussing the legality of the proposal, a number of senators stormed out of the meeting. They marched on the Capitol, collecting sticks as they went. A riot broke out and Tiberius, along with 300 of his followers, was clubbed to death.

Tiberius's ideas did not die, however: a land commission he set up survived and redistributed some land. In 123 his brother Gaius was elected tribune and carried on his brother's work, setting up new colonies for landless Romans and Italians and subsidizing the price of grain for the poor. The Senate's fears were again aroused and one of the consuls organized the suppression of Gaius and his followers in 121. After armed combat, and without a trial, about 3,000 men were killed.

The suppression of the Gracchus brothers marked a turning point in the political history of the Roman republic. Some senators remained sympathetic to reform but the majority had not only ignored the issues but had tried to defend their position by brutal force. The consensus which had given such stability to Rome's government for so long now began to break down.

The strains of war showed the true vulnerability of the Senate. In 112, Rome was at war with Jugurtha, the king of Numidia. An entire Roman army was forced to surrender to Jugurtha, and discontent with the Senate's

BELOW **Roman coin depicting a Gaul (not Vercingetorix as once thought), issued in celebration of Caesar's Gallic campaign in 48 BC.**

THE RISE OF ROMAN POWER
After defeating Carthage Rome ruled the Mediterranean. It then turned to the east, conquering Macedon and Greece by 146. Conquests in Asia followed. Marius eventually dealt with a serious threat from wandering Germanic peoples in the north in 102–101 BC.

LEFT **Carthaginian glass mask, of a bearded man, from the 4th century BC.**

Marius was married to Caesar's aunt. She died in 69 BC and had the unusual (for a woman) honor of a public oration by her nephew.

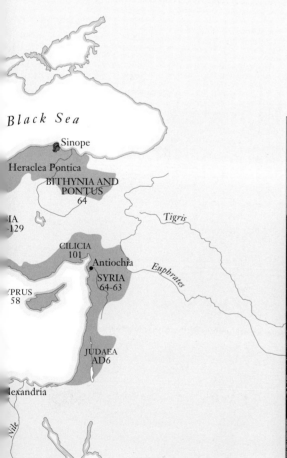

LEFT **Victory, so vital to the Roman way of thinking, was often personified. She was generally depicted as a winged goddess.**

conduct of the war grew. Gaius Marius, a political outsider, exploited popular feeling to win the consulship and gain authority from the Popular Assembly to conduct the war. This was a humiliating blow for the Senate which traditionally controlled all military commands. Marius then returned to Africa to bring the war to a successful conclusion. In a great triumph in Rome, Jugurtha was dragged in chains through the streets.

Next Marius was called upon to deal with migrating German tribes who had been threatening Rome's territories in the north. He was reelected consul for five consecutive years to deal with the emergency. By 101 the Germans were crushed and Marius was back in Rome celebrating a second triumph.

Marius's career had again shown that military crisis could elevate a popular general, giving him his powers through the Popular Assembly and overriding the restrictions on repeated tenure. During the war Marius also had to raise new recruits. With no support from the Senate, who would normally have ordered a levy, he had

drawn on landless volunteers. At the end of the war, these men had nowhere to return. Marius sought to get them settled in veterans' colonies overseas but it was clear that in ambitious hands such an army, led by a popular general, might prove a potent political weapon.

Rome grants citizenship to people in other parts of Italy

The next disruption was in Italy itself. In all its wars Rome had been heavily dependent on its allies, the local cities and peoples of Italy who loyally provided troops. The relationship had suffered increasing strain. In 90 BC they rebelled, and a short but bloody "Social War" ensued. Rome quickly pacified some of them by offering them Roman citizenship, with the right to participate fully in political life. Others continued their resistance and were defeated, yet they received citizens' rights eventually. This unified Italy politically and over following generations this ensured a sense of common identity and increasing involvement of men of Italian origin in Roman social, political and cultural life at the highest levels.

More immediately, out of the Social War rose another general: Lucius Sulla. He had secured a consulship in 88 and was then awarded the command of the Roman armies which were being sent east to fight off an invasion by King Mithridates of Pontus. Before departing, Sulla was challenged by Marius who, at 70, was confident that he could

The term **Social War** comes from the Latin word *socii*, or allies. Pompeii was one of the cities involved. The city was besieged by Sulla in 89 and it was later romanized.

BELOW **The city of Corinth was on a site that had been inhabited since at least 3000 BC. The town was sacked by the Romans in 146 BC.**

still lead armies to victory. Sulla responded by marching on Rome, driving out Marius and his supporters and installing his own. He then went east.

When Sulla returned, having defeated Mithridates, he learned that he had been declared a public enemy. His house had been destroyed and his laws repealed. Sulla took revenge, killing thousands of men, and seizing the land of his opponents in the countryside to give to his veterans. As dictator, he attempted to restore the Senate's power – doubling its size to 600 and packing it with his supporters – and deprived the post of tribune of most of its powers.

Sulla retired voluntarily in 79 but his legacy was a bitter one. He had bullied his way to power with the help of his army, setting a dangerous precedent. His confiscations of land had increased rural unrest, his ruthless treatment of his enemies left a legacy of political bitterness and the gulf between Senate and people widened still further. The way was open for ambitious men to use the traditional avenue to popularity – military victory – to force their way to power.

The first of these ambitious men was Gaius Pompeius, or Pompey the Great. Pompey had started his career as one of Sulla's commanders and had defeated Sulla's enemies in Africa so effectively that he was called a young executioner. In the 70s he enhanced his reputation by defeating a governor of Spain who had opposed Sulla;

BELOW **Mosaic from Ostia showing the distribution of the corn dole, introduced by Gaius Gracchus in 123 BC to feed the growing numbers of poor citizens in Rome.**

THE LAND REFORM OF THE GRACCHI
Gracchus's move to redistribute the land seized from areas that supported Hannibal led to his murder.

ETRURIA
UMBRIA
Tiber
Perusia
Asculum
Spoletium
Histonium
Alba Fucens
Caere
Rome
Marsi
Celenza Val Fortore
Praeneste
Aesernia
Samnites
Salapia
Interamna
Minturnae
Apuli
Sinuessa
Capua
Beneventum
Venusia
Sant Angelo
Arienzo
Campani
Lucani
Rocca San Felice
Mt Vesuvius
Tarentum
Sicignano
Polla
Barra
Heraclea
Sala Consilina

⚒ Gracchan colony
■ place with inscribed boundary stone
⚓ center of slave revolt
▨ ager publicus, 133BC
▨ rebel area, 91-89BC

0 _____ 150km
0 _____ 100mi

Bruttii

Minervium

Rhegium

Spartacus was a Thracian gladiator. His revolt took six legions, led by Crassus, to be suppressed. The punishment was harsh and over 6,000 of the rebellious slaves were captured and crucified.

Brundisium

he then returned home to help quell the remnants of a slave uprising begun in 71 BC and led by Spartacus. Pompey exploited his successes to win a consulship for the year 70, though he was six years underage and not a member of the Senate.

Pompey's fellow consul was Marcus Crassus, a wealthy noble who had made a fortune out of dealing in the confiscated land of Sulla's enemies. They were both shrewd men. Aristocrats at heart, they knew that their position as men of status depended on stability at home and they used their consulships to widen their political support – in particular by restoring full powers to the tribunes.

The Senate's rejection of Pompey aids Julius Caesar's bid for power

Not long after his consulship Pompey began to look for new commands which could sustain him as the central figure in Roman politics. In 67 he was given a three-year command to suppress the pirates who were menacing Roman shipping in the Mediterranean. In only three months the pirates were destroyed. Pompey then moved east to deal finally with the threat of Mithridates; in 63 Mithridates was forced into suicide.

Pompey undertook a major reorganization and expansion of Rome's empire in the east, incorporating Pontus and the collapsed kingdom of Syria. A number of client states were established – independent, but under strong Roman influence – to insulate Rome against its only serious challenger to the east, the empire of Parthia. The new acquisitions could now be taxed effectively and Pompey claimed that he had raised the revenue of Rome by 70 percent.

Pompey returned to Rome in 62 BC. It was a troubled time. A year before, a debt-ridden aristocrat, Catilina, had tried, and failed, to capitalize on popular discontent and seize power. Pompey's requests were simple and reasonable: recognition of his settlement in the east and land for his veterans. This was still too much for the Senate. Reluctant to confirm Pompey as the leading man of Roman politics they rebuffed him. This was a dangerous move, prompting Pompey to find new allies.

The most significant of these was an ambitious young man: Gaius Julius Caesar. Caesar (100–44 BC) was the descendant of an ancient patrician family of Rome but alongside traditional aristocratic methods of building support (such as the particularly lavish games he had put on as aedile), he had also made a number of gestures designed to establish firmly his credentials as a champion of popular rights.

On his return from his consulship in Spain in

60 BC, he was triumphantly elected to the consulship for 59. He strengthened his association with the older and more prestigious Pompey and reconciled him to Marcus Crassus. The three made an informal pact (the so-called, and unofficial, First Triumvirate) and agreed to work together to push through a contentious legislative program, above all a land bill.

Caesar made some attempt to work with the Senate but, facing considerable obstruction, he pushed his laws through the Popular Assembly. Land was gained for Pompey's armies and his reorganization of the east was ratified. The alliance between Caesar and Pompey was consolidated when Caesar's only child, his daughter Julia, was given in marriage to Pompey.

Caesar also secured a new military command for himself once his consulship ended. This included the provinces of Cisalpine Gaul in the north of Italy, Illyricum on the Adriatic coast and, later, southern Gaul. In 58 Caesar led a campaign from southern Gaul to conquer the whole of the country. This brought him yet more acclaim.

Crassus and Pompey were consuls again in 55 and they renewed Caesar's commands but their agreement was about to end. In 54, Julia died and the personal link between Caesar and Pompey was broken. In 53 Crassus, attempting to emulate the military achievements of Pompey and Caesar, rashly led an army into the Parthian empire and was humiliatingly defeated and killed.

The empire was now at the mercy of two strong men: Pompey, still with immense prestige after his earlier achievements, and Caesar, now bringing to a close a brilliant campaign in Gaul. The relationship between the two gradually began to break down. Pompey had stayed in Rome. Conservative senators began to realize that Caesar was the main threat to their power in Rome and they moved closer to Pompey. With their support Pompey was elected sole consul in 52.

This consolidation of Pompey's power left Caesar on the defensive. His period of command was almost at an end. Despite desperate negotiations to find a solution which would avoid civil war Caesar was finally asked to lay down his arms when his command ended. He was trapped. Either he disbanded his armies and came to Rome as a private citizen – the sure end of his political career – or he defied the Senate and resorted to force.

There was a small river, the Rubicon, which marked the border between Cisalpine Gaul, where Caesar had command, and the rest of Italy where Pompey was supreme. Caesar made his decision. On 10 January 49 BC, he led his armies across the Rubicon to begin a civil war.

The official triumvirates, boards of three officials, had existed since about 289 BC. Their duties varied from dealing with crime to running the mint and supervising a banquet of Jupiter.

ABOVE Marius (top), a political outsider, and Sulla, an aristocrat. The class-based rivalry of these men caused a great deal of bloodshed.

ABOVE Land was marked out into 100 squares of 50 hectares and then distributed to Roman colonists. This was called centuriation.

At first Pompey seemed to have all the advantages. He controlled Italy and Spain and could draw on the resources of the east. However, in Italy fewer people than expected were prepared to rise on his behalf and Pompey was forced to move east. In an extraordinary series of campaigns Caesar overran Italy, defeated seven legions in Spain loyal to Pompey and then, in the winter of 48, shipped an army of 11 legions across the Adriatic to confront Pompey. The final showdown came in Greece, at Pharsalus. It was Caesar's greatest victory. Pompey fled the battlefield, leaving 6,000 of his men dead and another 24,000 as prisoners. He escaped to Egypt but, as he stepped ashore, he was murdered on the orders of the Egyptian king.

Caesar had pursued Pompey to Egypt and here enjoyed an unexpected interlude in the war. This hardened soldier became bewitched by Queen Cleopatra who ruled Egypt jointly with her brother. For two months Caesar and Cleopatra cruised together along the Nile and Cleopatra later gave birth to a son, Caesarion, rumored to be Caesar's. Then Caesar's ambitions called him back to duty. He faced campaigns in the east, in Africa and against Pompey's two sons who held out in Spain before he was able to return home to Rome, the undisputed ruler of the empire, in October 45.

Caesar had overthrown the senatorial government which had ruled Rome for centuries. The process which had begun with the refusal of the Senate to deal peacefully with the reforms of the

Gracchi had now culminated in the eclipse of the Senate itself at the hands of an ambitious general.

Could Caesar establish a new form of government around his own person? He tried to but he seemed to have no creative ideas for constitutional reform. In 46, he made himself dictator for 10 years and then, in 44, for life. This was quite unprecedented, and such a position of supreme power was not compatible with the tradition of aristocratic power-sharing. The Senate was packed with his own supporters who loaded him with various honors. The appointment of governorships and magistracies fell under his control. Caesar now appeared in public on a gilded chair, dressed in a triumphal purple robe. He was the first living Roman to appear on coins.

This growing aloofness touched a raw nerve in the depth of Roman aristocratic consciousness: the fear of a restoration of the monarchy. In 44 a conspiracy was hatched to remove this threat to aristocratic freedom. There were about 70 men involved, led by Gaius Cassius Longinus and Marcus Junius Brutus. They chose the date 15 March – the Ides of March – shortly before Caesar left Rome for the east. He was set upon and publicly stabbed to death.

Caesar's murder rekindles the struggle for personal political power

The conspirators proclaimed that Caesar had been killed in the name of republican liberty. They meant aristocratic liberty, but this aroused little enthusiasm. There was no outburst of joy, only a shocked silence from the surrounding crowds and the conspirators had to hurry off to hide on the Capitoline Hill. Eventually Brutus and Cassius were forced to flee the city.

With the republic dead, the struggle for personal political power became more fierce. One contender was Mark Antony, consul with Caesar in the final year of his life. He had the support of the legions in Italy and the masses of Rome. However, when Caesar's will was read, it was learned that he had adopted as his son and heir his 18-year-old great-nephew, Gaius Octavianus. Octavian soon demonstrated that he could be as ruthless and ambitious as anyone else, quickly proving wrong those senators who considered him a boy who could easily be manipulated. By the age of 19 Octavian was a consul. He also made a deal with Antony and, after the defeat and death of Brutus and Cassius at Philippi in 42, they progressively shared the empire between them. Cleopatra was the central figure in the drama that followed.

ABOVE **Pompey (top) and Mithridates, whose policy of conquest brought him into conflict with Rome. He was finally defeated by Pompey.**

RIGHT **Terracotta gladiator. The first known gladiatorial contest was in 264 BC, with three pairs of contestants, but the numbers of fighters gradually increased. Gladiators were originally slaves and criminals, but in later years women also fought in the arena.**

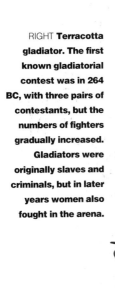

RIGHT **Balcony of a Roman villa by the sea. The recorded history of Rome is the history of the small but powerful landed aristocracy. Power, prestige and pleasure were the preserve of a privileged minority.**

RIGHT **Marble statue of a consul in the republic. Consular status was, for a long time, the privilege solely of the wealthy and educated elite of the Roman republic.**

Cleopatra VII (69–31 BC), daugher of Ptolemy XII, was Macedonian, not Egyptian. She inherited the throne along with her husband-brother but they fell out and started a civil war.

Antony had summoned her to meet him and she soon became his mistress and bore him three children. Who exploited whom is not clear. Cleopatra needed the support of Rome to survive as queen of Egypt; Antony needed Egypt's wealth if he was to maintain his armies.

In a magnificent ceremony in Alexandria in 34, Antony threw down his challenge to Octavian. He declared that Caesarion was the true heir of Caesar. Octavian had to respond. He exploited the Roman distrust of the east, and played on rumors that Antony intended to move the capital from Rome to Alexandria. It was Octavian, not Antony, who represented true Roman traditions.

The final break came when Antony and Cleopatra began moving troops to Greece. Octavian could now claim that Cleopatra was a foreign ruler invading Roman territory. Both sides gathered their forces. In 31 Octavian crossed to Greece. Antony brought his army close to his fleet in a defensive position at Actium, a cape off the western coast of Greece. Octavian moved to trap him and cut his supplies. In a scrappy naval battle Antony tried to break out but his fleet was destroyed. Antony and Cleopatra fled back to Egypt where both committed suicide. Their leaderless army surrendered.

Gaius Julius Caesar Octavianus, still only 32, was the undisputed master of the entire Roman world. A new phase in Roman history had begun.

Mark Antony (c82–30 BC) was once a friend of Octavian and was even married to Octavian's sister. When Antony divorced his wife for Cleopatra, Octavian declared war against him.

JULIUS CAESAR · POLITICAL GENIUS

In the troubled world of the Roman republic in the 1st century BC only the toughest, most ambitious of men could achieve a position of supreme power. Such a man was Julius Caesar. He was a political genius who clawed his way up with a shrewd manipulation of public discontent and a clever set of political alliances. Military success was the most obvious means to political power and prestige and here, too, Caesar excelled. He was a brilliant commander, decisive and ruthless. His first military campaigns – in Spain in 60 BC

and in Gaul in the 50s – were designed to bring him prestige and plunder as much as Roman conquest. It was incidental that he also built up a loyal army which, when civil war came in 49, he was to use to destroy his enemies. The civil wars show Caesar's extraordinary energy as well as his military genius. His campaigns took him from Asia to Spain and from Greece to the African provinces. In between he enjoyed his celebrated relationship with Cleopatra.

At the time of Caesar's assassination, when he was only 55, he was planning a military expedition to the east to deal with

ABOVE **The dying Gaul: a 2nd-century Roman statue in honor of a victory over the Gauls.**

× battle, with date
→ campaign of Caesar, with date
⬭ conquests of Caesar
▨ approximate extent of empire at Caesar's death 44BC

0 _____ 600 km
0 _____ 400 mi

LEFT **The Julian calendar, still in use today, after only slight modifications.**

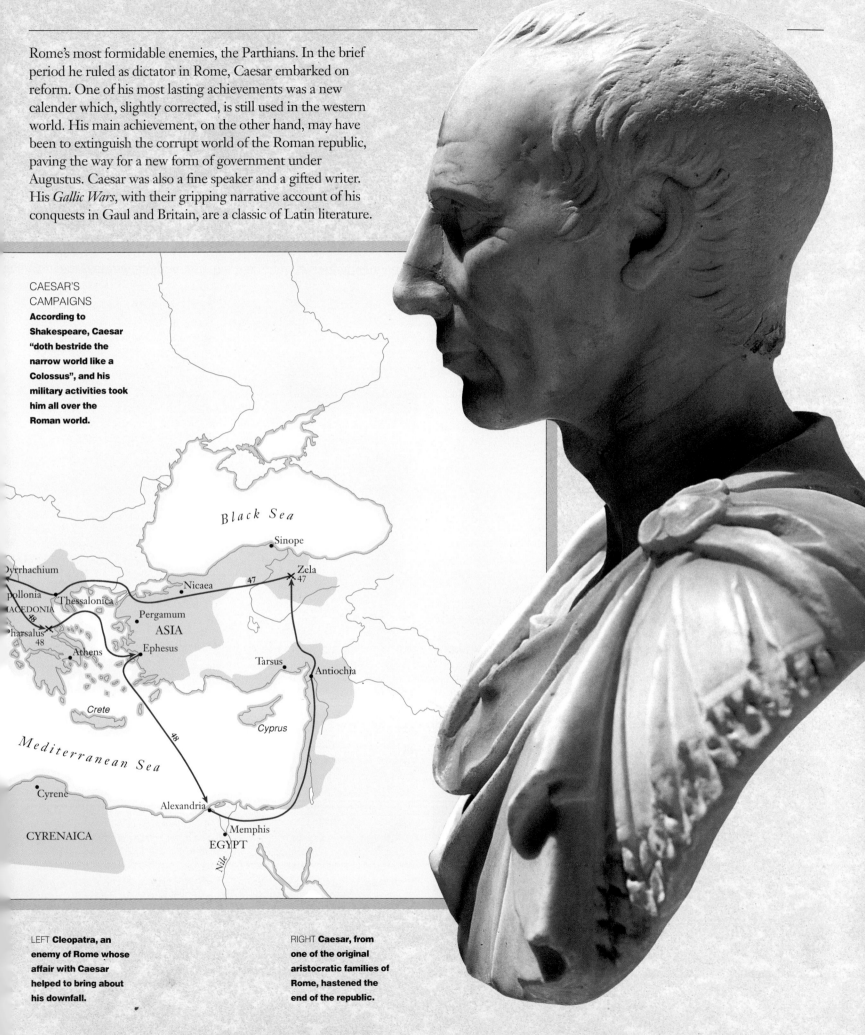

Rome's most formidable enemies, the Parthians. In the brief period he ruled as dictator in Rome, Caesar embarked on reform. One of his most lasting achievements was a new calender which, slightly corrected, is still used in the western world. His main achievement, on the other hand, may have been to extinguish the corrupt world of the Roman republic, paving the way for a new form of government under Augustus. Caesar was also a fine speaker and a gifted writer. His *Gallic Wars*, with their gripping narrative account of his conquests in Gaul and Britain, are a classic of Latin literature.

CAESAR'S CAMPAIGNS
According to Shakespeare, Caesar "doth bestride the narrow world like a Colossus", and his military activities took him all over the Roman world.

Black Sea

Sinope

Zela
47
47

Dyrrhachium

Apollonia   Thessalonica   Nicaea

MACEDONIA

48   Pergamum   ASIA

Pharsalus   48

Athens   Ephesus

Tarsus

Antiochia

Crete

Cyprus

Mediterranean Sea

48

Cyrene

Alexandria

Memphis

CYRENAICA   EGYPT

Nile

LEFT **Cleopatra, an enemy of Rome whose affair with Caesar helped to bring about his downfall.**

RIGHT **Caesar, from one of the original aristocratic families of Rome, hastened the end of the republic.**

23

THE SPIRITS OF ROME

Romans took a great deal of care to perform the correct rituals to ensure the *pax deorum* – the goodwill of the gods. Some worship was a family affair, aimed at obtaining purely private benefits, but public worship was needed to ensure the goodwill of the gods toward city and state. To propitiate the gods and ensure a prosperous outcome to Rome's political and military affairs, a complex calendar of religious ceremonies had to be performed in exactly the prescribed manner: a mistake debased the whole ritual, which then had to be repeated from the beginning. There were priests responsible for divination to discover whether or not the gods approved of a proposed course of action. Divination might take the form of examining animal entrails or the behavior of birds. Skepticism was costly for some people, as one consul discovered. According to the historian Suetonius, "Claudius Pulcher showed his scorn of religion during a naval engagement off Sicily. When he took the auspices and discovered that the sacred chickens were not eating, he threw them into the sea, saying, 'If they don't want to eat, let them drink', and then he engaged the enemy in a naval battle. He lost the battle."

The sacred six

Vesta was the goddess who presided over the hearth – the center of the Roman home – and was propitiated by private family worship. The temple of Vesta in the Forum contained the sacred hearth, tended continuously by the six Vestal Virgins. Vestals were recruited at the age of seven from good families and spent 30 years in the service of Vesta. After that time they were free to marry if they wished, though few did. Romans believed disaster would strike the state if the sacred hearth's fire went out; any Vestal who allowed that to happen was whipped. An even greater punishment was meted out to a Vestal who was unchaste: she would be buried alive. In the 1,000-year history of the temple only 18 Vestals received this punishment.

The temple of Vesta in the Roman Forum.

Gods of the Capitol

The most important of Rome's temples was that, on the Capitoline Hill, to the trio of Jupiter, Juno and Minerva – three of the most important deities in the early history of the Roman world. Builders began construction in the time of Rome's monarchy, and the temple was dedicated in the first year of the new republic.

Jupiter was god of the sky and lightning. He symbolized good faith, justice and honor, and the Romans swore their most binding oaths in Jupiter's name. Jupiter was also a war god. His aid was invoked before military expeditions and he was always offered part of any riches won in battle. Annual games were held in his honor. In time Jupiter became associated with the Greek god Zeus and took on his attributes as supreme ruler of the universe.

Juno, Jupiter's consort, was goddess of the moon and eventually became the principal female divinity of the state. She too played a role in protecting the city: the legendary cackling of her sacred geese warned of a Gaulish attack in 390 BC and saved the Capitol. Juno was later given the title *moneta*, the warner. The first Roman coins were produced in the temple of Juno Moneta; the word later came to mean mint and then money. Juno was eventually associated with

The watcher at the gate

Doorways and gates were guarded by the god Janus, who was worshiped at an ancient gateway in the Forum. From here he watched over all the doors and gateways of the city of Rome. In legend, Janus's intervention saved Rome after the Capitol had been betrayed to the Sabines by Tarpeia, a Vestal Virgin. Tarpeia did not profit from her treason: she was killed by the Sabines who flung her body from a crag on the Capitoline Hill. The rock became known as the Tarpeian Rock and became the execution place for traitors. Because of his timely intervention in this crisis, the gates of Janus's temple were always left open in times of war so that he could go instantly to the aid of the Romans. One of the few occasions when the gates were closed was in 29 BC, at the end of the civil wars. Prayers could reach other gods only through Janus, as he presided over all gateways; in religious ceremonies his name was always invoked first. Janus had knowledge of both the past and the future and was portrayed with two faces. He also gave his name to the first month of the year, January.

A bronze coin showing Janus. Unlike many Roman gods, Janus had no Greek equivalent.

Rome's river god

ABOVE **Bronze figurines of Jupiter (center) and Minerva, and a terracotta figure of Juno.**

the Greek Hera, consort of Zeus.

Minerva, daughter of Jupiter, was the goddess of wisdom and mental activity and presided over the trade and industry of Rome. She was also patron to writers, doctors, schoolmasters and craftsmen. Minerva became identified with the Greek goddess Athena who was said to have sprung fully armed from the head of her father Zeus. She later became a goddess of war, and Pompey built a statue to Minerva out of the spoils of his conquests.

ABOVE **The Pons Amilius, spanning the Tiber, is the oldest stone bridge across the river.**

Travel in mountainous central Italy was difficult and the valley of the Tiber was an important natural routeway. The lowest crossing place of the river was an important strategic location and it was on hills overlooking this point that the city of Rome grew up. The Tiber was navigable, giving Rome good trade links, but its strong current and winding course kept the city safe from surprise attacks from the sea.

The Romans understood the benefits the Tiber brought them and invested the river with a divine spirit. Father Tiber was usually portrayed as an old bearded man but, though he was thought to show his anger by flooding, he was not the object of formal worship.

Every May, however, a procession of priests and Vestal Virgins cast human effigies into the Tiber as an act of purification. This was an ancient ceremony, so old that the Romans of republican times had forgotten both its origins and its significance. It was, perhaps, thought that the Tiber could divert the anger of the gods.

LEFT **The Tiber river personified: a statue from the emperor Hadrian's villa in modern Tivoli.**

REPUBLICAN SOCIETY

At the beginning of the 3rd century BC Rome was essentially still an agricultural community. Almost all Roman citizens were peasant freeholders working small farms of just a few hectares. Though the nobility dominated society, their wealth – and the basis of their power and influence – lay mostly in land rather than slaves or treasure. Indeed the nobility's professed moral code was austere and disapproved of luxury: as late as 275 BC a senator was expelled for possessing silver vessels weighing over 4 kilograms. However, the rapid growth of Rome's empire after the Second Punic War brought major social changes. The small farmers suffered economically as a result of war damage and their liability for military service and many sold up to big landowners and left the land to swell the ranks of the urban poor who came to make up the majority of the citizen body. At the same time wealth and captives flooded into Rome, greatly enriching the nobility and leading to a vast increase in the numbers of slaves.

The basic unit of Roman society was the extended noble family, presided over by its authoritarian male head, the *paterfamilias*, and its dependent clients. The institution of clienthood formed the basis of aristocratic political power and influence but it also helped create bonds of common interest across society. It was a mutually supportive relationship between a weaker party – the client, and a stronger – the patron. The patron gave legal protection and other benefits in return for the client's support for his political ambitions.

RIGHT **The idealized patrician: Lucius Brutus, a (possibly mythical) founder of the republic.**

The town and country divide

Leisured Roman poets left an idyllic view of rural life, but in reality the lives of ordinary country folk were often hard. In good years the smallholder had surplus food to sell in the city markets, but the unreliable rainfall of peninsular Italy made his living insecure. Slave labor made life even harder for the landless laborer. The rural unemployment was so serious that Julius Caesar tried to alleviate the

Starving goats search for food just outside the walls of Rome.

situation by requiring large landowners to recruit a third of their workforce from free laborers. Banditry was common and country people suffered more in wartime than town-dwellers. People could find refuge in the city but they might return home to find their houses and crops burned or looted.

Patrician and plebeian

BELOW **How to wear a toga; a privilege once belonging only to citizens.**

The distinction between patrician and plebeian was one of blood rather than wealth. Patricians were members of an ancient hereditary aristocracy; plebeians were all citizens, rich or poor, who were not patricians. The early republic was marked by aristocratic privilege and it was the

4th century before plebeians won the right to become magistrates and senators. Any plebeian who was elected to the consulship became ennobled. Anyone who joined the nobility in this way was called *novus homo* - a new man - but by the 3rd century a new business class, the equestrian order, had emerged.

Governing the republic

Although the republic was not a democracy, decision-making was collective. The popular legislative assemblies annually elected magistrates, the executive officers of the state. The senior magistrates were two consuls, with equal authority, who commanded the army in time of war. Below the consuls was a range of magistracies. Most junior was the quaestorship, a treasury post. After the quaestors came aediles, responsible for public works; censors, who drew up the lists of voters; and praetors, senior judges and deputies to the consuls. Magistrates exercised authority in the name of the people, but their actions were controlled by the Senate. The Senate, 300 ex-magistrates, was dominated by the nobility and did not always consider the interests of the whole community. Magisterial authority, though, was limited by the tribune of the plebs whose rights of veto over magistrates gave the lower classes some protection.

List of consuls and triumphant generals at the entrance to the Forum.

"The just application of laws"

It is the duty of a magistrate to understand that he represents the whole citizen body and that he must therefore uphold the dignity and honor of the state, defend its laws, render justice, and remember that all these powers have been entrusted to him as a sacred trust... he who holds public office must especially see to it that each man keeps what belongs to him and that private citizens suffer no loss of property through public legislation ...it was particularly for this reason that governments and states were established: so that each man might keep what belonged to him...men who...try to pass some agrarian law, in order that occupants may be driven away from their residencies ...are undermining the foundations of our society...therefore men who hold public office must steer clear of that kind of generosity which takes property from one group and gives it to another. And they will especially take care that each man keeps what belongs to him through the just application of laws and legal decisions.

Cicero, De Officiis (An Essay about Duties).

Wall painting of a court scene with magistrates.

"Provoco": every citizen's right of appeal to the people.

ROMANS AND THE SEA

Early Rome was a farming community and had little to do with the nearby sea. Even during their conquest of Italy, the Romans gained little experience of naval warfare: their early attempts at fleet actions were dismal failures. Although Rome had gained unchallenged mastery of the western Mediterranean by 241, it did not maintain its fleet. Once the Greek states of the east had been conquered Roman naval power declined so far that by 70 BC pirates threatened Rome's food supplies. A vigorous campaign by Pompey in 67 BC eradicated the pirates and thereafter the empire kept a standing navy to patrol the Mediterranean sea lanes. The fleet also played an important role in defending the frontiers of the empire.

A winning invention

Romans made few innovations in their warships, which closely followed Greek designs. Rome's early naval victories against Carthage, however, were due in part to one Roman invention: the *corvus* (the crow), a drawbridge, fitted with an iron spike, which could be lowered onto the deck of an enemy ship. This enabled the strongly armed Roman marines to board and overwhelm the enemy ship. The corvus was an effective weapon, but it made Roman ships top-heavy and unseaworthy and was later abandoned.

Building a navy from scratch

Having started a war with Carthage, the Romans soon realized they needed a navy. Using a captured Carthaginian warship as a model, a fleet of 120 warships was completed in only 60 days. The Romans benefited little from their victories. Roman seamen were so inexperienced that hundreds of ships were lost in bad weather. However, Roman seamanship improved as the war progressed while Carthaginian seamanship declined as they recruited more and more inexperienced men to replace their losses. In 241 the Romans won a decisive naval battle off Sicily and forced Carthage out of the war.

Carthage harbor, destroyed by the Romans in 146 BC.

Warships of the Roman fleet

Ship design

R oman ships were built in the Mediterranean tradition that dated back at least to the time of Homer. The keel was laid first, then the planks of the hull were added. These were carefully shaped to fit each other exactly and joined edge-to-edge with mortise and tenon joints. When the hull was complete, strengthening ribs, known as frames, were fitted to the inside and a deck built on top. This was a time-consuming and expensive method of shipbuilding but, with the number of slaves available to work, time was of little concern to the Romans. The high cost was also compensated for by the fact that the resulting vessels were extremely strong and watertight. Some ships were treated

Rough seas were a hazard for shippers as well as piracy.

with wax to protect the timber; others had tarred fabric and lead sheets tacked to the hull to protect against the shipworms which could bore through the wood. This made some merchant ships difficult to maneuver, especially in stormy weather, as they could not sail very close to the wind. Nevertheless, they were extremely sturdy and able to transport a great deal.

The most common type of Roman merchant ship was the *corbita*, a clumsy, round-hulled sailing ship with curving prow and stern and a cargo-carrying capacity of 70 to 350 tonnes. Under average conditions, corbitas could make only about 3.5 knots, but they were seaworthy and made trading voyages as far afield as India. The largest cargo ships were the grain carriers that brought Rome's corn supplies from Egypt. When used for carrying passengers, grain ships could accommodate over 600 people.

Cross-section of a ship showing the tight-fitting planks with mortise and tenon joints.

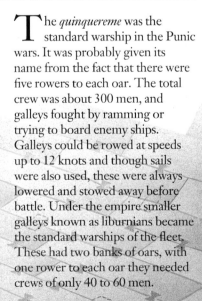

T he *quinquereme* was the standard warship in the Punic wars. It was probably given its name from the fact that there were five rowers to each oar. The total crew was about 300 men, and galleys fought by ramming or trying to board enemy ships. Galleys could be rowed at speeds up to 12 knots and though sails were also used, these were always lowered and stowed away before battle. Under the empire smaller galleys known as liburnians became the standard warships of the fleet. These had two banks of oars, with one rower to each oar they needed crews of only 40 to 60 men.

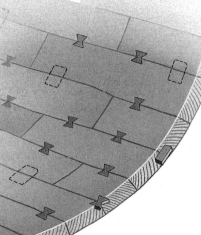

This Pompeiian wall painting shows four small galleys.

THE REPUBLICAN ARMY

Rome's rise to greatness was due to military organization and the fighting qualities of foot soldiers; cavalry was never a great Roman strength. In the early republic, men served according to their wealth: soldiers received no pay and had to provide their own arms. The poorest citizens were excluded from military service as they were considered not to have sufficient incentive to defend the state.

At first the Greek influence was strong and the army fought as a phalanx of armored spearmen. Wars with the Celts and the Italian hill tribes taught the Romans to adopt more flexible formation, while the spear was replaced by the javelin and the sword.

The Roman soldier had no equal in the Mediterranean world. Pay was introduced in 396 BC but for years the Roman army remained a conscripted citizen army, serving only when needed. In 107 BC, recruitment was finally opened to poorer citizens, and the army became increasingly made up of career soldiers. By 14 BC, although conscription was still practiced, Augustus had organized the first professional standing army.

Dressing for battle

The armor of the Roman legionary varied from age to age. Legionaries wore a coat of chain mail until Claudius's reign (AD 41–54) when this was replaced by armor made of overlapping iron plates. A century later more flexible armor made of iron scales was introduced. A bronze helmet, copied from the Celts, protected the head and neck and served as dentification. According to the Greek historian Polybius, the light-armed troops, *velites*, who were not legionaries, were "equipped with a plain helmet, sometimes covering it with a wolf's skin or something of this sort, both to protect it and at the same time to make it distinct so that those men who are stoutly

Symbols of war

The early legions carried five standards – the eagle, the wolf, the minotaur, the horse and the boar – but in 104 BC Marius abolished all standards except the eagle, the symbol of Jupiter.

The eagle standard was the standard of the whole legion and never left the camp unless the whole legion was on the move. By the time of Caesar the eagle standards were made of silver and gold. The eagle was an important rallying point in battle and to lose it was a huge disgrace. Enormous efforts were made to recover the eagles lost at Carrhae in 53 BC when Crassus was humiliatingly defeated. Legions also adopted identifying symbols: for example, the Ninth legion, which helped win the sea battle at Actium, took Neptune as its symbol.

BELOW **Etruscan-style bronze** *cornu*, **or military horn, used to call troops to battle.**

TOP **Each legion had an** *aquilifer* **to carry the eagle standard into battle.**

Organizing the troops

The basic unit of the Roman army was the legion. Originally the term was applied to the whole army and it was not until the 4th century BC that it took on the more familiar meaning of a regiment of heavy infantrymen.

The secret of the success of the legion was its flexible organization. By the 1st century BC a full-strength legion consisted of 5,120 men divided into 10 cohorts. Normal cohorts had 480 men divided into six centuries of 80 men, but the first cohort of the legion, which contained the best soldiers, had five double centuries of 160 men. Each century was led by a centurion who was promoted

1. Legion	5. Legionary
2. Cohort	6. Centurion
3. Century	7. Tribunes
4. Contubernium	8. Legate

Siege engineering

bearing the brunt of battle, and those who are not, will be clearly visible to their officers."

The shields were oval, made of wood and covered with linen and calfskin. Iron strips on the shield provided protection against sword thrusts. The main weapons were the *pilum*, a heavy javelin designed to break on impact so that it could not be thrown back by the enemy, and the *gladius*, a short thrusting sword ideal for more close-quarter fighting.

FAR LEFT **Helmets were made either of bronze, like this one, or iron.**

Arrowheads and bullets for a ballista: iron bolts and stones.

from the ranks on merit.

The smallest unit which could take independent action was the *maniple*, or "handful", made up of two centuries. Centuries were themselves divided into 10 "tents", or *contubernia*, of eight men each. The commander of the legion, the legate, who was generally a senator, had an officer staff of one prefect and six tribunes. The tribunes were the men responsible for choosing their soldiers.

Siege engineering was one of the Roman army's great strengths, and required a combination of fighting and engineering skills. A besieged fortress would be surrounded by a double line of earthworks: an inner line to kept besieged force in, an outer to keep relief forces out. Siege towers were built to mount archers or catapults for covering fire. Soldiers then advanced under shields in the *testudo*, or tortoise, formation to build a ramp for a battering ram, housed in a strong wheeled shed. This was moved up

Testudo formation – literally, tortoise.

to the base of the walls to smash a breach in them. Walls were also scaled using a mobile siege tower with a drawbridge on top. This was moved up to the walls under covering fire, then troops stormed across the bridge. Catapults were widely used in siege warfare. The largest, known as the *onager* (wild ass – after its kicking action), could hurl a 50-kilogram boulder over a distance of 400 meters. The *ballista*, a smaller catapult, was used to give covering fire for assault troops.

The Roman army's weapons for short- and long-range fighting.

Onager	Crossbow	Ballista	Bow	Javelin	30m	60m	180m

Chapter 2

Republican Life and Culture

The Romans are often portrayed as stern and unbending but, in the late republic, a very different picture of Roman society emerges from the work of the poet Catullus (c 84–54 BC). Catullus came from Verona in northern Italy: a typical rich, young Italian going to Rome to enjoy himself. His poems are personal, immediate and often irreverent, and the depth and directness of his feelings are like nothing else in Roman literature.

The most memorable poems are those Catullus wrote to his lover, Lesbia. Lesbia was actually Clodia, an educated, sophisticated – and married – aristocratic woman. The affair begins in rapture, and Catullus offers her as many kisses as there are grains of Libyan sand or stars in the sky. As she betrays him for younger lovers his disillusion is bitter.

"Give her my good-bye, her and all her lovers, whom she embraces in their hundreds...and let her not this time count on my love which has collapsed through her fault like a flower on the field's edge when touched by a passing plowshare."

The private beliefs and feelings of many Romans were greatly at odds with the public image of unflinching courage and dignity, cultivated by so many aristocratic families of the republic. Superstition was as much a part of the Roman character as was pragmatism and magic served side by side with science. Romans were not cold and formal individuals but real people with strong and desperate passions.

The education of Dionysus: this Pompeian wall painting, part of a series, shows the life of the Greek god worshiped in Rome as Bacchus.

When one of the great aristocrats of Rome died, it was the custom to display his body publicly in the Forum before it was carried off for burial. A leading member of the family would proclaim the virtues of the dead man and set his exploits alongside those of his ancestors. It was a treasured opportunity for the family to reassert its identity and its achievements.

When the aristocrat Lucius Caecilius Metellus died in 221 BC his son highlighted his exploits. Caecilius had been an impressive warrior and a valiant commander. He had excelled as an orator and had taken a major role in public affairs as a leading member of the Senate. He had gained great wealth – honorably – and left many children. Although much of this may have been exaggeration, these were the achievements that Romans generally applauded and by which each family judged its own success.

Courage in war – *virtus* – was paramount. The most prestigious rewards the state could give were for military valor: crowns for being the first into a besieged city or for saving the life of a Roman citizen. The most cherished crown was that of oak leaves, considered a greater honor than crowns of gold or silver. The greatest reward of all was the triumph, providing an unrivaled opportunity for a victor and his family to be placed on public display. Many people, unable to qualify for a triumph, would celebrate privately outside the city.

Success in war led naturally to prestige and success in a political career. Up to the 2nd century, 10 years of military service had been the minimum legal requirement for a political post. Although it was possible by the 1st century to enter public life without a career in the army, lack of military achievement remained a serious handicap. Pompey and Caesar owed their position to success in war; Marcus Crassus set out on his ill-fated expedition to Persia in 55 BC in the attempt to boost his political position through military victory and subsequent public acclaim.

While achievement in public life conferred the highest status, a Roman aristocrat could not simply rest on the acclaim of his military achievements. He was also expected to conform to certain values. One was *pietas*, the correct attitude toward the gods, shown through the observance of ritual both in the home and in public life. Another was *fides*, good faith, which defined the standards for relationships between patrons and their clients and even extended to the correct treatment of allies. The public observance of these values combined with other achievements to form a man's *dignitas*: his status or glory.

Men in public service often abuse their authority for private gain

Those whose careers took them out of Rome could do very well financially. As soon as a foreign territory had been pacified, its governors, selected for a year at a time, had every opportunity for private gain, not least from the generous allowances awarded by the Senate. As late as 61–60 BC, Julius Caesar was able to restore his depleted fortune by a successful military expedition in northwest Spain. Cicero, governor of the province of Cilicia

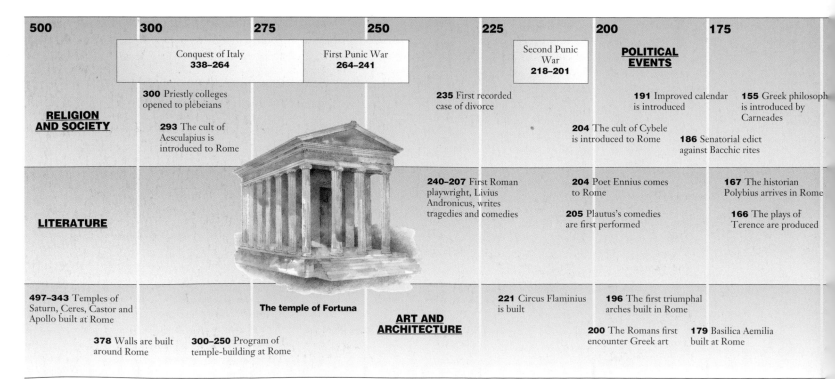

500	300	275	250	225	200	175
	Conquest of Italy 338–264		First Punic War 264–241	Second Punic War 218–201	**POLITICAL EVENTS**	

RELIGION AND SOCIETY

300 Priestly colleges opened to plebeians

293 The cult of Aesculapius is introduced to Rome

235 First recorded case of divorce

204 The cult of Cybele is introduced to Rome

191 Improved calendar is introduced

186 Senatorial edict against Bacchic rites

155 Greek philosoph is introduced by Carneades

LITERATURE

240–207 First Roman playwright, Livius Andronicus, writes tragedies and comedies

205 Plautus's comedies are first performed

204 Poet Ennius comes to Rome

167 The historian Polybius arrives in Rome

166 The plays of Terence are produced

497–343 Temples of Saturn, Ceres, Castor and Apollo built at Rome

378 Walls are built around Rome

300–250 Program of temple-building at Rome

The temple of Fortuna

ART AND ARCHITECTURE

221 Circus Flaminius is built

200 The Romans first encounter Greek art

196 The first triumphal arches built in Rome

179 Basilica Aemilia built at Rome

LEFT **Stone jars in Ostia mark where the ashes of Roman slaves are buried. A favorite slave's jar may have been paid for by his master.**

FAR LEFT **This marble memorial relief of Antistius Sarcula and his wife was erected in their honor by two of their former slaves, now freedmen.**

150	125	100	75	50	25	1BC	AD 100

3rd Punic War **149–146**

Social conflicts in Rome **133–80**

Civil wars **48–44**

139 Astrologers and Jews banished from Rome

c100 Cults of Serapis and Isis are brought to Rome

58 Altars to Isis on the Capitol are destroyed

18 Legislation against celibacy and adultery

46 The Julian calendar is introduced

12 Augustus is given the title *pontifex maximus*

149 Publication of Cato's history of Rome

55 Death of the poet Lucretius

37–30 Virgil's *Georgics* are written

19 Virgil's *Aeneid* is published

8 Ovid is banished to the Black Sea

145 Alexandrian scholars flee Ptolemy VIII; many settle in Rome

51 Caesar's *Gallic Wars* is published

35–30 Horace's *Satires* are published

77 Pliny's *Natural History* is published

62 The poet Catullus arrives in Rome

45–44 Cicero's main philosophical works are published

M. Tullius Cicero

120 Sanctuary of Fortuna at Praeneste built

80 Architectural style of wall-painting develops

55 Pompey's theater, Rome's first, is built

28–23 Vitruvius *On Architecture* is published

c50 Impressionistic style of painting develops

120 Circular temple in Forum Boarium built

80 Circular temple of Mater Matua built in Rome

50–40 Murals at Pompeii's Villa of the Mysteries painted

13 Dedication of the Theater of Marcellus

for a year, prided himself on his correct dealings but still ended up over two million sesterces richer. The unscrupulous could profit on a truly massive scale: Verres, the governor of Sicily, was accused by Cicero of having accumulated 40 million sesterces in three years.

These senior posts were not open to the equestrian class and, in addition to the rewards of military service, the main financial benefits to them came from public contracts. These contracts covered everything from the working of provincial mines and the supply of food and clothing for the army to the collection of certain taxes on behalf of the state. In addition, such activities put many equestrians in a strong position to engage in moneylending to provincial communities and client kings, sometimes at extortionate rates of interest.

ABOVE **Strewing nuts, symbolic of the casting off of childish toys and of fertility, is an important part of any wedding.**

RIGHT **Clasping hands means that a couple is now married. Here, the groom is holding a wedding contract drawn up before the ceremony.**

Marcus Porcius Cato (234–149 BC) was known as Cato the Elder. He supported the idea that Rome should completely destroy Carthage.

These new riches transformed the lives of Rome's affluent citizens. The wealth that flooded in from the east after the conquest of Greece was dazzling: gold and silver to be melted down, and slaves in their thousands to run the households of the rich. As many as 75,000 slaves may have come from the First Punic War, and another 250,000 during the first half of the 2nd century.

Much of the new wealth was lavished on conspicuous consumption. Rome became a glorious showpiece for the new empire, adorned with the plunder of the east. Grand homes were built for the first time in the city, and the old tradition of banqueting gained new life as hosts competed to provide the most ostentatious silverware and sought-after delicacies. Some people would spend more for a single pot of Black Sea caviar than for a yoke of oxen.

Old-fashioned Romans, such as Cato the Elder, railed against the new wealth. Extravagant living, he claimed, made Romans unfit to be soldiers and dissipated their family fortunes. The ancient values of Roman life were being undermined by frivolous habits, such as Greek drinking parties, imported from the east. Cato believed that Rome's traditional values developed from the land and he urged Romans to go back to living and working on their own estates.

Few people followed Cato's advice, and most of the work on the land was provided by slaves for absentee landowners. The main advantage of slaves, from the point of view of the landlord, was that they were not permitted to serve in the Roman armies. Work on the land could not stop, even during times of war.

Conditions for slaves on the land were harsh. Often they were made to work together in chains and could be dispensed with as easily as broken tools. "Sell old and unhealthy slaves," recommends Cato in *De Agricultura*, his handbook for farmers. It was largely the rural slaves who were involved in the major slave risings of the republic: one of 70,000 slaves in Sicily in 135, another in 104, and that of Spartacus in 73 BC. Spartacus was a slave from Thrace who was being trained as a gladiator in Capua. He escaped and built up a force of 70,000 slaves from the surrounding countryside. Eight Roman legions were needed to defeat him and his army.

The lot of domestic slaves was far easier. Although most slaves held menial jobs, some were highly educated people – often more so than their Roman masters. If they were lucky, they would be used as tutors, secretaries or doctors. Others who had saved a specified sum of money or who enjoyed the special favor of their masters could be given their freedom, and the ease with which slaves could be freed was a remarkable feature of Roman society. The freedmen, often with the support of their former masters, set up their own businesses as butchers, bakers or small traders. Some, however, chose to remain within their masters' families.

The family was the most important unit in Roman society, and the word *familia* referred to more than a mother and father and their children. For the upper-class Roman it was a household, with its slaves and freedmen who continued to work for the family, as well as close relatives. Caesar's mother lived in his home for at least 20 years after she became a widow. Apart from the family members who lived with him, a great man would also have, and pride himself on, numerous supporters, many of them clients hoping for favors in return for offering social support.

Roman fathers possess the power to have their sons executed

Traditionally, the Roman father (*paterfamilias*) was a figure of impressive power. In the case of divorce the father, not the mother, kept custody of the children. Fathers had the right to arrange marriages for their children, to whip or imprison their sons, to execute them or even to sell them into slavery. This "father's power" (*patria potestas*) was believed by the Romans to have originally been defined by Romulus. It was legally valid until

ABOVE **Once a couple were engaged, they would exchange gifts to signify their devotion. Rings like these, with clasped hands, and pendants with similar patterns were commonly given.**

The *paterfamilias* was the oldest male relative in a family and could be a grandfather or an uncle. If he died, a guardian was appointed for the single women.

BELOW **Some women of republican times were so inhibited about nudity they would not take off all their clothes, even to make love. The woman in this mosaic has kept on her brassiere.**

the death of the father, however old the children.

Few fathers were so harsh as to enslave or execute their children; more often they were deeply affectionate toward their children and wives. Cato, stern and unbending though he appeared in public, never missed a chance of being at his baby son's bath time. Cicero was grief-stricken when his daughter Tullia died in childbirth.

By the 1st century BC, many women retained some independence after their marriage. The most common form of marriage by this time was that of *sine manu* – without authority – in which the wife remained part of her own family and did not come formally under the authority of her hus-

band. A woman's family could even recover her dowry if her marriage ended in divorce.

However, many women began married life at a disadvantage. By custom a first marriage took place when the bride was barely past puberty, but bridegrooms often tended to be much older. Sometimes this could lead to the total domination by an older husband of his young, inexperienced bride. One 1st-century BC epitaph even tells of a woman married at the age of seven.

RIGHT **Unlike modern houses, Roman houses faced inward. Light and air came through openings in the roof above the central atrium and the peristyle. To ensure maximum privacy, none of the windows faced outward and the front rooms of a house were often rented out as shops.**

1	Ornamental pool *impluvium*	5	Kitchen
2	Atrium	6	Bedrooms
3	Living room *tablinum*	7	Master staircase
4	Dining room *triclinium*	8	Servants' staircase
		9	Upper dining room *cenaculum*
		10	Garden with peristyle
		11	Household shrine
		12	Shop

Many marriage contracts stipulated that the main aim of marriage was to produce children and, in a state where the main business was war, population growth was of great concern to the government. In 181 BC a censor, Metellus Macedonicus, publicly urged male citizens to marry and Julius Caesar, in his consulship of 59 BC, was prepared to make land available to fathers of more than three children.

However, families still remained small. Sometimes this was deliberate: all children had equal rights of inheritance and a large family could break up the family fortune. In genuine cases of infertility, which was always assumed to be on the part of the woman, a man could divorce his wife. Not every husband took advantage of this right: in a touching 1st-century BC eulogy, a husband speaks of his horror at his wife's suggestion that he divorce her, and let her help him find another wife, because she was unable to bear children. A family with daughters only could adopt a young man as heir – a useful device to ensure the continuance of the *nomen*, the family name.

One form of **birth control**, says Pliny, is two worms found in the head of a hairy spider. Tied to a woman with deerhide, the worms act as a contraceptive.

Appeasement of the gods is central to Roman private and public life

One of the most important functions of the paterfamilias was to oversee the religious rites required to maintain the well-being of the family. The origins of these rites went back to the days when families still lived off the land. Vesta was the goddess of the hearth, involved in the preservation of the household fire on which the farmers were so dependent. The cupboards of stored food had their own spirits, the Penates. Then there were gods of the household, the Lares, who traditionally guarded the boundaries of a home and all those who lived within it.

The only way for a family to keep the *pax deorum* was to follow a correct ritual. A sacred salted cake was thrown into the fire at the chief meal each day to appease Vesta. Misfortune followed when a ritual was not performed properly and the only way to regain the favor of the gods was to carry out the ritual again or discover a new formula of appeasement.

This dependence on the gods was incorporated into the public religion of Rome, and religious life was inextricably intertwined with political life. The sanction of the gods would be sought before any major public action was taken, such as the holding of an assembly or the departure of a commander for war. Temples could also serve other public functions: state treasure, for example, was housed in the temple of the god Saturn.

The priests of the state-approved cults were responsible for making sure that all rituals were carried out correctly. These priests were not chosen because they possessed any special religious authority or expertise: they were political figures. The most important priesthood, that of *pontifex maximus*, had an influential role in political decisions and was particularly prized for its prestige. Julius Caesar's election to this post in 63 BC was his first major career achievement.

There was always room for new gods. From at least the 6th century BC, as Rome progressively absorbed the culture of Greece, it assimilated and

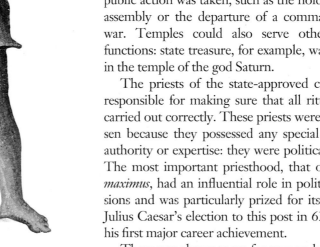

BELOW **Romans considered having no slaves at all to be a sign of extreme poverty; many people would take three slaves just to go to the baths. This young lad is an indoor slave.**

LEFT **Scrubbing brush and jug used by indoor slaves to clean floors.**

ABOVE **Slaves often had identity tags with their masters' names and addresses.**

Cybele was imported into Rome because of a Sibylline prophecy, during the invasion of Hannibal, which said that Rome would be victorious if Cybele and her sacred symbol were taken to Rome.

incorporated some of its gods as well. Romans assumed that the Greek gods, Zeus and Hera, for instance, were simply local variants of their own Jupiter and Juno. Some gods such as Aesculapius, the god of healing, were totally new to Rome.

The Greeks, on the other hand, readily gave divine status to their rulers and many Roman leaders were surprised to find themselves treated as gods. As early as 195 BC, the Greek city of Smyrna was worshiping a goddess Roma: the city of Rome itself, made a goddess. In later years a cult of Roma, linked to a prominent Roman – such as Julius Caesar – became popular throughout the empire.

One new cult imported to Rome was that of the goddess Cybele – *magna mater*, the great mother deity – adopted officially during the Second Punic War to boost Rome's morale. However, once the cult had been instituted, the Romans were horrified to discover that her worship involved frenzied initiation rites and her priests had to castrate themselves before entering her service. The cult was placed under the strict supervision of the state and Roman citizens were not allowed to become priests.

The Roman attitude to religion also led to the downfall of the cult of Bacchus – the god of wine – introduced to Rome from the east by traders. It, too, involved initiation rites, and it was alleged that the secret meetings of its devotees were drunken orgies. In 186 BC the state acted forcefully to suppress many of the ceremonies. Thereafter only the private worship of Bacchus in groups of not more than five was allowed.

The allegations of scandalous conduct, together with the distrust for forms of religious organization and authority which lay outside the control of the state authorities, were enough to arouse suspicion. Roman formal religious rituals did not require much emotional involvement, though; the popularity of the imported cults may have indicated a demand for new and more personal forms of religious activity and experience.

Following the Mithradatic Wars in the 80s, hundreds of Greeks fled in exile to Rome and so it was easy to receive direct instruction from a native in language, philosophy or rhetoric. Many young men also went abroad for a year of study in Athens or other centers in the Greek east.

Marcus Fulvius Nobilor sponsored a games in 185 which, apart from the usual program of Greek actors and wild animals, also had athletic contests, seen for the first time in Rome.

Art is the first branch of Greek culture to take hold in Rome

The more traditional Romans of the 2nd century viewed the culture of Greece with suspicion. Generally the Romans had to accept that they were second in creative skills to a people whom they had easily subdued in war, but in some areas – particularly literature – Romans did build on Greek models to create works of genius.

Art was the first facet of the new culture to reach Rome: the capture of each major eastern city provided the Romans with hundreds of new works of art. Marcus Fulvius, returning

ABOVE LEFT **The presence of bees, sacred messengers of the gods, was seen as a sign of good luck.**

LEFT **A pig-sheep-bull sacrifice was common for land purification ceremonies. The animals were garlanded and slaughtered with a special knife.**

ABOVE **A household shrine depicting the *Genius*, guardian spirit of the home, with two Lares.**

from a campaign against the Aetolians in 187, brought with him 785 bronze and 250 marble statues. In the 2nd century BC thousands of statues, bronzes and pieces of silver plate – much of it direct plunder – poured into Rome.

These riches were also widely distributed to cities throughout Italy and as far as Spain. Statues became increasingly popular as decorations for public spaces and private homes. Greek workshops turned, increasingly, to satisfying the Italian market and Greek sculptors came to seek their fortunes in Rome. By the 1st century BC they were being commissioned by Romans to create the fine character portraits of leading citizens which are a major artistic legacy of the late republic.

Greece also provided new concepts of city life, such as the city as a showplace for grand public buildings. Some of the types of buildings and materials, as

LEFT **The cult of Jupiter Optimus Maximus – the Best and the Greatest – was originally introduced to Rome by the Etruscans. The Romans adopted him as their chief god and special protector. Jupiter was responsible for weather, especially storms.**

Terence – Publius Terentius Afer (c195–c159BC) – was born in Carthage and taken to Rome as slave to a senator. He so impressed his master that he was educated and then freed.

well as structural techniques and decorative schemes, were Greek. Marble, long used by the Greeks for sculpture, was used for the first time in Rome, on a temple, in 146.

Just as important was the influence of Greece on literature: almost every form of Latin literature is based on Greek models. Early Roman playwrights introduced theater to Rome through the direct translation of Greek plays. Plautus, writing between 205 and 184 BC, is the first Roman playwright whose work survives. He had a genius for transforming original Greek plays into sparkling and witty scripts easily understood by a Roman audience. His successor was Terence, writing in the 160s. Terence used Greek originals with perennial themes: fathers' problems with their adolescent sons, sexual fulfillment versus married respectability, the status of women in society.

Greek philosophy brings peace of mind to many troubled Romans

One result of the impact of Greece was to bring the Romans face-to-face with a culture in which questioning and debate were an integral part of life. The first Greek philosophers who visited Rome were greeted with suspicion, but with Roman society undergoing profound social change, old ideas were bound to be questioned. Soon an intense interest in Greek philosophy developed among a small cultured elite, with two schools of thought proving particularly attractive to the educated Roman sophisticate.

The first of these was Epicureanism. This philosophy was developed by Epicurus, a Greek from the island of Samos who had settled to teach in Athens where he died in 270 BC. Epicurus believed that human beings were no more than a

collection of atoms which would dissolve on death. There was no afterlife, either for body or soul, and living in fear of the gods was nothing but superstition. Instead, argued Epicurus, people should live for the present world with the goal of finding peace of mind. This could be done by learning to understand and live at one with the material world which was the only reality. Epicurus also advised his followers to withdraw from the strains of public life and cultivate private friendships instead.

In the troubled society of the 1st century, Epicureanism appealed to many, and the Romans produced the most persuasive advocate of Epicureanism – the poet Lucretius. In his *De Rerum Natura* (*On the Nature of the Universe*) Lucretius applauds Epicurus for freeing men from the tyranny of superstition and then goes on to explore the meaning of a world which is made up of no more than atoms. For many philosophers this would be a sterile notion but Lucretius had an enormous appetite for the beauties of nature and the glory of all living things. His poetry is rich and sensuous and he shows a deep faith in human qualities such as affection and mutual support.

The other popular school of thought was Stoicism. Stoicism derived from the teachings of the philosopher Zeno who taught in a *stoa*, or roofed colonnade, in Athens from about

Lucretius – Titus Lucretius Carus - (c99–c55 BC) - was rumored to have been killed by a love potion which drove him mad. Very little is actually known about his life.

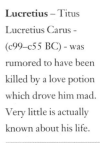

RIGHT **Music was important to Roman life; instruments such as cymbals and flutes were common.**

BELOW **Apollo, son of Jupiter and god of the sun, was the only Greek deity who retained his name and identity. He was also the god of music and poetry and is depicted here on a small fragment of a fresco, playing the lyre.**

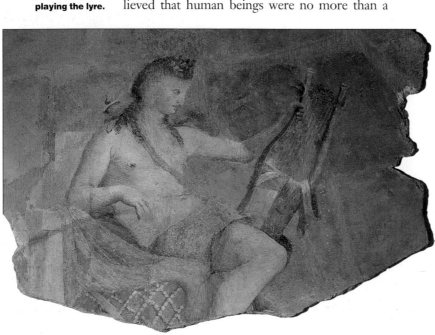

300 BC. For the Stoics, the universe was controlled by a divine power, often called Reason, which allowed it to evolve according to a defined plan. People could only find happiness if they accepted their place within this plan and learned to live in harmony with it. Misfortunes, pain and death, as part of the divine order, were to be endured without complaint and the Stoics showed how this could be achieved without sacrificing inner calm and contentment. Stoicism appealed to many Romans because it seemed at one with traditional Roman virtues of hardiness, endurance and frugal living.

By the 1st century BC the full breadth of Greek and Hellenistic culture had permeated educated Roman society. The private thoughts and public achievements of one individual – Marcus Tullius Cicero (106–43 BC) – demonstrate clearly how these two distinct cultures combined to form a completely new identity.

BELOW **Greek philosophy greatly encouraged civilized gatherings as many Romans participated in philosophical discussions.**

CICERO · WRITER AND STATESMAN

Cicero, educated in Greece and Rome, was the first Roman to achieve political success not through noble birth or military success, but through oratory alone. For him, oratory became an art in itself and he took pride in being able to construct an argument to suit any case. Cicero always acknowledged his debt to Greece, and when he wrote his handbooks on oratory he strongly recommended a study of Greek philosophy as an essential foundation for good speaking. He saw himself not as an original philosopher, but as an instructor passing on the ideas of others. As he withdrew from the political scene, he produced works in which Greek ideas were given Latin forms of expression and introduced to Roman readers.

On religion

Cicero did not believe in the literal existence of the traditional Roman gods, and considered the belief that gods had even human forms was absurd. To a Stoic, the only god was a universal principle of Reason. Similarly, Cicero was cynical about the motives for worship of the conventionally and publicly pious.

If the traditional gods whom we worship are really divine, what reason can you give why we should not include Isis and Osiris in the same category? And if we do so, why should we repudiate the gods of the barbarians? We shall therefore have to admit to the list of gods oxen and horses, ibises, hawks, asps, crocodiles, fishes, dogs, wolves, cats and many beasts besides…Either therefore this process will go on indefinitely, or we shall admit none of these and this unlimited claim of superstition will not be accepted; therefore none of these is to be accepted.

Did anyone ever render thanks to the gods because he was a good man? No, but because he was rich, honored, secure. The reason why men give to Jupiter the titles of Best and Greatest is not that they think he makes us just, temperate or wise, but safe, secure, wealthy and opulent.

LEFT **The Egyptian dog-headed god Anubis, dressed in the Roman fashion. He was sometimes combined with the Greek Hermes and called Hermanubis.**

On politics

Here, on the brink of civil war in 50 BC, Cicero compares the strengths of Caesar and Pompey.

BELOW **A coin depicting a cap of liberty and two daggers. The legend *Ides of March* refers to Caesar's murder.**

EID·MAR

About my own position I am at loss what to decide; to the Caesarians as men I am bound by ties of gratitude and friendship, while I favor the Senate's cause but hate its champions. You will of course realize that, in a case of internal dissension, men should support the side that is in the right so long as it is a matter of politics and not fighting, but the stronger side when it comes to open warfare, considering then that might is right. Now in this dispute I perceive that Pompey will have with him the Senate and the judiciary in general, while all those who have anything to fear or nothing to hope will rally to Caesar. The latter's army is incomparably the better. I only hope that we have time enough to survey the forces of each, and to choose sides.

On public life

Cicero was apparently opposed to corruption in public life, and used his considerable legal skills to bring the guilty to trial in Rome and the provinces. He was equally capable, however, of turning his skills to defending the corrupt. Here he shows his skills at their best as he attacks Gaius Verres, the corrupt governor of Sicily, in court.

I must record a fact which many witnesses can corroborate. When Gaius Verres was in Sicily, a number of people heard him saying this sort of thing on various occasions: "I have a powerful friend! Whatever I steal from the province, I am sure he will protect me. My intention is not just to make money for myself; I have mapped out the three years of my Sicilian governorship like this. I shall consider myself to be doing nicely if I can earmark one year's profit for my own use, the second year's for my protectors and counsel, and the whole of the third year's - the richest and most lucrative - for the judges who try me!"

On old age

Cicero had an unfearing attitude to death. His own death was brutal, however: he was hacked to death by Mark Antony's agents and his head and hands were nailed to the Forum's *rostra*.

All things in keeping with nature must be classified as good; and nothing is so completely in keeping with nature than that the old should die. When the same fate sometimes attacks the young, nature resists and rebels: the death of a young person reminds me of a flame extinguished by a deluge. But the death of the old is like a fire sinking and going out of its own accord, without external impulsion. In the same manner as apples, while green can only be picked by force, but after ripening to maturity fall off by themselves, so death comes to the young with violence but to old people when the time is ripe. And the thought of this ripeness so greatly attracts me that as I approach death I feel like a man nearing harbor after a long voyage: I seem to be catching sight of land.

THE ROMAN LADY

The married, upper-class Roman woman of the republic spent much of her time on domestic affairs. She was responsible for running a large household with many slaves and this involved considerable time and effort, especially if her husband was away on military service. Although early in Rome's history women were largely confined to the home, by the late republic women were much more able to appear in public and relationships between the sexes were relaxed.

The dictator Sulla's sixth wife, Valeria, for instance, did not wait for him to make the advances: she approached him at the theater and tried to draw out a thread of gold from his cloak. The Romans, however, had distinct double standards for sexual behavior. Jealous husbands often used the household slaves to spy on their wives, and penalties for adulterous women were far harsher than for men.

"If husbands suffered for their wenching in the same way as women were divorced for theirs, there would be a lot more lonely men than women about," remarks an old slave woman in one of Plautus's plays.

To sew a fine seam

Lanam Fecit – "she made the wool" – was a compliment carved on the tombstones of virtuous wives. At weddings a spindle and distaff were carried by the bride's attendants as symbols of the wife's role in charge of the home's spinning, weaving and clothmaking. It was one for which young Roman girls were trained from an early age.

Augustus reaffirmed old values by wearing clothes made only of homespun wool and his wife Livia carried on the old custom of supervising the household's weaving. By AD 50, however, these customs had died out in richer homes and the wealthy Romans bought their clothes from shops.

Roman women would use silver spindles and glass whorls, like the one below right, for spinning.

Glass, bone and bronze needles, used with the modern-looking thimbles to the far right.

Reading and writing

A young girl chews her pen in the search for just the right word.

Many women of the late republic were highly educated, but most Roman men resented women who were too intelligent or well-read. Sempronia, a well-educated, upper-class Roman matron who supported Cataline in his attempt to overthrow Cicero's government in 63-62 BC, was described in highly disapproving terms by the historian Sallust.

"Sempronia had often in the past acted with a masculine daring and boldness…She had studied Greek and Latin literature. She could play the lyre and dance, although with more skill than is necessary for an honest woman." Sallust, who was himself expelled from the Senate for immorality, adds, "and she had other talents which lead to moral dissipation", but grudgingly admits that Sempronia was "a woman of great wit and great charm."

A Roman wife needed at least elementary mathematics and writing skills so that she could run the household. A later convention was to portray women with a *stylus* (pen) and a *diptych*, a two-leaved wooden tablet spread with wax and used to send messages.

Ovid took it as a matter of course that his lovers would write him love letters and appreciate his own poetry, but there were drawbacks. "I need sympathy. That wretched writing-tablet is back, with a dismal 'No, I can't make it today'," he laments at his rejection by a lover.

Powders and paints

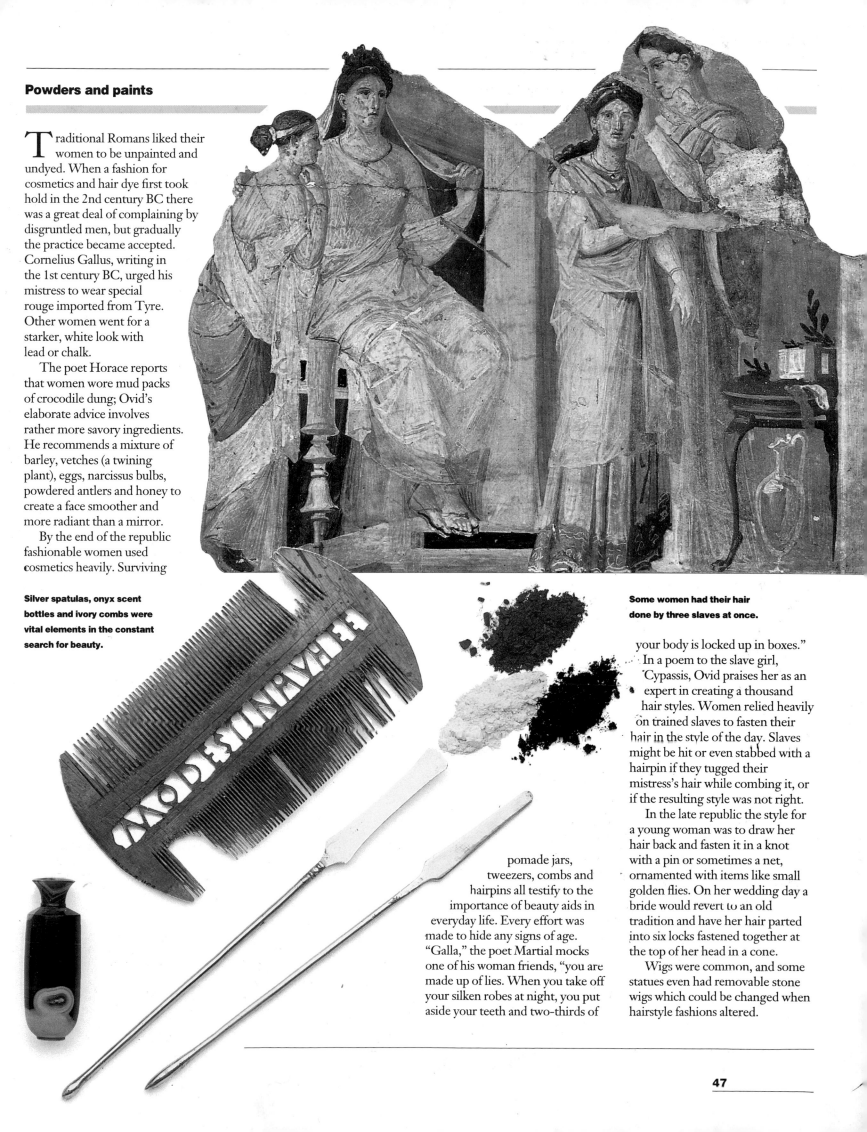

Traditional Romans liked their women to be unpainted and undyed. When a fashion for cosmetics and hair dye first took hold in the 2nd century BC there was a great deal of complaining by disgruntled men, but gradually the practice became accepted. Cornelius Gallus, writing in the 1st century BC, urged his mistress to wear special rouge imported from Tyre. Other women went for a starker, white look with lead or chalk.

The poet Horace reports that women wore mud packs of crocodile dung; Ovid's elaborate advice involves rather more savory ingredients. He recommends a mixture of barley, vetches (a twining plant), eggs, narcissus bulbs, powdered antlers and honey to create a face smoother and more radiant than a mirror.

By the end of the republic fashionable women used cosmetics heavily. Surviving

Silver spatulas, onyx scent bottles and ivory combs were vital elements in the constant search for beauty.

Some women had their hair done by three slaves at once.

pomade jars, tweezers, combs and hairpins all testify to the importance of beauty aids in everyday life. Every effort was made to hide any signs of age. "Galla," the poet Martial mocks one of his woman friends, "you are made up of lies. When you take off your silken robes at night, you put aside your teeth and two-thirds of your body is locked up in boxes."

In a poem to the slave girl, Cypassis, Ovid praises her as an expert in creating a thousand hair styles. Women relied heavily on trained slaves to fasten their hair in the style of the day. Slaves might be hit or even stabbed with a hairpin if they tugged their mistress's hair while combing it, or if the resulting style was not right.

In the late republic the style for a young woman was to draw her hair back and fasten it in a knot with a pin or sometimes a net, ornamented with items like small golden flies. On her wedding day a bride would revert to an old tradition and have her hair parted into six locks fastened together at the top of her head in a cone.

Wigs were common, and some statues even had removable stone wigs which could be changed when hairstyle fashions altered.

47

GROWING UP

"I want you to give your daughter Attica a kiss in my name," wrote Cicero to a friend, "since she is a cheerful little girl, the best thing in children." In richer households children were often regarded with pride and affection and Cicero mentioned children as something he would miss most when he went into exile. There was no doubt, however, that parents in republican times were concerned to mold their children to fit society. Behavior was carefully monitored and corrective treatment applied at the earliest sign of weakness or character defect.

The legal status of children was carefully defined. Below the age of 7 children were held not to be responsible for their own actions; girls under 12 and boys under 14 could not marry or be guilty of adultery. For a boy the crucial age was 17, the age at which he could learn to fight. A year before this he gave up the clothing of boyhood, the *toga praetexta*, and put on the *toga virilis*, the symbol of manhood, at a special ceremony and then prepared for military training. To call him a *puer* (boy) after this age was a terrible insult. This was one of the ways in which Mark Antony referred to the young Octavian, who later issued a decree forbidding any reference to himself as *puer*.

The newborn Roman

When a baby was born it was customary for the father to lift him or her from the ground into the air, a sign that the father had taken responsibility for the child as his own. A child not recognized could be left to die. In a wealthy family, a birth might be greeted with rejoicing, but in poorer families it was often the harbinger of added financial burden.

Unwanted children, especially sick male babies or girls, might be taken to lonely hillsides and left to die. In a letter from a man called Hilarion to his wife Alis, he writes, "If you have the baby before I return, if it is a boy, let it live; if it is a girl, expose it."

Swaddling in tight linen

Swaddling may not have helped the high infant mortality rates.

bands was common for newborns. "After their first experience of daylight," wrote Pliny the Elder, "children have all their limbs swaddled, a severer bondage than that of any domestic animal…there he lies crying with his hand and feet tied, the creature who is going to govern the rest."

Many women died giving birth and the infant mortality rates were extremely high. The mother of Tiberius and Gaius Gracchus bore 12 children in all but only three survived to adulthood. Women might have six or seven babies and still end up childless.

This meant there was no end of suggestions on the best way to look after young children. Cato urged that babies should be bathed in the warmed-up urine produced by an adult who had eaten cabbage. If a child would not settle to sleep, he recommended placing goat dung in its diaper. This unusual remedy was, apparently, particularly effective for girls.

Back to school

In early republican Rome most children of wealthy families were educated entirely at home, often by pedagogues – tutors who were slaves. Cato the Elder was an exception: he insisted that he do all the teaching himself. He taught his son reading, law, athletics, riding and swimming; when he began writing his *History* he copied it out in large handwriting especially so that his son could read it. For Cato only the home could provide the molding of character that was essential for a Roman citizen.

By the 1st century BC it was more common to be educated outside the home. Schools varied enormously in quality and most teachers earned little. The first school a child attended taught elementary reading, writing and mathematics. Wealthier children would move on at the age of 11 to a *grammaticus* where they would

learn poetry by heart. Clear speaking and pronunciation were enouraged, and it was at this stage that the child would learn Greek. Later training with a *rhetor* would set up the young upper-class Roman as an orator able to make his way in the courts. For a lucky few, education might be completed with some time in Greece.

Wax tablets, used with a bone stylus; reed pens took ink.

ABOVE **Glass and pottery marbles.**

LEFT **Four knucklebone faces provided 35 game combinations.**

Boys at play with nuts, marbles and knucklebones.

The life of the Roman child was rich in games and play was regarded as a natural part of growing up. The first toy was usually a *sistrum*, a rattle, often made in pottery in the shape of a bird with pebbles inside. Older babies had a collection of playthings, *crepundia*, threaded onto a string for them to handle. These toys were often tied round the shoulder.

For older children there was a wide range of activities: as Horace says, "building toy houses, harnessing mice to a little cart, playing odds and evens, riding a long stick." Boys enjoyed playing at imitating adult occupations: gladiators, soldiers and judges.

Nuts were often used like marbles, and were particularly popular. They were rolled together and thrown into the necks of pottery vases or onto marked gaming boards. Nut games were so common that the phrase "giving up your nuts" was used to describe the moment when a child formally started going to school.

Girls were given dolls though few survive apart from some rag dolls preserved in Egypt. These are not baby dolls; they are more like women of marriageable age, as if providing a role model for young girls. Just before girls married they dedicated their dolls to Venus to acknowledge the fact that they were now moving to a new status.

A child's well-loved rag doll.

SUPERSTITIONS AND RELIGIOUS RITUALS

Superstition, according to the historian Polybius, was an important facet of the Roman state and character: "The quality in which the Roman commonwealth is most distinctly superior is in my opinion the nature of their religious convictions…Since every multitude is fickle, full of lawless desires, unreasoned passion, and violent anger, the multitude must be held in by invisible terrors and suchlike pageantry."

There were no gods exclusive to Rome: the major state gods of the city had their origins in the ancient part of the Italian peninsula and throughout Italy minor gods and goddesses continued to hold local appeal. So long as Roman gods were not mocked, or state control threatened, the government and priesthood were tolerant of local beliefs.

The priesthood was not a professional body, but was chosen from among the aristocracy. The most important priests were the pontiffs, who supervised the calendar and the state festivals, and the augurs, who were responsible for divination – by means of animal entrails – to discover whether or not the gods approved of any proposed course of action.

The cult of the earth mother

The traditional religion of republican Rome was overwhelmingly masculine, rational and ritualistic. Despite the presence of many ancient Italian goddesses there remained a deep need for a celebration of the feminine. This is perhaps why the cult of the great Mother Goddess Cybele, brought to Rome at the height of the First Punic War, was so popular.

Cybele's homeland was Anatolia – the land of Troy and the original home of Aeneas, forefather of Rome. This is one reason why the Romans were so drawn to her.

The great mother goddess was worshiped alongside her consort Attis. According to legend, Attis, a shepherd, loved by Cybele, had betrayed her by falling in love with a nymph. In her fury Cybele made him fall into a fit of madness during which he castrated himself and bled to death under a pine tree. Attis was later reborn and he was then reunited with Cybele.

Cybele's annual festival took place in March and the most fervent of her worshipers proved their devotion by castrating themselves under a pine tree to celebrate Attis's rebirth.

Elaborate clamps, perhaps for use in a castration ritual.

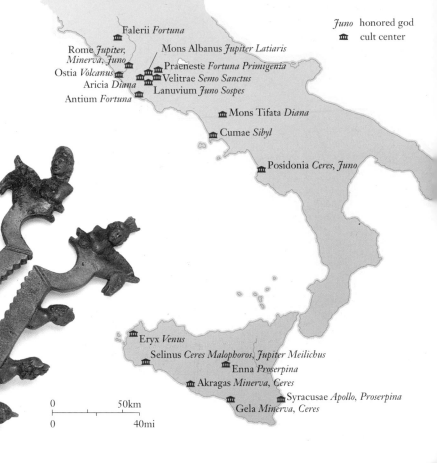

Provincial cult centers

Southern Italy had a wide variety of cults, including shrines to the main Roman deities. The many ancient Italian goddesses, such as Fortuna, a goddess of fertility, Ceres, the corn goddess, and Diana, the wood goddess, had their own centers for local worship.

Despite their tolerance, the Romans preferred to maintain the primacy of Rome in Italy; the state set up a major temple for each cult in Rome, thus undermining the popularity of local shrines.

Juno honored god
🏛 cult center

Falerii *Fortuna*
Rome *Jupiter, Minerva, Juno*
Mons Albanus *Jupiter Latiaris*
Praeneste *Fortuna Primigenia*
Ostia *Volcanus*
Velitrae *Semo Sanctus*
Aricia *Diana*
Lanuvium *Juno Sospes*
Antium *Fortuna*
Mons Tifata *Diana*
Cumae *Sibyl*
Posidonia *Ceres, Juno*

Eryx *Venus*
Selinus *Ceres Malophoros, Jupiter Meilichus*
Enna *Proserpina*
Akragas *Minerva, Ceres*
Syracusae *Apollo, Proserpina*
Gela *Minerva, Ceres*

0   50km
0   40mi

"Depravities of every kind"

When the wine had inflamed their minds, and the dark night and the intermingling of men and women, young and old, had smothered every feeling of modesty, depravities of every kind began to take place because each person had ready access to whatever perversion his mind so inclined him…The violence was concealed, however, because the shrieks of those tortured by deviant sex or murder could not be heard over the loud wails and the crash of drums and cymbals.

Livy, in *A History of Rome*, with a traditional view of Bacchanalia.

Making decisions by the book

Sibyl, or Sibylla, was a mythical prophetess of ancient Greece, originally a royal Trojan maiden. Apollo endowed her with a prophetic ability and when she spoke her sayings were recorded on a palm leaf. According to Roman legend, a collection of her sayings – the Sibylline books – was sold to Tarquinius Superbus, the last king of the Roman world.

In later years many sites were associated with her oracles. The most famous of the shrines from which she was said to have prophesied was the cave at Cumae in southern Italy, and she continued to be venerated there.

The Sibylline Books were housed in the temple of Jupiter on the Capitoline Hill, with 15 priests assigned to look after them. At times of state emergency – war, civil disorder, plague – the Senate could order them to be consulted.

It was the Sibylline books' recommendation that the cults of Cybele and Aesculapius be brought to Rome and, according to the Greek historian Dionysius, "…the Romans guard no other possession, whether sacred or profane, as they guard the Sibylline oracles."

By the end of the republic the practice of consulting the books had almost completely died out.

ABOVE **The rock-hewn entrance to the cave of Sibyl at Cumae.**

RIGHT **Peonies were thought to have magic curative powers.**

This 1st-century AD wall-painting from a *columbarium*, a building for funeral urns, depicts a Bacchanalian revel.

THE GREEK IDEAL

The first Roman response to the riches of the Greek world was cautious. The new culture was totally alien to traditional Romans; it appeared to be based on materialism and the active pursuit of pleasure for its own sake – a direct threat to the more frugal Roman way of life. Even Greek philosophy, according to Plutarch, was viewed with alarm by Cato: "As soon as this passion for discussion came flowing into the city, Cato was concerned that the youth, by diverting their ambitions toward philosophy, would prefer to gain a reputation as men of words rather than of deeds and military campaigns."

However, the lure of this massive wealth of the east soon proved irresistible. Greek art became so popular as a badge of culture and fashion that Greek craftsmen were soon in a position to exploit the Roman market, and many collectors of things Greek accumulated what they could, often with little appreciation of the culture which had produced it.

Theater was one of the many cultural imports from Greece. Greek plays – especially the comedies adapted for Roman audiences – became highly popular, and were usually presented as part of festivals or games. The theater itself would be a temporary building of wood faced by wooden seats. It was not until 55 BC that Pompey gave Rome its first stone theater.

The body beautiful

Rome shared with Greece an old tradition of commemorating its most successful men with public statues. Part of the tradition which Rome did not originally share was to portray these men in the nude. In the first century BC, once the passion for all things Greek swept Rome, the tradition began to change, and by the end of the century nude statues were much more acceptable.

A common practice of the Greek sculptors working for the Roman market was simply to add the head of the subject to a mass-produced nude body. Most statues were simply copies, others were faked originals, but all seem to have found a ready market in Rome.

Nude statue, possibly of Marcellus, nephew of Augustus.

Art and mythology

Triton, half man, half fish, was the son of Poseidon, lord of the sea. This demigod was also adopted by the Romans, and in this sculpture he is shown carrying off a hapless sea nymph.

Architecture and Roman styles

The influence of Greece on Rome was as profound in architecture as it was in the rest of art. The Greek temple style, using columns and porticos, was adopted for Roman use; decorative columns – the Greek orders of architcture – were also borrowed.

The original two orders were Doric and Ionic, developed by the two main Greek peoples. The later and more elaborate Corinthian order was first brought to Rome by Sulla when he looted columns from the temple of Olympian Zeus in Athens.

Although created by the Greeks, and first used in the 5th century BC on a temple to Apollo at Bassae, the Corinthian order proved more popular among the Romans as the Greeks found the more intricate patterns too awkward to carve.

The Romans made this order even more elaborate than the original Greek concept. The resulting Composite style was later raised to a formal order at the end of the 1st century BC.

The Composite order: Corinthian in style with Ionic scrolls.

Lucius Calpurnius Piso, consul in 58 BC, and father to Caesar's third wife, Calpurnia, had served a command in Macedonia and it may have been there that he acquired an interest in Greek and Hellenistic art. In his home in Herculaneum, he kept no fewer than 87 bronze statues and 1,000 scrolls of papyri. This Villa of the Papyri, as it is known, served centuries later as a model for the J Paul Getty museum in California.

The statues in Piso's home provide a vivid record of a rich and cultivated republican Roman's taste in Greek art. There were copies of classical Greek statues and of others in the earlier Archaic style. There was a set of 18 busts of Greek philosophers, poets and orators and a group of portraits of Hellenistic kings and generals. There were only two – unattributed – portraits

of Romans and not a single statue of anyone from Piso's family.

Piso, like so many republican Romans, was anxious to impress his visitors with his appreciation and knowledge of Greek culture to the virtual exclusion of anything Roman. Later in the century the obsession with statues had begun to fade and attention turned instead to wall painting.

In the villa at Boscoreale near Pompeii (about 40 BC) the 3rd-century Greek philosopher Menedemos is portrayed in such a way as to suggest that philosophy could inspire good government – a novel concept for traditional, pragmatic Romans.

A house in Rome of the same date had a whole set of scenes from Homer's *Odyssey,* a popular theme with Romans seeking Greek culture. Other painters – almost all Greek – reproduced famous Greek classical originals on the walls of provincial villas. By now the legends and mythology of Greece had become fully assimilated into Roman culture.

"Your support of the theater"

Now, listen politely to my request. I am again introducing Terence's play The Mother-in-Law, although I have never yet been able to find a quiet attentive audience for it. Bad luck has dogged it. A favorable response from you, however, and your support of my efforts, will put an end to this bad luck.

The first time I tried to present this play, my rivals for an audience were some famous boxers and then a tightrope walker as well. People gathered in noisy groups; there were shouts, and women's shrieks, and all this commotion forced us off the stage before the play was over.

So, in order to give this new play another chance, I tried an old trick: I staged it a second time. And I was successful in holding the audience – at least to the end of the first act. But then a rumor spread that some gladiators were going to perform – and my audience flew off in a huge crowd, pushing, shouting, fighting to get a good spot at the gladiator performance. Well, I really couldn't keep my show going.

Today, however, there is no unruly mob. Everything is calm and quiet. I have been given a golden opportunity to stage this play, and you have been given the chance to pay honor to the dramatic arts. Don't allow, by your neglect, music and drama to fade away, appreciated by only a few. Let your support of the theater promote and encourage my own.

As I have never greedily put a price value on my own talent, as I have always maintained adamantly that my greatest concern was how best to serve your pleasure, so then now allow me this request. Terence, the playwright, has on good faith entrusted his work, indeed his very self, to my care and to your attention. Don't let wicked critics laugh wickedly at him, attacking him on all sides.

Please, understand his situation and give us your undivided attention, so that other playwrights may be willing to write and to that I may be encouraged in the future to buy and produce new plays.

Terence, *Hecrya* (*The Mother-in-Law*). This play was performed at a funeral games in 160 BC.

An informal atmosphere: this mosaic depicts actors rehearsing for a performance.

Chapter 3

The Emperors of Rome

After Octavian's victory at Actium in 31 BC, he was the undisputed ruler of the Roman world. Although he was formally known as *princeps* – first citizen – and his adopted forename of Imperator was not used as a title for over half a century, he was the first emperor of Rome, and he established the most enduring institutions of the new regime.

A successful emperor had to be many things: a conscientious administrator, a successful commander in chief and the fountain of justice, accessible to petitioners from all over the empire. Some emperors also took on the role of public benefactor: providing free grain, encouraging public building and sponsoring shows. Ultimately, in a predominantly rural and undeveloped economy, an emperor could do little more than keep the machinery of government working smoothly and coordinate opposition to Rome's enemies. The best carried out this task efficiently; some exploited their position for personal gain. Only a few emperors made dramatic changes to the policies and structures that underpinned the empire.

The post of first citizen was quickly accepted as hereditary. When an emperor had a son, the title passed to him – sometimes with disastrous results. If he had no son, he could adopt one who then became heir to the title, making the process of succession smoother. For three centuries, the emperor embodied the most powerful symbol of the unity of the empire. During his life he was given a near-divine status, and after his death the Senate could declare him a god.

Detail from the *Ara Pacis Augustae*, the altar of peace proclaiming the greatness of Augustus. Here (far left) he is shown as a father figure.

By 30 BC, the wars which had torn the Roman world apart for 20 years were over. Octavian, at the age of 33, controlled an army of 280,000 men and had amassed vast personal wealth, seized from the collapsed dynasty of Egypt. He returned to Rome in 29 BC and celebrated the defeat of his enemies in three days of triumph.

The rejoicing did not prevent the wealthy senatorial families of the city from being uneasy about Octavian's return with his armies. These great families had, through their control in the Senate, dominated the running of the republic. It had been made clear, from the rule of Julius Caesar, that a military dictatorship was a threat to their power and prestige. Octavian appeared to be on the brink of becoming another dictator.

Octavian's claim of a "restored republic" is a clever tactical bid for power

However, Octavian appeared to have no such ambitions. He soon disbanded a large part of his army, using his personal wealth to find land for the discharged soldiers. He continued as consul, one of the traditional posts of the republic, offering himself for reelection each year. Then, in 27 BC, in an unexpected move, he offered all his powers back to the Senate with the claim that he was actually restoring the republic.

It was not a selfless offer. Octavian was a clever politician. His sole power was based on extraordinary measures which could not be maintained indefinitely. He wanted to keep that power, but could not easily proclaim himself king or dictator,

and he realized the need for a new approach.

The concept of the "restored republic" was a brilliant solution. Octavian knew that he had an enormously strong position as the man who brought the civil wars to an end and restored peace. He was indispensable, and counted on the Senate having to define for him some central role in the government of the empire.

The Senate's first response was to offer this savior of the state the direct administration of the provinces of Gaul, Syria and Spain, in addition to Egypt, for the next 10 years. It was in these provinces that the bulk of the Roman army was stationed and so, indirectly, the Senate was confirming Octavian as supreme military commander. A few days later a new name – Augustus, or revered one – was devised especially for the purpose and bestowed on Octavian. The eighth month of the year was also renamed in his honor.

New powers came in 23 BC, a year in which Augustus fell ill and nearly died. He surrendered the post of consul with its heavy burden of administrative duties and, in return, he was given power as proconsul to intervene over the heads of any provincial governors and also to exercise direct authority over the whole army. Another power followed: that of tribune of the people. This had been one of the most important posts in the republic, representing the interests of the people rather than the Senate. It included the right to summon the Senate and to veto any of its laws. Augustus particularly valued the power of this post because it gave the illusion that his leadership rested on the will of the people.

Augustus's position now rested upon a clever combination of his wartime authority and the

The word **republic** comes from the Latin *res publica*: public matter, or the affairs of the people. Institutions of republican Rome were actually biased heavily in favor of the aristocratic minority.

LEFT **The snake was a common image in Roman art and jewelry and was believed to have powers over a family's well-being.**

100 BC		AD 1		50		100		150
DYNASTIES		The Julio-Claudian dynasty **27 BC–AD 68**			The Flavian dynasty **69–138**			
THE EMPERORS OF ROME	**46–44** Julius Caesar is dictator in Rome	**14** Death of Augustus and accession of Tiberius	**54–68** Nero is emperor of Rome; in 59 he orders the execution of his mother Agrippina	**79–81** Titus is emperor, succeeded by Domitian	**117–138** After the death of Trajan, Hadrian succeeds			
	27 Octavian becomes emperor and is granted the title of Augustus	**27** Tiberius retires to Capri		**97–98** After the death of Domitian, Nerva is emperor. He is followed by Trajan	**138–161** Antoninus Pius rules in Rome			
	2BC Augustus adopts Tiberius as his heir	**37** Caligula is emperor, followed by Claudius in 41	**68–69** The year of four emperors (Galba, Otho, Vitellius, Vespasian)					
			69–79 Vespasian is undisputed emperor					
WARS AND MONUMENTS	**58–51** Caesar's conquest of Gaul	**9** Defeat of Roman army by Germans, but by 16 the defeat is reversed	**43** Invasion of Britain, led by Claudius	**70** Siege and destruction of Jerusalem	**105–106** Conquest of Dacia by Trajan			
	49–48 Civil war between Caesar and Pompey		**61** Revolt of the Iceni in Britain under Boudicca	**113** Trajan's Column is erected in Rome				
	31 Defeat of Cleopatra of Egypt and Antony by Octavian at Actium		**80** Inauguration of the Colosseum in Rome	**114–116** Conquest of Armenia and Mesopotamia				

bundle of political powers granted to him by the Senate. In perpetuating his monarchical rule within the framework of the "restored republic", he had avoided the charge of kingship or tyranny, and had created for himself an unassailable position of legitimate leadership.

Augustus's formal title was that of *princeps*, which meant no more than first citizen and had been given to prominent citizens before, but he was in effect, emperor. He set up house on the Palatine Hill overlooking the Forum, and kept a household of personal servants, close friends and acquaintances to conduct his business.

Augustus was scrupulous in the way he treated the Senate. He addressed its members by their correct titles and attended their family celebrations. He consulted leading members on issues of policy, giving the impression that he valued their opinions. He rarely advertised his military powers and the Senate's effective loss of power to the emperor was a painless process which few senators appeared to contest.

Further honors were bestowed on Augustus. He became *pontifex maximus*, the religious head of state, in 12 BC and was acclaimed *pater patriae*, father of the country, in 2 BC. Augustus manipulated his image carefully. Although he was reluctant to allow adulation to go too far, he was increasingly revered as a god figure, particularly in the east of the empire. A cult of Rome and Augustus spread from the east as far as Gaul in the west. His statues were designed for the maximum propaganda effect. Particularly important was his role as bringer of peace, one which was commemo-

RIGHT **The Gemma Augustea: a beautiful carved sardonyx cameo, made for propaganda purposes, shows Tiberius and the deified Augustus.**

rated in the *Ara Pacis*, his altar of peace in Rome.

With his position consolidated Augustus set about transforming the administration of his empire, and in this he showed his true genius. He reformed the Senate, purging it of unworthy members and choosing most of the provincial governors and army commanders from the remainder. Determined to find able administrators he also drew on the equestrians, using their talents in the administration of the empire.

Augustus was conservative; he honored the customs and traditions of the past, ones rooted in

Augustus carried out a rebuilding program in the city of Rome. This program included the restoration of over 80 temples to the old gods.

150	200	250	300	500

The Antonine dynasty **139–192**	The Severan dynasty **193–235**		**306** Constantine becomes Augustus of the western empire	
161 Marcus Aurelius becomes emperor	**193–211** Septimius Severus rules as emperor of Rome	**222–235** Alexander Severus is emperor	**270** After 13 emperors in 35 years, Aurelian succeeds	**323** Constantine establishes himself as sole ruler of the empire
180–192 Commodus is emperor	**212–217** Caracalla is emperor, followed by Elagabalus (until 222)		**275** Aurelian is followed by six emperors in nine years	**395** The empire is permanently divided into east and west
			284 Accession of Diocletian (until 305); he sets up a tetrarchy (system of four rulers)	**476** Deposition of the last western emperor, Romulus Augustulus
164–166 The equestrian statue of Marcus Aurelius is erected	**217** The Baths of Caracalla are completed	**249** Defeat of the Goths in Thrace relieves the threat to the eastern empire temporarily	**270** Eastern Dacia is abandoned to the Goths	**315** The Arch of Constantine is built in Rome
167 Invasions of the northern and eastern provinces of the empire by barbarians	**222** Sasanian dynasty succeeds in Persia	**253** Wars against German invaders	**270** New walls are built around Rome by Aurelian	**410** Sack of Rome by the Visigothic leader Alaric
		259 Emperor Valerian captured by the Persians		**455** Sack of Rome by the Vandals

his own childhood, and aimed to restore them. Worship of the older gods of Rome was encouraged and many temples restored. Augustus extolled the stability of marriage and passed harsh new laws against adulterers. Many Romans resented these intrusions into their private lives but the emphasis on the past was valuable in consolidating the new regime. To Roman thinking, restoration was the best kind of reform.

Augustus now had to turn to Rome's extensive possessions overseas. He was reluctant to follow the republican policy of brutal expansion into new territories and exploitation of their resources. He knew that continuous warfare would threaten his carefully constructed political settlement and could also encourage challengers to his own position. The Roman legions were not, however, idle.

Augustus ensures his choice of heir to the position of emperor

The Spanish interior was ruthlessly conquered and there was a major military expansion north in an attempt to establish a stable frontier for the empire along the Elbe and Danube. This ended in disaster in AD 9 when a Roman general, Varus, and three legions were caught by German tribes in the dense Teutoburg forest and massacred.

Augustus, now an old man, was badly shocked by the experience. Expansion was halted and a border established farther west along the Rhine. He avoided conflict in the east because a war with Rome's most powerful enemy, Parthia, would be costly and ultimately futile.

Augustus died in AD 14. His achievements had been extraordinary: he had created a stable, well-administered empire that was to last for centuries. The major problem was that of the succession. Augustus's powers had been granted to him by the Senate for life; would his power be passed, on his death, to another single figure, thus creating a new institution as a permanent part of the Roman constitution? Augustus had made several attempts to nominate a recognized successor. After many setbacks, including the deaths of his two grandsons, Gaius and Lucius, he forced his stepson Tiberius into a loveless marriage with his daughter Julia. He then adopted Tiberius as his son and made it quite clear that he was to be the successor. In AD 13, the year before Augustus died, Tiberius had been made the emperor's equal in terms of political power. He was highly experienced and a good administrator: no one had been consul more often or commanded more armies and provinces. However, Tiberius lacked the confidence and personal touch of

Augustus and his relations with the Senate soon broke down. In AD 26, aging and saddened by the death of his son Drusus, Tiberius withdrew to the island of Capri – amid much speculation about depraved behavior in the privacy of his secluded villa. Back in Rome plots and tensions flourished in the political vacuum that was created.

When Tiberius died in 37 there was undisguised – but very short-lived – relief. Tiberius's successor was a great-nephew, Gaius Julius, known as Caligula. He was 24 when he succeeded, a welcome contrast, at first, to Tiberius. It soon became clear, though, that he was not emotionally equipped to handle virtually limitless power.

Caligula claimed that he was already a god, and squandered the vast riches of the treasury to indulge his whims to the full. There was no constitutional way of withdrawing an emperor's powers: the only way to remove Caligula was murder. In AD 41 he was stabbed to death by his bodyguard.

The experience of Caligula was so sobering that there was, briefly, talk in the Senate of restoring the republic. Before a decision was made the Praetorian Guard stepped in – as personal bodyguards to the emperor, they had most to lose if the republic was restored. It was in their interests to find a new emperor quickly and they did: Claudius, an uncle of Caligula, who was discovered cowering behind a curtain in the imperial palace. The Praetorians then forced the Senate to accept their choice of emperor.

Claudius was not an obvious first choice for emperor. Handicapped as a child and left with a shaking head and a bad limp, he had always been treated with contempt by the imperial household. Left to himself, he had time to study and develop an interest in the problems of the empire. His initial position as emperor was weak as he had no links with the army. He immediately set about planning an invasion of Britain. It took place in 43 and Claudius hurried north to be at the head of his troops for their final victories. He then returned to Rome to claim a triumph.

Claudius consolidated the position of the emperor at the center of government by appointing a group of freedmen as secretaries of state, each of them responsible for a particular area of administration. The countless petitions which came in from all over the empire could now be handled more efficiently and matters of justice and finance attended to. Claudius also took a great interest in the provinces. He knew that the human resources from the provinces were vital and he encouraged wealthy provincials to become romanized and seek their fortunes in the capital.

Despite his public achievements, Claudius's private life was a shambles. He had his third wife, Messalina, executed for conspiracies and sexual excesses, and was probably poisoned by his fourth wife, Agrippina, who was determined to ease her own son Nero onto the imperial throne.

The choice of emperor moves clearly from the Senate to the army

Nero was only 16 when he became emperor and at first was influenced by sober advisers such as Seneca, the Spanish philosopher. A change came in 59 when Nero arranged for the murder of his dominating mother, and then his megalomania was allowed full play. When a fire devastated Rome in AD 64 Nero built an enormous palace in the ruins of the city. The Domus Aurea, or Golden House, had a 35-meter-high statue of him in its hall and, with its grounds, covered an area one-third the size of Central Park in modern New York. He also embarrassed more traditional senators by performing in music and drama competitions in Greece and Rome, fixing the results so that he was always the winner.

Nero's greatest mistake was to neglect the army. In 68, one of the provincial governors of Gaul revolted and was joined by the governor of northern Spain, Sulpicius Galba, whose troops proclaimed him emperor. Nero committed suicide and the family of Augustus died with him.

With the extinction of the first imperial family of Rome there was a vacuum at the center of the empire. No one seriously considered abolishing the post of emperor but the choice now rested with the armies, not the Senate, which simply gave formal recognition to the latest successful military nominee. Despite being accepted by the Senate, Galba lasted less than seven months. Two other generals, Otho and Vitellius, reigned briefly in 69. The final victor was another general, Titus Flavius Vespasianus, who won the support of the armies of the east and along the Danube frontier. Vespasian controlled Egypt and threatened to cut off the grain supply to Rome. The senators accepted him as emperor, but Vespasian showed where power really lay by dating his rule not from when the Senate first recognized him but from when he had first been acclaimed by his troops.

He was the first of the "Flavian" emperors,

When the young **Nero** first had to sign death warrants, he lamented, "Why did they teach me to write?"

BELOW **Tiberius, in his youth, was nicknamed Biberius Caldius Mero (a play on his own name of Tiberius Claudius Nero) meaning, literally, "drinker of wine with no water added".**

LEFT **Gaius Caesar's nickname of Caligula came from the miniature** *caligae* **or military boots he wore as a child; it meant "little boots", or "bootikins".**

along with his sons Titus (79–81) and Domitian (81–96). Vespasian was experienced and energetic, working tirelessly to reform the finances of the empire and restore discipline to the army after the breakdown of 68 to 69. Both he and Domitian campaigned along the borders of the empire defeating troublesome tribes and establishing forts and watchtowers along the more vulnerable areas.

Vespasian was the first in his family to become a senator. The Flavians remained outsiders to the old ruling circles of Rome, but although their power rested with the armies, Vespasian went out of his way to retain the support of the Senate. The tension between the ideals of a republic and the actuality of a monarchy still increased, and under Domitian the relationship between Senate and emperor broke down completely. Domitian was far more interested in maintaining efficient administration than in trying to mollify the senatorial aristocracy. When he was murdered in AD 96 the Senate immediately erased his name from all the public monuments he had built and quickly moved in one of its more distinguished members, Nerva, as the new emperor.

Nerva was 60 when he succeeded and he had no links with the army. The Senate had created a precarious situation which was unlikely to last. However, Nerva cleverly designated as his successor an experienced army commander, Marcus Ulpius Traianus (Trajan), who was known to the Senate, having been a consul in 91. Trajan was remarkable in that he was the first emperor to come from outside Italy. His family, though Italian in origin, had settled in Spain generations before.

Trajan was a man of action who could lead without force or cruelty. He conceded to the members of the senatorial classes their traditional status in imperial administration – but there was never any doubt that power ultimately lay in his hands. He intervened so much in the running of the empire that he may have stifled local initiative.

As commanders in chief of the army, the emperors had the duty of defining military policy. It was in line with Trajan's adventurous nature that he launched campaigns of expansion. The most immediate threat to the empire came from the Dacians, north of the Danube. Under an able leader, Decabalus, they had proved a match for Domitian. Trajan determined to destroy them, but it took two hard-fought campaigns for Roman victory. Trajan created a new province from the land, moving settlers into the area to make it one of the most romanized parts of the empire. The gold of Dacia was brought back in triumph to Rome and used by Trajan to build a vast forum and marketplace, dominated by a column decorated with reliefs glorifying his campaigns.

Trajan's final campaigns were less successful. He was determined to crush that old enemy of Rome, Parthia. At first all went well. Trajan annexed Armenia, the traditional buffer between the two empires, and then moved into Parthia itself.

BELOW **Claudius, who limped and slobbered, and whose mother called him a monster. This head, broken from a full-figure statue, shows him in a more flattering light.**

Trajan propounded the theory that a person was innocent until proven guilty. It was better, he said, for a guilty person to go unpunished than for an innocent person to be condemned on suspicion alone.

BELOW **Nero, who was suspected of setting fire to Rome himself so that he would gain glory and the acclaim of the people by rebuilding the city.**

Its western capital, Ctesiphon, surrendered as he approached. Moving down the Tigris river, Trajan reached the Persian Gulf and was said to have lamented that he was too old to move further eastward in the steps of Alexander the Great. He was exhausted. It soon became clear that his conquests could not be held and that the Romans had established no effective control over the vast plains of Mesopotamia. Trajan died in 117.

The next emperor, Hadrian (117–38), followed a very different policy. He realized that the empire was overstretched and needed to be consolidated within stable and defensible borders. The most famous of these borders was Hadrian's Wall in the north of Britain, but the same policy was followed throughout the empire. Legions and ancillary troops were given permanent bases in vulnerable areas.

Hadrian was a restless man and indulged his love of Greek culture by traveling widely in his empire. It was a peaceful and well-administered empire that he left to his chosen successor and adopted son, Antoninus Pius (138–161). Antoninus Pius, from a Roman family settled in southern Gaul, was quiet and mild-mannered. He preferred to stay in Rome, ruling the empire cautiously along the lines established by Hadrian.

In the middle years of the 2nd century the empire seemed to have achieved a perfect balance. The emperor was obeyed without question as supreme lawgiver, commander of the armies, controller of administration and maker of imperial policy. Talent was drawn in from the provinces, as the backgrounds of the emperors themselves showed, and the abler members of the equestrian class were increasingly used in administration. Under Antoninus the Senate was still accorded respect though its institutional role was minimal. Individual senators were still called on as army

THE GROWTH OF THE EMPIRE

Though most of the land area conquered by Rome had already been won in republican times, expansion continued up to the reign of Trajan. The mingling of the diverse peoples of the empire was stimulated by army service and the settling of veterans in special colonies.

- ■ provincial capital
- ● Augustan colony
- — province boundary
- Roman empire 44BC
- acquisitions to AD13
- acquisitions to AD96
- acquisitions to AD117

0 ——— 600 km
0 ——— 400 mi

North Sea

BRITANNIA
Londinium ■

Colonia Agrippina ■
GERMANIA INFERIOR
Rhine
Moguntiacum ■
BELGICA
GALLIA LUGDUNENSIS
Durocortorum ■
GERMANIA SUPERIOR
Augusta Vindelicorum ■
RAETIA
NORICUM
Virunum ■
Carnuntum ■
AQUITANIA
Lugdunum ■
Burdigala ●
Axima ■
Segusio
ALPES POENINAE
ALPES COTTIAE
ALPES MARITIMAE
PANNONIA
Aquinc
Sirmizeg
NARBONENSIS
Narbo ■
Cemenelum ■
ITALIA
Viminacium ■
Salonae
MO SUPE
TARRACONENSIS
CORSICA
Aleria ■
DALMATIA
Rome
LUSITANIA
Tarraco ■
Emerita Augusta ■
MACEDO
BAETICA
Corduba ■
SARDINIA
Carales ■
Tingi ■
Caesarea ■
Carthage ●
Syracuse
EPIR
ACI
MAURETANIA TINGITANA
MAURETANIA CAESARIENSIS
SICILIA
AFRICA
Cy
Mediterranean S

LEFT **Hadrian's policy was consolidation, rather than expansion, of the Roman empire.**

commanders and provincial governors.

However, everything depended on peace. The frontiers of the empire were so extended and – in relation to their length – so weakly guarded that any major threat could bring disaster. Shrewd emperors realized this and concentrated their efforts on keeping the tribes outside either divided or pacified by Roman money. On Antoninus's death storm clouds began to gather. In the east the Parthians were on the move. Along the frontier of the Upper Danube tribes were settling their differences and uniting to threaten the borders. The emperor who was called on to confront Rome's enemies was Antoninus's adopted son, Marcus Aurelius (161–80), who ruled at first with an adoptive brother, Lucius Verus.

At the time of his accession, Marcus Aurelius had no military experience. However, his reign was one of almost continual warfare and he struggled heroically to maintain the frontiers of the empire against incessant attack. The cost was enormous, but these frontiers were still intact when he died. Marcus Aurelius was one of the great emperors.

In strong contrast to Marcus Aurelius was his son, Commodus, who was proclaimed Caesar in 166 and became sole emperor following his father's death in 180. Commodus spent his 12-year reign largely in Rome. He claimed the city as his private property, renaming it Commodiana, and lived a life of debauchery. His particular obsession was showing off his physical strength against wild beasts in the arena. Favorites fought over the spoils of power until Commodus was strangled by one of his wrestling partners.

Commodus was so hated that, after his death, the people pulled down statues of him and removed his name from any public inscriptions.

Septimius Severus conquers the final province of Rome

There was another power struggle between opposing generals, and the victor was Septimius Severus, a provincial Roman aristocrat from Leptis Magna in Africa. He was a senator and, at the time of Commodus's death, governor and commander of the troops in Pannonia, one of the provinces along the Danube border. It took four years of civil war, however, before he was firmly in control.

LEFT **Trajan's campaigns brought new territories to Rome, though not permanently.**

BELOW **A detail from Trajan's Column in Rome, a monument to his victories, depicts him in talks with the defeated Dacians.**

63

Shortly before **Septimius Severus** became emperor, the Praetorian Guards auctioned off the title of emperor. The highest bidder, Marcus Didius Julianus, was murdered soon after.

Septimius Severus was a realist. He knew that the empire was faced by strong enemies and needed to be strengthened. This meant encouraging talent from the provinces and his administration drew heavily on fellow Africans. His particular concern was the army. He added two new legions, raised soldiers' pay and opened up higher commands to those from the ranks. He believed in going on the offensive against Rome's enemies: in the east, he added Rome's final province, Mesopotamia, in 199 and died while campaigning in northern Britain in 211. His final words to his sons Caracalla and Geta were, "Stick together, pay the soldiers and forget all the rest."

Caracalla (211–17) murdered his brother, who had been appointed emperor with him, and was himself eventually assassinated by his own troops. A usurper, Macrinus, followed before the Severan dynasty regained control with Elagabalus in 218. Elagabalus took his name from an eastern sun god whom he used, unsuccessfully, to raise support.

Elagabalus was also murdered and was succeeded by a cousin, the 14-year-old Severus Alexander (222–35). The empire still had the security to allow a minor from the reigning dynasty to assume power but Alexander was killed in his turn when his policy of negotiating with the German tribes was rejected by his troops.

In the 230s Rome faced a new threat from the Sasanids who reconquered Mesopotamia. By the 240s the German tribes, now organized in far larger units, were massing on the northern borders. It was the threats from both north and east that put enormous strains on the empire. For the Romans to fight effectively on two fronts at once was almost impossible. If invaders breached the frontier and bypassed the overstretched army they could use the Roman road system to move hundreds of kilometers into Roman territory.

The continual invasions of the 3rd century, and the resulting social and economic disruption, placed great stress on the emperor. He now had to be a military man above all, ranging the empire from one broken frontier to another. The opportunities for political struggles between ambitious commanders multiplied. Few emperors could maintain a position as undisputed leader of the scattered Roman armies and fight off invaders.

There were at least 20 emperors between 235 and 284, many of whom died violent deaths. One, Valerian, suffered the humiliation of being captured by the Persians, the greatest disgrace that could befall an emperor, and he died in captivity. His son,

LEFT **Concern about continued invasions from the north led to the construction of the Aurelian wall, nearly 20 kilometers long, around the entire city of Rome. Towers were erected every 300 meters.**

ABOVE **The ill-fated family of Septimius Severus. One son, Caracalla, murdered his own brother Geta (who has been painted out of this portrait) and later ordered all representations of Geta to be destroyed.**

Gallienus, who ruled alone from 260 to 268, began the fight back, creating mobile forces which could respond to the continuous breaches of the frontiers. It was Gallienus who finally excluded senators from all army commands, using equestrians instead. With the emperor far from Rome, the Senate became little more than an observer of events. From 282 it did not even give formal recognition to a new emperor. Many of its members, still wealthy – if politically impotent – left Rome for their landed estates.

The saviors of the empire are men who come from the provinces

The salvation of the empire came from the Balkans: the vital land bridge between the east and west of the empire. Holding the Balkans was essential if the empire was not to fragment. The area also bred tough and hardy men who had proved fine recruits for the armies. The demands of the crisis brought rapid promotions for men who could lead, and opened up the possibility of the highest prize of all, the post of emperor .

Outstanding among the first emperors to emerge from the Balkan armies were Aurelian and Probus. The success of Aurelian (270–75) was extraordinary. A man of unflinching courage, he surrendered Dacia, drew a shorter, more defensible frontier along the Danube, and moved east to crush an independent state which had emerged around the great eastern trading city of Palmyra, and then returned west to bring Gaul back into the empire. "Restorer of the World" was the proud but justified legend on his coins.

Probus, emperor from 276 to 282, concentrated on restoring order within the empire, clearing out the lingering invaders and reclaiming land that had been abandoned in the turmoil. When Probus died, the victim of a mutiny against his strict discipline, it looked as if chaos would never end. The short reign of Carus (282–83) precipitated a confrontation between his son, Carinus, emperor in the west, and Diocles, a Balkan general who had been proclaimed emperor by the troops of the east in 284.

In 285 Diocletian, as he became known, emerged as sole ruler, but his position was precarious: there was no reason why stability should return. Yet Diocletian was able to hold the frontiers of the empire and reorganize it to face the challenges of the centuries that followed.

Lucius Domitius Aurelian was murdered by officers who believed that he planned to execute them. For six months after Aurelian's death, his widow was the nominal head of state.

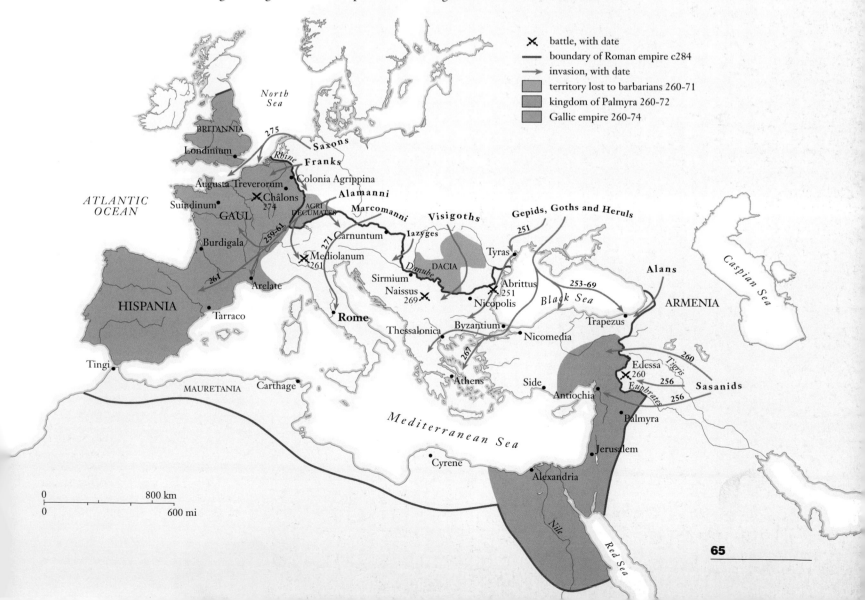

✕	battle, with date
—	boundary of Roman empire c284
→	invasion, with date
	territory lost to barbarians 260-71
	kingdom of Palmyra 260-72
	Gallic empire 260-74

ROME · CITY OF MARBLE

Imperial Rome was a splendid but crowded city. Spreading well beyond the three square kilometers encompassed by the ancient fortifications, the population overflowed even the much more extensive walls of AD 274. The city contained no fewer than 11 public baths and over 1,000 pools and fountains fed by 19 aqueducts; two circuses as well as two amphitheaters; 36 arches and many thousands of statues. Palaces numbered almost 2,000. Many public buildings were vast, reducing still further the living space available for the mass of the people.

At the heart of the city was the Forum. In this complex of temples, processional ways, triumphal arches, basilicas, council halls, rostra and open spaces all the most important aspects of urban life had been conducted since republican times. The Forum had thronged with merchants and tradesmen, senators and orators, and the imposing marble temples housed the rituals and sacrifices that Roman religion demanded.

Emperors knew the prestige to be gained by embellishing the Forum, and added to it with temples, arches and marketplaces; some even built their palaces to overlook the Forum itself. But as the new markets attracted the traders, so the old Forum became less frequented, used mainly by those with business in the temples and law courts, and rarely crowded except for the celebration of each new military triumph.

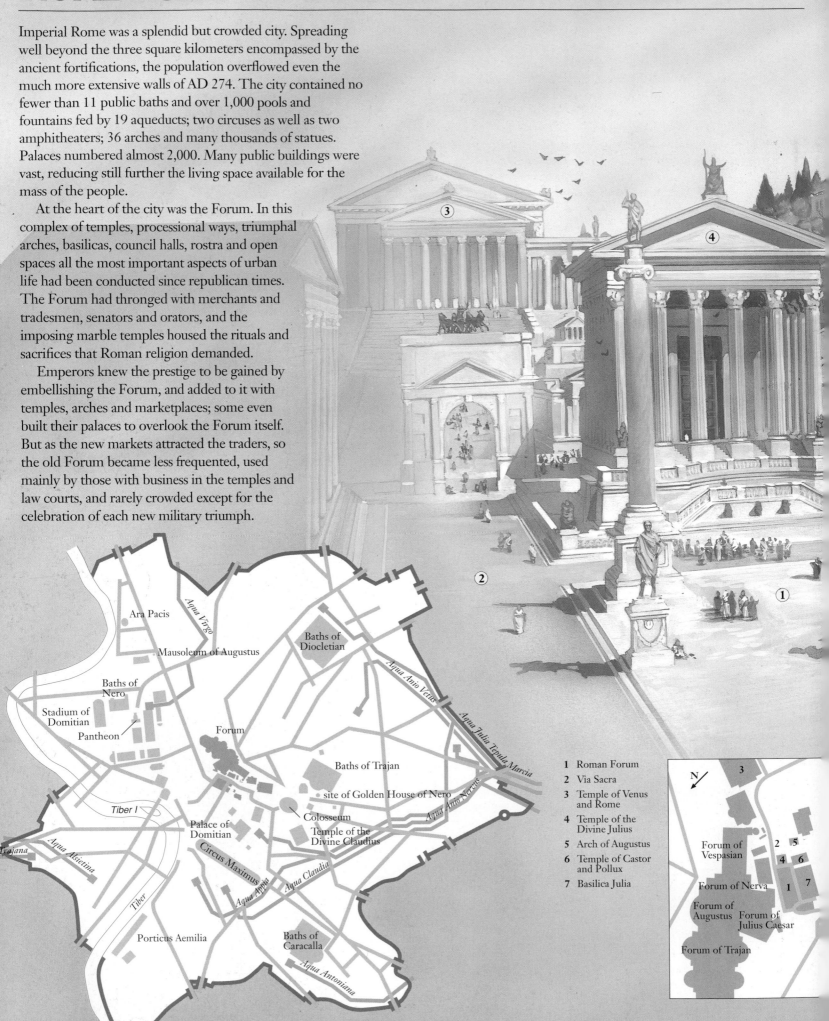

1 Roman Forum
2 Via Sacra
3 Temple of Venus and Rome
4 Temple of the Divine Julius
5 Arch of Augustus
6 Temple of Castor and Pollux
7 Basilica Julia

Forum of Vespasian

Forum of Nerva

Forum of Augustus   Forum of Julius Caesar

Forum of Trajan

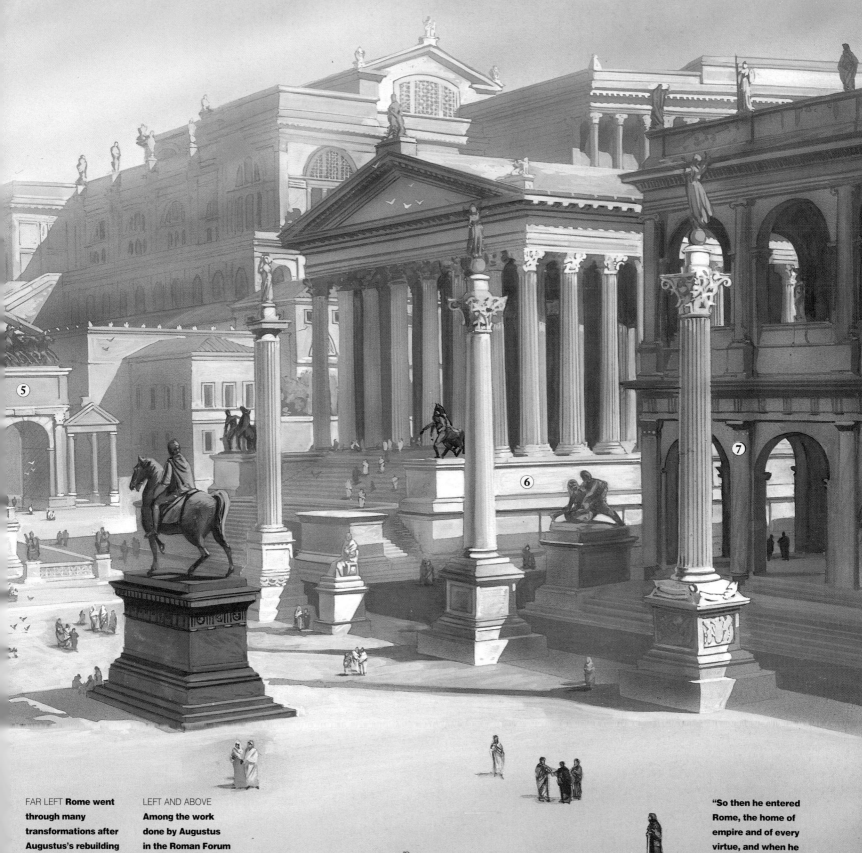

FAR LEFT **Rome went through many transformations after Augustus's rebuilding program. Fires devasted the city in AD 64 and 104; the extensive rebuilding at those times resulted in some of the most opulent of Roman architecture, such as Nero's Golden House and the baths of Trajan, Caracalla and Diocletian.**

LEFT AND ABOVE **Among the work done by Augustus in the Roman Forum was the refurbishment of the temple of Castor and Pollux and the completion of the temple of the divine Julius and the Basilica Julia. Looming above the Forum were the imperial residences on the Palatine Hill. The temple of Venus and Rome was added in Hadrian's reign.**

"So then he entered Rome, the home of empire and of every virtue, and when he had come to the Rostra, the most renowned Forum of ancient dominion, he stood amazed: and on every side on which his eyes rested he was dazzled by the array of the marvelous sights."
AD 357: Ammianus Marcellinus on Constantius II.

THE CULT OF THE EMPEROR

The political powers enjoyed by Roman emperors were formally conferred on them by the Senate. They also needed the support of the armies, often gained in the course of a successful military career. Soldiers carried an image of the emperor and took a personal oath of loyalty to him.

The emperor's power also had a religious aspect. In the eastern part of the empire, power implied divine status. In Egypt the emperor was considered to be following in the tradition of the pharaohs and was treated automatically as a god. Delegations to the emperor from eastern cities would address him as if he were divine, and some emperors requested the deification of their predecessors.

It was left to each emperor to make what he wanted of this impulse for worship. Some were embarrassed by it while others reveled in the adulation, doing all they could to promote it. Most were quietly aware that it was one more way in which their position as supreme ruler of the empire could be ensured and they did little actively to discourage veneration.

Becoming a god

The Romans believed that men with merit would ascend to a heaven set above the earth. The model was Hercules, who had spent his time on Earth laboring for humanity and was then rewarded by becoming a god.

Those emperors who, in the eyes of the Senate, had successfully fulfilled their role on Earth, were proclaimed gods: a process known as apotheosis. Apotheosis was even more believable, if as in the case of Augustus, a senator came forward to say he had actually seen the form of the dead emperor ascending to heaven complete with laurel crown and an accompanying eagle.

Deified emperors would have temples dedicated to them throughout the empire. A favorite was a dedication to Augustus and Rome. In the east these temples were built without any prompting from Rome, but in many parts of the west they were imposed as part of the general spread of Roman culture.

Ivory triptych of an apotheosis, possibly Antoninus Pius.

Divine attributes

In the Greek world – the east of the empire – the main attribute of the gods was that they were more powerful than men. Consequently, men who had great power on earth were seen as gods, and emperors were treated as if they were divine beings.

Many emperors were unhappy with their divine status. Augustus did little to foster his own cult, and Tiberius actively discouraged

Postumus, usurping emperor of the west (260–268), chose to be portrayed as Hercules on coins.

people from worshiping him. In direct contrast, Caligula insisted that he be treated as a god while he was still alive. At Olympia he ordered his features to be placed on the body of a statue of Zeus, the god of the Olympic games, and he offended the Jews by having a similar statue set up in the temple in Jerusalem.

Hadrian, a great benefactor of Greek cities, received widespread worship in the east. In Athens alone, 95 altars were dedicated to him and throughout Asia he was identified with Zeus. When his favorite companion, Antinoüs, drowned, Hadrian's grief was so great that he encouraged people, especially in Greece, to worship Antinoüs as a god.

The power brokers

Eagles were a symbol of war and imperial strength. An eagle, released at the cremation of an emperor, bore his soul to heaven.

The trappings of power

Laurel and oak leaves were symbols of bravery and power: laurels were associated with the older priesthoods of Rome and oak wreaths with bravery in battle.

The color purple, the most expensive of dyes, was used mainly for the emperor's clothes. Although senators' togas had a purple border and the *toga praetexta* of a young boy had a purple hem, it later became treason for anyone but the emperor to dress all in purple.

The image of the emperor was transmitted across the whole empire through coins and statues. Augustus was pictured on coins with an oak wreath woven into a crown on his head in a form similar to that of Hellenistic kings. The most common form of statue was of the emperor in body armor, in keeping with the cult of war. Augustus's most famous

The murex shell provided the dye used by the Romans for the emperors' imperial purple.

statue portrays him in this fashion, and Domitian, Trajan and Hadrian all used the same image. Emperors were also represented as a god, or in a toga as an ordinary citizen.

At first most emperors mixed easily with their people, but later some began to distance themselves from their subjects. Aurelian, meeting a delegation of Germans, dressed himself in imperial purple and sat on a high throne surrounded by his commanders. Diocletian introduced elaborate court rituals and ensured the elevation, seclusion – and inaccessibility – of the emperor.

Augustus founded the Praetorian Guard as an imperial bodyguard: an elite force of some 4,500 men with distinctive uniforms, superior rates of pay and the privilege of serving only 16 years instead of the 20 or 25 of the ordinary legionaries.

The Guard was stationed in barracks at the edge of Rome and in towns throughout Italy. For 200 years they were the only troops in Italy; so long as they remained loyal to the emperor his position was strong. The key position was held by the prefects, men whom the emperor had to trust implicitly.

The day-to-day activities of the Guard were to act as a personal bodyguard to the emperor. They

This 2nd-century relief depicts five Praetorian Guards.

would have accompanied him to the games, to the Senate and on his travels around the city.

In the last resort the Guard helped to keep order. In AD 61, for instance, Nero ordered that 400 slaves from one household be executed following the murder of their master by one of them. When there were protests from citizens, the Guard was brought in to round up all the slaves and lead them all off to execution.

The Praetorians' greatest influence followed the death of an emperor. If they could quickly establish their own choice of emperor, as they did with Claudius, they might hold him in power. However, if their choice was unpopular to the army as a whole, he would eventually be overthrown by the generals.

TYRANTS AND PHILOSOPHERS

Many Roman emperors were of exceptional ability, either as soldiers (Vespasian and Trajan), administrators (Augustus, Claudius, Domitian) or men of culture (Hadrian and Marcus Aurelius), and rose admirably to the challenges of the post. Others, such as Caligula, Nero and Commodus, were unable to cope with the enormous problem of the virtually limitless power they suddenly acquired. In these reigns intrigue flourished and administration atrophied. There was no constitutional way of removing an emperor and assassination was by no means unknown as a last resort.

As the empire became more secure, the skills needed by an emperor also changed. It was the major achievement of Hadrian and his successor Antoninus Pius to realize that aggressive expansion was not the best policy, and that the future of the empire lay in peace and consolidation.

In later reigns the empire was threatened by invaders and tough realistic men were needed as rulers – such as Septimius Severus, who reformed the armies to meet the growing threats. By the middle of the 3rd century the emperors had to be accomplished soldiers if they were to survive at all.

Mushrooms, used to kill Claudius.

All in the family

The accession of Claudius, forced upon the Senate by the Praetorian Guard, reflected the importance of succession. If there was a son or close male relative within the ruling family he would be the natural successor but intensive intrigue often occurred behind the scenes. For the women of the court, otherwise deprived of political power, this was one of the few ways in which they could hope to exercise any influence. A central figure in the reign of Claudius was Agrippina, his fourth wife, whom he married in 49. Agrippina was Claudius's niece and had, according to Suetonius, "a niece's privilege of kissing and caressing Claudius, and exercised it with a noticeable effect on his passions". This relationship was legally considered incest, and Claudius had the law changed to enable him to marry his niece.

Agrippina was also a great-granddaughter, by adoption, of Augustus and daughter of a brilliant and popular military commander,

Agrippina, wife of Claudius.

Men of action

During the crisis of the later 3rd century, when the empire was under attack from both north and east, it was an advantage for emperors to be military men. They were tough, far from the cultured ideal of the previous century, such as Marcus Aurelius, and they were exposed to the dangers of continual warfare. Decius was killed by the Goths in 251, the first emperor to fall in battle against a foreign enemy, and

Valerian died after being captured by the Persians in 260.

An even greater danger for an emperor was death at the hands of rebellious troops or rivals for power. Gordian III (238–44) was murdered by his troops while in Persia. His successor, Philip I, was killed on the order of Decius, who then took over as emperor. Gallienus (253–68), one of the most brilliant and resourceful of the emperors of these years, was finally killed by his own chiefs of staff.

Later emperors of the century – Aurelius, Probus and Diocletian – all came from the

Balkans, a breeding ground of hardy men determined to save the empire, whatever the cost.

One result of continual campaigning was to take the emperor away from Rome. Its importance as an administrative center declined as the emperors consolidated their own personal courts outside of the city.

Philip I, known as Philip the Arab: a new, non-Roman type of warrior and emperor.

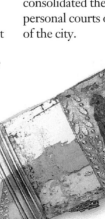

Germanicus – the brother of Claudius. By marrying Agrippina, Claudius improved his political position, but he faced danger from her own driving ambitions.

Although Claudius already had a son and heir – Britannicus, by his third wife, Messalina – Agrippina was determined to secure the succession for her own son, Nero, three years older than Britannicus.

Agrippina worked carefully on Claudius, intent, in the first instance, on establishing Nero as joint emperor with Britannicus. Britannicus could not succeed until he reached the age of 14 and took the toga of manhood in March 55. In October 54, Claudius died after a banquet, taken ill in suspicious

Coin depicting Caligula's three sisters, with whom he had incestuous relationships.

circumstances. Among many rumors was one that Agrippina had given him poisonous mushrooms. Two months later, with Nero now acclaimed as emperor, Britannicus died too, poisoned publicly at a banquet. Nero, who was present, claimed that Britannicus had long suffered from epileptic fits, one of which had finally killed him. Agrippina's triumph did not last. Four years later her own son claimed that she was plotting to kill him. According to Tacitus, Nero tried several methods of murdering his mother: from poison to arranging panels of her bedroom ceiling to fall on her, and even dispatching her in a collapsible boat. She was finally stabbed to death. Nero later suffered from nightmares; he imagined that he was haunted by his mother's ghost, and his behavior became increasingly erratic.

This sword, with its elaborately decorated scabbard depicting Tiberius as Jupiter, was owned by an officer who served Tiberius.

The sensitive soldier

The reign of Marcus Aurelius (161–180) marked a turning point in the history of the empire. The long years of peace of the mid 2nd century were shattered as Rome came under attack from both north and east, and the emperor faced with the task of repelling the enemies was a man who had no military experience, and who hated court life. However, Marcus Aurelius struggled to find a personal morality which would help him resist the temptations of court life and enable him to deal with the continual pressures placed on him when he became emperor at the age of 40. He gradually evolved his own philosophy, based on Stoicism, which taught him that duty must never be avoided.

Marcus Aurelius would, on his own admission, have been happier living quietly in the peace of the mountains or the seaside but his duty called him to the battlefield. This sensitive, cultured man spent his reign fighting to preserve the empire's frontiers for his successors. In his own words, "Be like the headland on which the waves continually break, but which stands firm and about which the boiling waters sink to sleep." In later centuries Marcus Aurelius became known for these *Meditations* – his thoughts, written in Greek, which he jotted down at random over his years of power. This personal diary, never intended for publication, shows a man who, even in the darkest days of war, was able to ponder the wider meaning of the world around him. For him, a human being was small and insignificant in comparison with the universe. Life was a ceaseless pattern of activity after which death would bring oblivion, even for an emperor. "Up and down, to and fro, round and round: this is the monotonous and

meaningless rhythm of the universe…whatever happens to you was prepared for you beforehand from eternity."

These melancholy thoughts are made appealing by his appreciation of the unity of all living things. "Meditate on the bonds between all things in the universe," he advised,"…for all things are in a way woven together and all are because of this dear to one another."

In one of his jottings, at Carnuntum on the banks of the Danube, Marcus Aurelius summed up his philosophy of life:

"If you do the work on hand following the rule of right with enthusiasm, manfully and with kindheartedness…and preserve the divinity within you pure and upright, then you will live a happy life and there is no one who can prevent this."

Those who saw Aurelius in action believed he carried out these aims to the end and for many he was the model emperor.

This bronze equestrian statue of Aurelius was the only one of its kind to survive from antiquity.

CIRCUS AND SPECTACLE

Life in the city of Rome was punctuated by great festivals: ancient religious festivals, anniversaries of emperors' victories, celebrations of important dates in Rome's own history – in total, probably over 130 days in a year. They were originally religious festivals – such as the *Ludi Romani* dedicated to Juno, Jupiter and Minerva – but gradually lost their religious significance for many people. About half of these festivals were celebrated by a wide variety of games and spectacles: chariot races in the Circus Maximus; gladiator and wild beast fighting in the Colosseum and other amphitheaters; athletics, poetry and music in the Greek games founded by Domitian in 86.

Festivals were an important safety valve for the people; the games were generally the only means by which public feeling could be voiced. In AD 33, for instance, when corn supplies were threatened, Tiberius's visits to the theater were disturbed by shouts of protest. With the huge numbers of poor and unemployed people, diversion was vital if public order was to be kept, and and the emperors were always careful to take responsibility for the festivals.

The games were also useful as a propaganda tool for an emperor, providing the opportunity of interacting with the people. Julius Caesar had been criticized for conducting business from his box, so Augustus always gave entertainments his full attention. At the climax of a gladiatorial contest the crowd would shout their verdict on defeated – but still living – men; and the emperor could please the people by responding to their demands.

The Colosseum

The Colosseum was built, incredibly, in only 10 years. This magnificent setting for mass entertainment could hold 50,000 spectators and the arena itself covered 3,500 square meters. Underneath were cages in which the wild animals were kept. In AD 80, on the inauguration day, 5,000 beasts were there to be killed.

A wide variety in the shows was essential to please the crowds. There were gladiatorial fights, a bewildering range of contests beween beasts, and the occasional speciality act – panthers drawing a chariot, or an elephant kneeling before the emperor. The arena could be flooded to provide mock sea battles. In the interval, criminals were often brought out to kill each other and later Christians were sent in, defenseless, to face lions and other wild animals.

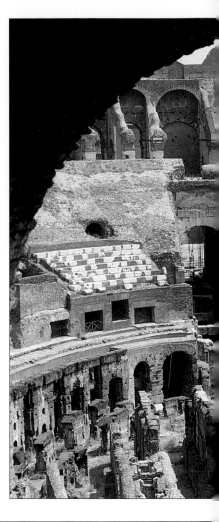

RIGHT **Vespasian built the Colosseum on land which Nero had taken for his Golden House.**

LEFT **Coin commemorating the Colosseum, formerly known as the Flavian Amphitheater.**

A day at the races

A fight to the death

Watching men fight each other was a practice dating back at least to republican times, but under the emperors it was developed as a major public spectacle. Gladiators were so highly trained that death was not inevitable. In one show 15 out of 18 men survived; Nero staged shows in which senators took part, and even the emperor Commodus fought in gladiatorial contests.

The more skilled and successful gladiators became celebrities, attracting fans and inspiring graffiti such as this one at Pompeii: "Celadus, the Thracian, makes all the girls sigh". Many gladiators returned to fight again and again even when the emperor had granted them the wooden sword which signified their release from service.

The most repellent shows were those where unprotected criminals were sent in to kill each other, and Seneca paints a grim picture of the spectacle. "Now all niceties were put aside, and it was pure and simple murder. The combatants have absolutely no protection. Their whole bodies are exposed to one another's blows, and thus each never fails to injure his opponent."

Many condemned men, on their way to the amphitheater, would commit suicide in any way possible rather than face a prolonged and agonizing death in front of the bloodthirsty, cheering crowds.

An unknown gladiator, and not Marcus Aurelius, was rumored to be Commodus's real father.

Bronze gladiator's helmet with scenes from the sacking of Troy.

The races were the most prestigious and enduring of Roman entertainment: "All Rome is in the circus today," wrote Juvenal, capturing their popularity. Chariot racing took place in the vast Circus Maximus – 600 meters long, with space for about 250,000 spectators. Chariots, normally drawn by four horses, would race seven times around a circuit, maneuvering a tight turn at each end. It was a dangerous sport and accidents were frequent.

Pompeiian wall painting of the races.

There were four teams, or factions: Red, Green, Blue and White, each with its own horses and riders. Most charioteers began as slaves; successful ones could eventually buy their freedom. One, Gaius Appuleius Diocles, survived to retire – after 24 years of racing – with a fortune of more than 35 million sesterces.

Spectators supported their favorite teams with fierce enthusiasm and riots between fans often broke out. Races were also social occasions, though: for meeting new people or just for enjoying a day out.

"You watch the races and I'll watch you. Let's each watch the things we love most," as the poet Ovid put it to a girlfriend.

POWER AND PATRONAGE

The emperors were immensely rich men. Augustus had taken for himself the treasures of the entire Egyptian kingdom, and Tiberius was said to have amassed a fortune of 27 million gold pieces, which was later squandered by Caligula. Later emperors benefited from the inheritances left them by grateful – and fearful – subjects and from the fruits of military plunder. Some lived extravagantly, building private palaces or villas, others sought popularity by vast expenditure on games or public buildings. Most of the great public buildings of Rome, such as the Pantheon, built by Hadrian; the Colosseum, provided by Vespasian; Trajan's Market and Forum, and the baths of Caracalla and Diocletian, were gifts from emperors. Outside the capital, different emperors favored particular cities. Septimius Severus beautified his wealthy native city of Leptis Magna with a new quarter, complete with forum and basilica, of a grandeur that would not have been out of place in Rome itself. The grateful citizens hurriedly erected a triumphal arch to welcome him when he next visited them. In the later empire, as Rome's importance declined, new cities – supreme among them Constantinople – carried on the tradition of imperial patronage.

Measures of triumph

The baths of Caracalla

The bath-house was an enduring symbol of Roman civilization. It represented a relaxed, convivial approach to life as well as providing a chance to wash away the dust of the city. Many emperors provided the capital with baths – Trajan, Titus, Diocletian and Constantine among them.

The baths of Caracalla, built in the early 3rd century, represent the peak of achievement in Roman bath building. They were set in an enclosure covering about 130,000 square meters, with room for about 1,600 bathers.

The main building housed the *tepidarium* (warm room) and *caldarium* (hot room) with heated water and the *frigidarium* (cold room) with cold water baths. There were also sweating rooms, dressing rooms and *unctuaria*, where people could have their skin scraped and oiled, as well as rooms for exercise.

The rooms were designed with great skill so that small intimate rooms contrasted with the great vaulted halls of the hot and cold baths. The circular hot bath, with a dome higher than that of the Pantheon, was deliberately placed to exploit the warmth of the sun in the afternoon.

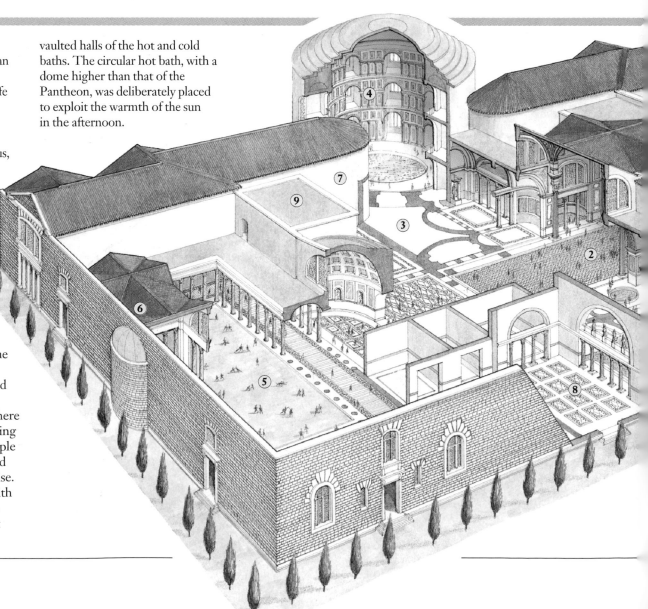

Hadrian's villa

Although the arch was known in ancient Greece and Egypt, it was considered too unstable a structure. The Romans, with their engineering ingenuity, were able to build large-scale arches without even the use of mortar. Arches were then used in bridges and aqueducts.

The triumphal arch had its origins in the celebration of military victories, and dates back to about 200 BC. They normally had no architectural connection with a city's gates or walls, and were erected across the road used for the procession of a victorious general's triumph. By the time of the empire, an arch was normally dedicated to an emperor, or at least to a member of his family. No other person would dare upstage the emperor by erecting his own arch.

In the later arch of Titus in Rome, Titus's victory over the Jews is commemorated with a relief of the sacred treasures of Jerusalem being carried back to Rome and another showing the emperor ascending to heaven as a god.

Tiberius added his own inscription to a triple arch built in France before his reign. This arch was erected in AD 26 to celebrate victory over Julius Sacrovir, a Gallic nobleman who led a rising against Roman rule. It was ahead of its time in having three openings – most had one or two – but otherwise was typical in being decorated with reliefs of the spoils of war.

The arch of Tiberius in Arausio (Orange).

1	Pool (*natatio*)	5	Athletics ground
2	Great hall		(*palaestra*)
	(*frigidarium*)	6	Gymnasium
3	Warm room	7	Bathrooms
	(*tepidarium*)	8	Anteroom
4	Hot room	9	Sweating room
	(*caldarium*)		(*sudatorium*)

Caracalla meant "cloak": he got his nickname from one he wore.

Several of the Roman emperors were attracted to the civilization of Greece, and none more so than Hadrian. He had a Greek education and traveled widely throughout the eastern provinces. Hadrian also bestowed immense patronage on Greek cities, above all Athens.

One of Hadrian's earliest and most spectacular building projects was his villa at Tibur (modern Tivoli), set in its own landscape with Rome just visible in the distance. Parts of this sprawling villa complex were named after buildings and places in the eastern world, particularly Greece. Many of the buildings were derived from Greek or Hellenistic models, and Greek sculptures lined the lakes and waterways which were such a prominent feature.

The villa marked the culmination of the luxurious villas that rich Romans had long enjoyed, and was also a revolution in architecture. Hadrian and his architects reveled in the play of light and shade, the uses of curves, space and color to create a harmonious whole.

Hadrian's villa, built on land that belonged to the his family, was virtually completed by 134, but he had little chance to enjoy it fully as he died four years later.

ABOVE **One of the elaborate lake settings in Hadrian's villa.**

Chapter 4

CULTURE AND RELIGION IN THE EMPIRE

The Romans were highly practical people: they could build bridges, win wars and administer an empire. They were less proficient in the creative arts, but they had the Greek world to influence them and provide models for inspiration.

The impact of Greece and the Hellenistic world of the east on the development of Roman culture was immense. Patterns of building, form of poetry, mystery religions: these came to Rome from the east, though they did not stifle Roman genius. Latin culture was sufficiently self-aware and flexible to be able to absorb and transform Greek ideas into masterpieces such as Virgil's *Aeneid*. Roman architects used the arch and the vault, learned from the east, to build the Pantheon with one of the largest domes in the ancient world. Culturally, it was a Greco-Roman empire.

In the 1st century, a new faith was born: Christianity, at first only one of many religious cults originating from the east of the empire. Although it passed virtually unnoticed by non-Christian writers for over 200 years, Christianity was to emerge as the dominant cultural force of the late empire.

Whether real or represented, gardens were an important part of Roman life, and served to imitate the gardens of Hellenistic princes.

One of the most accomplished sculptures of imperial Rome is the *Ara Pacis Augustae*, the altar of peace commissioned by Augustus. The reliefs on the altar portray a great procession which took place to commemorate the emperor's safe return from a provincial tour in 13 BC. The form of the altar is Greek, but the reliefs are a celebration of traditional Roman virtues.

Augustus is portrayed with his family in a way that would be immediately reassuring to traditional Romans. The old virtues of *gravitas* and *dignitas* are shown in the solemnity of the procession; *pietas*, the sense of duty to the gods and the state, is acted out by the participants.

The procession itself recalls the one recorded on the great frieze of the Parthenon in Athens. In the Ara Pacis Romans used the skills of Greece to breathe new life into their own traditions, and Augustus deliberately held himself up for favorable comparison with the great power of Athens in the 5th century BC.

The interplay between Greece and Rome was sustained by successive emperors. Nero insisted on traveling to Greece to take part in musical and dramatic festivals: "The Greeks alone are worthy of my efforts," he claimed, "they really listen to music." Domitian endowed Rome with its own Greek games, where music, poetry and rhetoric contests alternated with foot-races, boxing and discus-throwing. Hadrian showed the greatest enthusiasm and inspired a flood of Greek sculptors and craftsmen to pour into Rome.

The more astute Greeks realized that under Roman rule their cities enjoyed a protection impossible when the area was beset by intercity rivalries. As the 2nd-century Greek poet Aelius Aristides put it in his famous hymn of praise to Rome: "There is one pattern of government embracing all. What was originally thought impossible to join has been united under the rule of an empire at once strong and humane."

Greek models provide inspiration for Roman creativity in literature

One area in which the Romans took Greek models and made creative contributions of the highest order was literature. Augustus realized the importance of harnessing writers in his support and the age of Augustus saw a literary "golden age". Maecenas, a wealthy associate and close friend of Augustus, acted on behalf of the emperor, offering patronage to poets in the hope that they would repay the debt by praising the new regime.

One of the most talented of these poets was Quintus Horatius Flaccus, better known as Horace (65–8 BC). Horace studied in Athens and was steeped in the poetry of Greece. "Read the Greeks at night and read the Greeks by day," was his advice to aspiring writers. He was responsible for reviving the Greek art of lyric poetry. Horace desperately needed patronage: he had lost his family lands when he sided with Brutus – one of the assassins of Julius Caesar – in the civil wars. However, he feared that by accepting the support of the new regime he would compromise his independence. Horace's poetry treads a careful path: often praising Augustus but never succumbing to

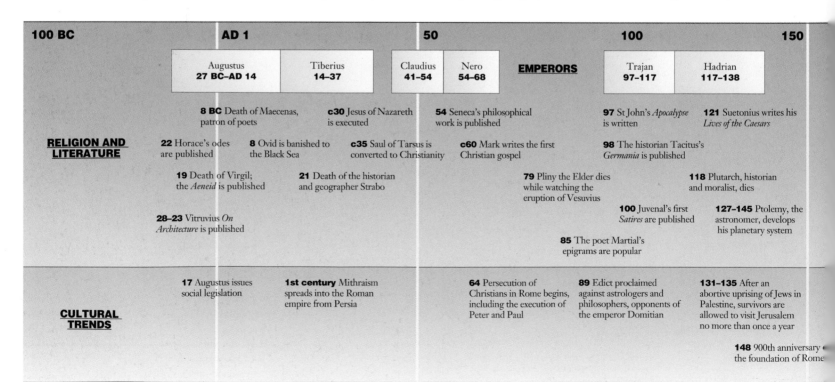

100 BC		AD 1			50				100		150

	Augustus 27 BC–AD 14	Tiberius 14–37	Claudius 41–54	Nero 54–68	**EMPERORS**	Trajan 97–117	Hadrian 117–138

RELIGION AND LITERATURE

8 BC Death of Maecenas, patron of poets
c30 Jesus of Nazareth is executed
54 Seneca's philosophical work is published
97 St John's *Apocalypse* is written
121 Suetonius writes his *Lives of the Caesars*

22 Horace's odes are published
8 Ovid is banished to the Black Sea
c35 Saul of Tarsus is converted to Christianity
c60 Mark writes the first Christian gospel
98 The historian Tacitus's *Germania* is published

19 Death of Virgil; the *Aeneid* is published
21 Death of the historian and geographer Strabo
79 Pliny the Elder dies while watching the eruption of Vesuvius
118 Plutarch, historian and moralist, dies

28–23 Vitruvius *On Architecture* is published
100 Juvenal's first *Satires* are published
127–145 Ptolemy, the astronomer, develops his planetary system

85 The poet Martial's epigrams are popular

CULTURAL TRENDS

17 Augustus issues social legislation
1st century Mithraism spreads into the Roman empire from Persia
64 Persecution of Christians in Rome begins, including the execution of Peter and Paul
89 Edict proclaimed against astrologers and philosophers, opponents of the emperor Domitian
131–135 After an abortive uprising of Jews in Palestine, survivors are allowed to visit Jerusalem no more than once a year

148 900th anniversary of the foundation of Rome

RIGHT **Atlas, brother of Prometheus in Greek mythology, held up the pillars which kept the earth and the heavens apart. Male figures, *atlantes*, used as architectural support features, take their names from him.**

complete and unquestioning adulation.

Part of the attraction of Horace's poetry lies in the self-portrait he provided: a genial, friendly man who loved the sun, wine, the company of women, and books. He was happiest talking with friends in Rome or relaxing on his farm – a gift from Maecenas – in the Sabine Hills. Horace was his own man, aware, after the turmoil of his early life, that he had got as much as anyone could expect and was determined to enjoy it all to the full.

Despite his prodigious talent, Horace was overshadowed by his contemporary and friend, Publius Vergilius Maro (70–19 BC), known as Virgil. Virgil, born in northern Italy, finished his education in Rome, where he studied rhetoric. He was a shy man whose only known interest was writing poetry. When his first work, the *Eclogues*, was published, Maecenas recognized an enormous talent and drew Virgil into his circle.

The *Eclogues* are a collection of poems about pastoral life and this is a theme that Virgil developed in a much more mature and sophisticated way in his first great work, the *Georgics* (36–29 BC). The four *Georgics*, each of some 500 lines, appear at first to comprise a handbook for Italian farmers: Virgil describes how to cultivate vines, grow grain, breed horses and cattle and care for bees. However, his interpretation of life on the land transforms the work into a poem.

"Here, in the countryside, men sleep secure, here is a life that never heard of lies, a life rich in goodness of every kind; here men pray to the gods, here men bow to the old; when Justice went out of the world, it was here that she left the last print of her foot."

Gaius Maecenas (c70–8 BC) was a wealthy diplomat and a valued adviser of Augustus. His personal life was unhappy, though, and his wife Terentia was said to be Augustus's mistress.

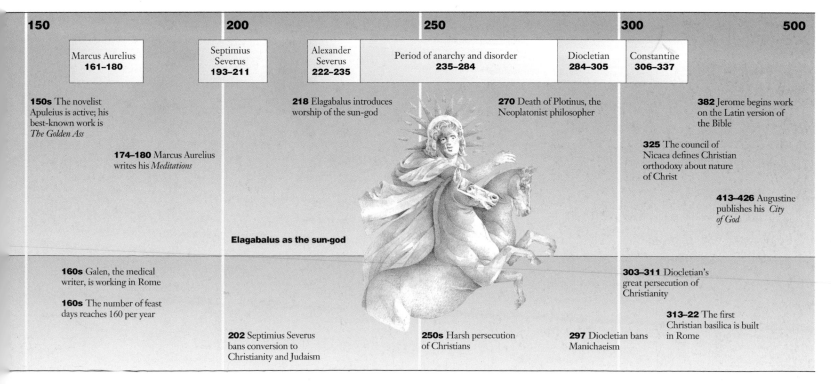

150		200		250		300	500

| Marcus Aurelius 161–180 | Septimius Severus 193–211 | Alexander Severus 222–235 | Period of anarchy and disorder 235–284 | Diocletian 284–305 | Constantine 306–337 |

150s The novelist Apuleius is active; his best-known work is *The Golden Ass*

218 Elagabalus introduces worship of the sun-god

270 Death of Plotinus, the Neoplatonist philosopher

382 Jerome begins work on the Latin version of the Bible

174–180 Marcus Aurelius writes his *Meditations*

325 The council of Nicaea defines Christian orthodoxy about nature of Christ

413–426 Augustine publishes his *City of God*

Elagabalus as the sun-god

160s Galen, the medical writer, is working in Rome

160s The number of feast days reaches 160 per year

303–311 Diocletian's great persecution of Christianity

313–22 The first Christian basilica is built in Rome

202 Septimius Severus bans conversion to Christianity and Judaism

250s Harsh persecution of Christians

297 Diocletian bans Manichaeism

Virgil was acutely aware of the prosperity enjoyed by an Italy united under Roman rule. He was also deeply conscious of what it meant to be Roman and the strength and value of the traditions of the Roman experience. For his last great work, the *Aeneid*, he sought these traditions in the remote past. Taking the story of Aeneas, a refugee from the fall of Troy – and the legendary founder of the dynasty that produced Romulus and Remus – Virgil created a poem which ranks as one of the masterpieces of western literature.

The *Aeneid* was written between 29 and 19 BC and was still unfinished at the time of Virgil's death. It is an epic, in a tradition going back to Homer, but its hero is very different from the warrior-heroes of Greece. Aeneas is a human being, often frail and uncertain, but watched over by the gods and driven forward by fate. His journeys, after the fall of Troy, are arduous and frustrating. Aeneas is often diverted, not least by his love for Dido, queen of Carthage, who kills herself when he leaves her and then reappears to reproach him when he visits the Underworld.

Virgil used Aeneas to reflect on the nature of Rome's imperial destiny. Romans had been chosen by fate to be the dominant power of the world but it was a difficult and lonely task. There was a great human cost to be borne before peace and security could be achieved, as Virgil clearly believed it had been under Augustus. The powerful impact of his ideas is largely due to the beauty of the poetry in which they are expressed.

The grandest style of Roman prose is used for writing histories

The Romans also showed an impressive mastery of prose. There were different styles, according to the audience addressed and the nature of the task. The grandest style, and one of the most effective, was that used in the writing of history. The great historian of the Augustan age was Titus Livius (59 BC–AD17), better known as Livy. The task Livy set himself was none other than to "record the achievement of the Roman people from the founding of the city". It took him the last 44 years of his life and about a quarter of the 142 books have survived.

Livy hoped, by recalling the achievements of the past, to inspire a revival of Rome's greatness. He had no scruples about inventing speeches and incidents from the past in order to develop his theme, and was brilliant at imagining how people must have felt – the soldier facing battle, for instance. Livy's imagination gave his narrative a compelling and inexhaustible power.

Livy's most important successor was Tacitus

(AD c55–120). Tacitus held office under the Flavians but after the tyranny of Domitian he became deeply suspicious of imperial power. Under Trajan he felt more at ease and was able to start writing his histories. They all deal with the 1st century AD, and his first major work was a biography of his father-in-law Agricola, the commander of the Roman armies in Britain. The theme Tacitus develops is in praise of the survival and achievement of a good man in bad times. In the same year, AD 98, he published the *Germania*, a study of the German tribes along the northern borders of the empire. His two other works, the *Annals* and the *Histories*, deal with the periods AD 14 to 68 and 69 to 96. Only parts of them survive.

It was his preoccupation with the way in which power works that makes Tacitus such an absorbing historian. What is the nature of tyranny? How does a dictator's mind work? Can a good man serve a bad emperor? Although Tacitus felt that, in the long run, Roman civilization would be beneficial, he could understand how the tribes that

BELOW **This illustration from Virgil's *Georgics*, with shepherds and farmyard animals, presents an idyllic picture of country life.**

Rome conquered might not agree. He sympathized with their struggles to maintain independence but disapproved when many gave up the struggle in exchange for the comforts of city life.

Many other works from these years show the complexity of the Roman character. The letters of Pliny the Younger (AD 61–c114) are those of a cultured and sensitive Roman of the senatorial class. Pliny wrote his letters specifically for publication and so gives rather an idealized picture of himself. His attitudes and feelings about people, his surroundings and the dilemmas of everyday life, however, still present a richly detailed picture of what it was to be an aristocratic Roman. Pliny's feelings for his third wife, Calpurnia, are deeply moving, particularly when he describes a miscarriage which leaves her sterile and him childless.

Roman literature was by no means all serious. In the *Satyricon*, written by Petronius in about AD 60, the adventures of a group of characters traveling round Italy are described with a vitality and humor which show another side of the Roman character. Petronius had no pretensions to write formal prose, but his work demonstrates that he had a natural ear for colloquial speech. The characters are down-to-earth and the cast list of the *Satyricon* includes prostitutes, witches and pickpockets. Most of the work is lost but in a surviving banquet scene at the house of a rich freedman, Trimalchio, there is a vivid and unforgettable picture of the different classes in Roman society drawn together by curiosity and greed.

A century later the same vitality surfaced in *The Golden Ass*, a novel by the African Lucius Apuleius. It is a racy story, full of eroticism, magic and hilarious happenings. The slightly autobio-

graphical hero of the novel, Lucius, is transformed into an ass and the only way he can regain his human form is to eat some roses. Most of the novel is taken up with his frustrating but eventually successful search for the flowers. *The Golden Ass* is written in an extraordinary variety of styles, unlike anything else in Roman literature. Although much of the story is fantasy, Apuleius brilliantly captured the atmosphere of the 2nd century, particularly its enthusiasm for the mystery religions of the east.

Greek ideas do not always inspire Romans to great creativity

Although the Greeks brought a new depth and vitality to Roman life, there were many areas in which Romans were seldom inspired to real creativity. A good example is Pliny the Elder (c23–79) who compiled a *Natural History* which was little more than a vast compendium of information and speculation about the world around him. The book is a mixture of fact, gossip and superstition; Pliny made no attempt to assess his information critically or even systematically.

In marked contrast was Ptolemy, the most impressive scientist of the Greek world. Ptolemy was Egyptian by birth and worked in the great cultural center of Alexandria between AD 127 and 145. His greatest work was in astronomy. Ptolemy believed wrongly – a common assumption among Greek astronomers – that the Earth was the center of the planetary system. Around it revolved the Moon, the Sun and the other planets; the whole system was thought to hold together in harmony with the movement of the planets being directly related to each other.

Earlier astronomers had realized that the paths of the planets were not exact circles, but could not work out what they were. Ptolemy used various observations about the planets to construct a system which made sense of them all. It required enormous ingenuity but he succeeded.

By starting with the belief that the earth was the center of the planetary system, however, Ptolemy's solution was inaccurate. His planetary system was a purely intellectual exercise but it showed his use of the greatest creation of the Greek mind – geometry – at its most sophisticated. His resulting work, *The Mathematical Connection* (in Arabic, the *Almagest*) remained the bible of astronomy for another 1,400 years.

The same contrast was to be found in medicine. The Romans made an important contribution to public health through the provision of

running water to cities and the efficient disposal of sewage. The army had medical officers and even military hospitals but Romans made no advances themselves in the understanding of how the human body actually worked. It was left to Greek doctors, such as Galen, who came to Rome from his native Pergamum in AD 161, to insist on the importance of careful observation and independent analysis of what was seen.

Greek culture also had a huge impact on the religion and philosopy of Rome, and the traditional state gods were similar to many gods of Greek mythology. "You neglected the gods and they heaped disasters on Italy," wrote Horace in one of his *Odes*. The "disasters" were the civil wars which had split the empire before Augustus came to power. Belief in the traditional gods of Rome had become hollow in the last years of the republic and the city was scattered with decayed temples which had fallen into disuse.

Augustus knew he could strengthen his position by associating himself with the traditional gods who had protected the city in earlier centuries. He particularly liked statues which showed him at sacrifice or in prayer, and he placed himself at the forefront of a religious revival.

There was a major program of temple-building with those gods to whom Augustus felt closest – Jupiter, Apollo and Mars Ultor, the god of war in his role of avenger – receiving the most lavish expenditure. This was followed by the rebuilding of the temples for the old state gods, Castor and Pollux and Concordia among them.

Once the traditional state religion had been

LEFT **When sick or injured people made appeals to the gods for a cure, votive offerings in the shape of the afflicted part were left, either in hope or, as this bronze leg, thanksgiving for being healed.**

BELOW **Aesculapius or Asklepios, the Greek god of healing, was brought to Rome in 293 BC following a plague. A temple, later a hospital, was established for him on a small island in the river Tiber.**

revived, the chief innovation was the cult of the emperor. The spread of imperial cults from Rome throughout the provinces did not necessarily diminish the importance of local cults, many of which fed a spiritual need unsatisfied by more traditional beliefs.

Many educated Romans felt the need for a more coherent philosophy of life. One mood which grew in intensity in the 2nd century was a feeling of the transitory nature of life and the tiny place in the universe occupied by man. The world is unreal, as if human beings are actors on a stage, and the true reality is elsewhere, to be found through deep introspection or in the search for some kind of higher order. This mood led to a revival of interest in the philosophy of the Greek thinker Plato (428–348 BC).

Plato believed that every concrete or abstract thing in the world – man, color, beauty or justice – had a perfect "form" existing in a spiritual realm. These forms are arranged in a hierarchy with the "form of the good" being the highest of all. This idea was developed by the Neoplatonists, of

LEFT **This marble relief shows the emperor Marcus Aurelius in the garb of a priest, paying homage to the god Jupiter. The bull was considered to be the god's special animal and white bulls with gilded horns were commonly used as sacrifices.**

Plotinus (AD 205–270) was interested in many schools of thought, from eastern philosopy to the occult. He died of a painful disease which could have been leprosy or tuberculosis.

whom the most prominent was Plotinus. Plotinus, probably Egyptian by birth, had studied at Alexandria before making his home in Rome. He believed that the form of the good, the "One" as he called it, could be grasped by the individual thinker who freed himself from the demands of his earthly body and tried to ascend toward an understanding of the One.

At the level of most profound understanding, Plotinus believed that a mystical union of the individual and the One could take place. "When in this state the soul would exchange its present condition for nothing in the world, though it were offered the kingdom of all the heavens…"

Neoplatonism suggested that there was one supreme divine entity, a concept alien to the traditional religions of both Greece and Rome. It was, however, the central belief of Judaism where a single protecting god had watched over the Jewish people and their territory, known to the Romans as Judaea, for centuries. Judaea had come under direct Roman control in AD 6 and relationships between Roman and Jew were, compared with the rest of the empire, uneasy. While the conservative priestly caste, the Sadducees, were prepared to collaborate with the Romans, many Jews were not. The political situation in Judaea was particularly tense.

It was in this world that a Jewish teacher, Jesus, began preaching in AD 28 or 29. His ministry was first largely in Galilee, an area still not under direct Roman control. He was a charismatic and approachable figure, mixing easily with all who came to hear him – including prostitutes, tax collectors and even Roman soldiers – and he soon built up an impressive following.

Jesus knew his Jewish texts well but he refused to be bound by them. He claimed a more immediate relationship with God than was traditional with orthodox Jews. He spoke of him intimately as Abba – "father". Moreover, he preached that God was already making his appearance in this world and would soon establish his kingdom.

This message raised both enthusiasm and fear. After a year or two of ministry, Jesus traveled south to Jerusalem, where the authorities moved to crush him. He was arrested and brought to trial as a dissident, because he was known as the "King of the Jews". The Roman governor, Pontius Pilate, and the Jewish authorities collaborated in his death by crucifixion, the traditional method reserved for rebels.

The shock to Jesus' followers was immense but, soon after his death, stories began to circulate that he was more than a man, he was a messiah. Jesus was not the traditional messiah of the Jews, who had always been portrayed as an earthly

ruler, but this did not prevent the word being used of him. The belief that he had risen from the dead shortly after his crucifixion was a sign for early Christians that Jesus enjoyed God's special favor, and it was a symbol of life after death.

The earliest Christian community was a Jewish one though no more than a tiny minority of Jews became Christians. The transformation of Christianity came with Paul, a Greek-speaking Jew from the city of Tarsus in Cilicia, converted, he said, by a vision of Christ. Paul believed that the message of Christ was for all men and women, slave and free, who showed faith in him. This was in contrast to Jesus' followers in Jerusalem who wished to reserve Christianity for Jews. There was a serious power struggle before Paul prevailed but once Christianity was open to the Gentiles (those who were not Jews), Christian communities began to spread throughout the eastern empire.

At first Christianity is viewed as another dangerous cult with secret ceremonies

The early Christian communities were based in towns and each elected their own leader, the bishop. Some bishops emerged naturally: they were the leading citizens who gathered a Christian community around them. Others were elected. The bishops baptized new Christians, corresponded with other churches and took responsibility for the ordination of fellow bishops. They provided a continuity for the Christian communities which proved vitally important for the survival of the faith. The bishops of those communities originally founded by Jesus' own apostles – Rome, Alexandria and Antioch – soon became the most prestigious. Rivalry between

ABOVE **"Judaea mourning"** — a coin celebrating the subjection of the area shows a woman with bound hands.

ABOVE **A ritual candelabrum, used in Jewish worship. The variable number of branches originally signified the seven days of creation.**

BELOW **A mithraeum, an underground shrine for the god Mithras. This cult, later suppressed, was so strong at one time that Mithras was honored as patron of the empire. There were at least 45 shrines in Rome alone dedicated to Mithras.**

Tertullian (born c155) became a Christian convert late in life and helped establish Latin as the language of the Christian church. He later felt the church to be too morally lax and founded his own sect.

them was fierce and continued for centuries.

What marked out the early Christian communities was their emphasis on shared living. "We Christians," said the theologian Tertullian, "have everything in common except our wives." Early Christians lived out their commitment as benefactors of the poor. By the middle of the 3rd century, 1,500 poor people were being supported by the church in Rome and in Antioch, a century later, the number being fed reached 3,000.

Like other eastern religions, Christianity required an initiation ceremony – baptism – and this gave followers a sense of exclusiveness which inevitably aroused suspicion. Many people viewed Christianity with the same uneasiness as the

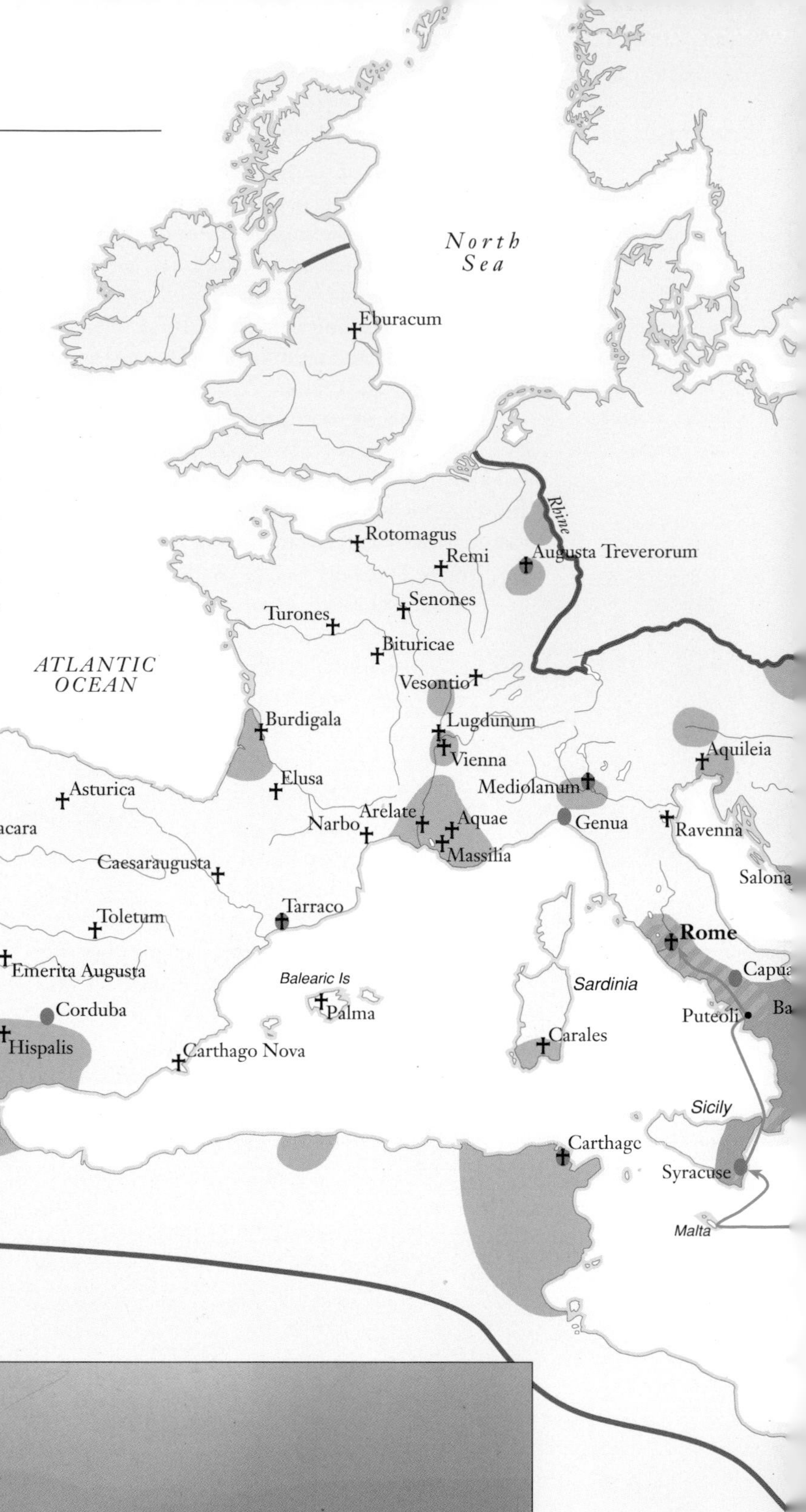

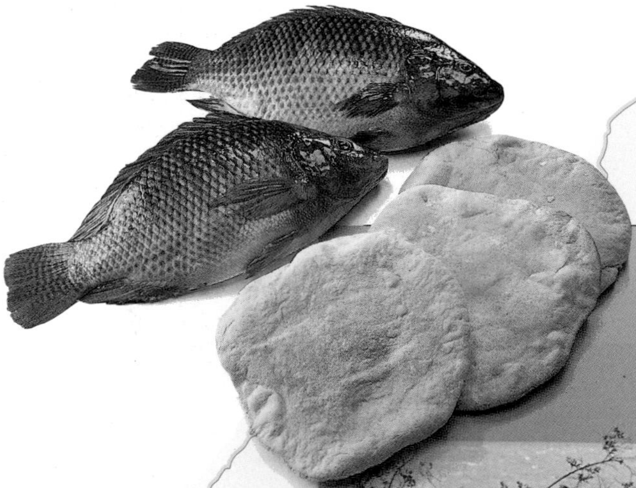

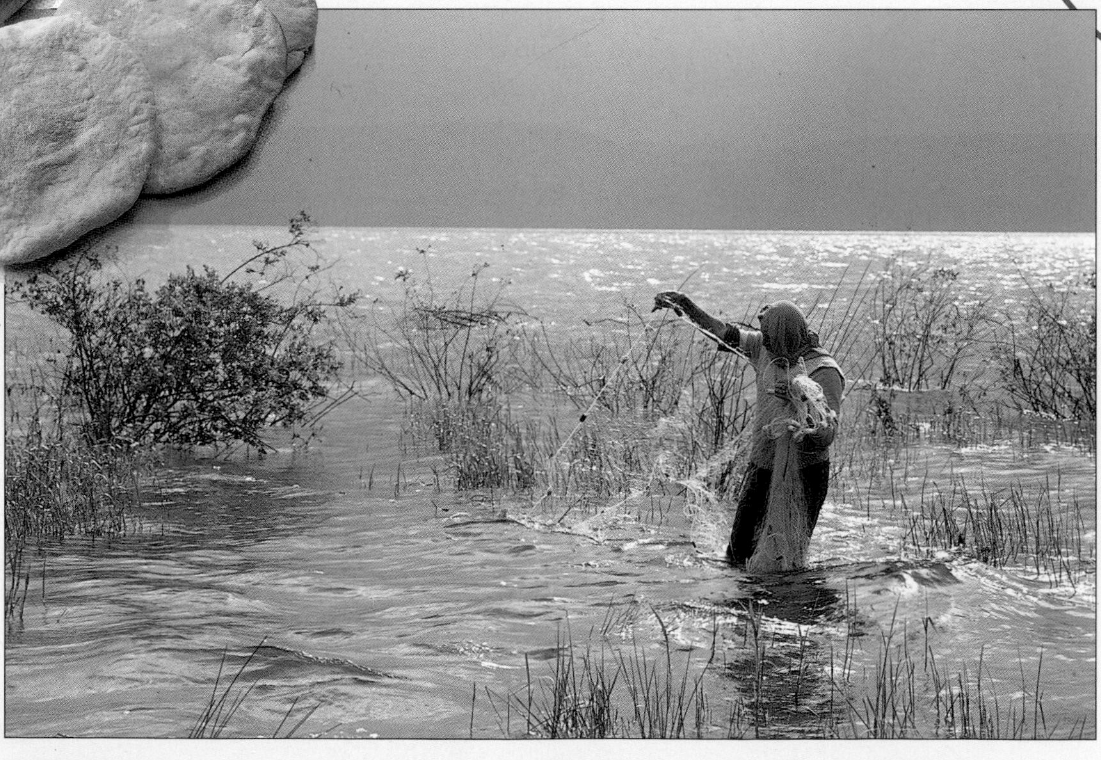

boundary of Roman empire AD325
St Paul's missionary journeys
1st, AD46-48
2nd, AD49-52
3rd, AD53-57
4th, AD59-62
archbishopric cAD300
Jewish settlement cAD300
Jewish area 300BC
Jewish area AD300
Christian area cAD300
0 400 km
0 300 mi
North Sea
ATLANTIC OCEAN
Eburacum
Rhine
Rotomagus
Remi
Augusta Treverorum
Senones
Turones
Bituricae
Vesontio
Burdigala
Lugdunum
Vienna
Aquileia
Mediolanum
Elusa
Asturica
Bracara
Arelate
Narbo
Aquae
Massilia
Genua
Ravenna
Caesaraugusta
Salona
Tarraco
Toletum
Rome
Emerita Augusta
Balearic Is
Sardinia
Capua
Palma
Corduba
Puteoli
Hispalis
Carthago Nova
Carales
Tingi
Sicily
Carthage
Syracuse
Malta

THE SPREAD OF JUDAISM AND CHRISTIANITY **Christianity spread throughout the Greek world and as far west as Rome under the guidance of St Paul; despite persecution, it was found all over the empire by AD 300. Judaism also spread in the eastern empire. It was often tolerated, and allowed to seek new converts.**

ABOVE **Christians used symbols drawn from everyday life. Fish were particularly popular as the Greek word *(ichthus)* began with the initial letters of the name Jesus Christ.**

LEFT **Jesus preached that the kingdom of God was like a net thrown into the sea to gather fish of every kind. This modern fisherman is very like the disciples of Jesus who became "fishers of men" and converted others to Christianity.**

republicans had viewed Bacchic rites, and were quick to report Christians to the authorities.

In a 2nd-century letter to the emperor Trajan, Pliny asks for an official position on Christianity. "An anonymous pamphlet was published which contained the names of many people. I thought that those who denied that they were or had been Christians should be dismissed, if they prayed to our gods, repeating the words after me, and if they dedicated incense and wine to your image…and if, moreover, they cursed Christ. It is said that those who are truly Christians cannot be forced to do any of these things."

Trajan's response was not to indulge in witch-hunts: "…these people are not to be searched out.

If they should be brought before you and proved guilty, they must be punished…But pamphlets published anonymously should have no place in a criminal proceeding, for this is a very bad prece-dent." The refusal of Christians to join in tradi-tional worship proved aggravating to many people, however, and at times of severe persecu-tion Trajan's letter was often used as the justifica-tion for executing people who did not recant.

Christianity was also challenged by intellectual debate. Christian apologists replied by claiming that Plato's form of the good was another term for the creator god whose son had been sent to earth as a sign of his care for all mankind. In this way a marriage took place between Christian faith and the intellectual discipline of the Greek world.

The breadth of the Roman empire facilitated the spread of religious belief, and the early Christian communities benefited from an unbro-ken tradition of spiritual leadership. No one could have predicted, however, that by the late 4th cen-tury Christianity would have become the official religion of the empire.

Trajan had outlawed secret societies and members of them were considered to be traitors. Christians, therefore, were legally guilty of treason, a crime which was punishable by death.

BELOW **Sarcophagus showing the arrest of St Paul. He escaped a flogging by virtue of the fact that he was a Roman citizen, but was imprisoned for two years. It is believed he died a martyr's death during the reign of Nero.**

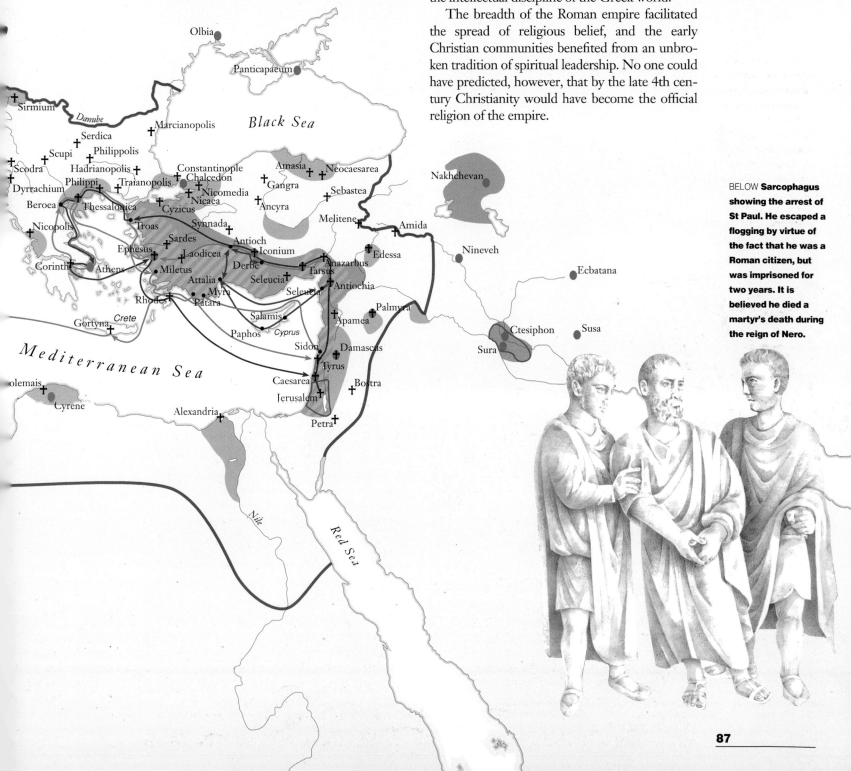

THE PANTHEON · FOR ALL THE GODS

The Pantheon, the temple to all the gods, was built between AD 118 and 125 and is the finest building of the Roman world to have survived in its original form. The mosaic floor, the interior columns and the great vaulted dome all remain as they were built. It is said that the Pantheon survived because a 7th-century pope believed it was a temple to the great Mother Goddess and, to avoid offending worshipers, changed the dedication to the Virgin Mary.

An earlier Pantheon was constructed by Marcus Agrippa, a devoted supporter of Augustus, and Agrippa's name still adorns the magnificent entrance porch. This building, though, is the work of the emperor Hadrian who was too modest to replace Agrippa's name with his own. No one knows for sure who was the architect but it is certain that Hadrian took a close interest in the construction.

Normally it was the exterior of a temple that was designed to impress. The superb pedimented porch of the Pantheon, with its 18 great Corinthian columns of gray and red Egyptian granite, is certainly spectacular but the interior amazed the world. There had been earlier domes in houses and baths but nothing on the scale of the Pantheon had ever been attempted and not in a temple – the concept of a temple as a domed rotunda was revolutionary. The dome, with a diameter of 43.30 meters, was the largest ever constructed until the 20th century.

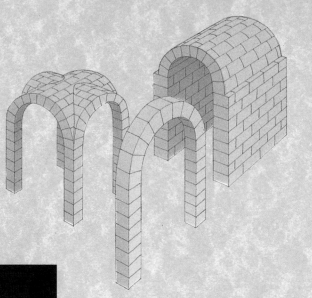

TOP **The traditional front porch of the Pantheon, similar to many Greek and Roman temples, hides what was a revolution in temple design.**

ABOVE **Expertise in building arches and vaults helped Roman architects with the monumental task of building the ancient world's largest dome.**

LEFT **Even if all the bronze doors of the Pantheon are closed, the single central opening of the dome can provide enough daylight to illuminate the entire building.**

RIGHT **Despite its impressive exterior, the Pantheon was probably the first monumental building to be designed with the interior as the primary concern.**

Constructing the Pantheon was one of the most impressive feats of Roman architecture, and a task that would have been impossible without concrete. For the lower walls it was mixed with travertine, the tough building stone quarried near Rome, while the dome itself was made up of concrete mixed with the lighter tufa and pumice rocks. Even so, the dome weighed over 5,000 tonnes and had to be built up layer by layer until the great central opening, 8 meters across, was reached. The walls of the foundations, 7.30 meters thick and

set 4.50 meters into the ground, were massively built to support the whole enormous structure.

The inside of the Pantheon is full of recesses, both in chambers leading off the ground floor and in the pattern of the dome. Those in the dome were built mainly to lighten the weight of the dome and allowing the concrete to dry out more quickly. Today, the main impact is aesthetic: the recesses give a feeling of airy spaciousness which is increased by the light pouring down through the central opening.

RIGHT **The diameter of the dome is exactly the same as the distance from the central opening to the ground, giving the building its elegant, distinctive harmony.**

89

MEDICINE AND MAGIC

The Roman healed the sick through a mixture of practical common sense, trust in the gods, and magic. When Ovid's mistress, Corinna, was dangerously ill after an abortion, Ovid's immediate response was to call on an Egyptian goddess of childbirth, Ilythia, promising her every kind of gift if Corinna survived. Superstition was rife. Goats' dung was mixed in wine and placed on fractured ribs, saliva was used as a protection against snakes.

The most important preventive measures, however, were those of good sense: the Romans' main contribution to medical history. Celsus, in his 1st-century treatise on medicine, advised a regime of exercise and a sensible diet as the best way to keep healthy. The Romans were well aware of the importance of good hygiene, such as regular bathing in clean water. Latrines were flushed, usually with water from the bath-house.

However, Romans had little knowledge of anatomy, and doctors from the east made the most systematic attempts to understand the working of the human body. Soranus, a physician from Ephesus who worked in Rome under Trajan and Hadrian, specialized in gynecology and Galen, the founding father of experimental physiology, built up an impressive knowledge of the human body through the dissection of apes. Many diseases remained untreatable, but these pioneers established the importance of careful observation. Their work, however, was not fully appreciated until the 16th century.

The Roman dispensary

Many of the treatments recommended by doctors were herbal, and concoctions of herbs were made up to treat every ailment. In his *Natural History*, Pliny the Elder gives a full description of the herbs used by the Romans with the names of over 40 of them. Garlic was included in 61 remedies for ailments ranging from leprosy to insanity. Mustard infused in cucumber sauce cured epilepsy, while asphodel could be used as a treatment for ulcers and warts.

Many of Pliny's remedies were even more exotic. For fevers, cat's dung should be put together with the toe of an owl and tied to the body of a cat which had been killed just before the moon waned. The whole was to be preserved in salt and taken mixed with wine.

Roman pharmacists collected herbs and provided them for doctors who would select different ones and mix them according to their own prescriptions.

ABOVE RIGHT **A rare job for a woman: running a pharmacy.**

BELOW **Herbal remedies: saffron for eyes and fennel for nerves.**

Leading the newborn to the light of day

Childbirth in Roman times was hazardous both for mother and baby. When confinement was close, Juno, as Lucina, the one who leads the newborn to the light of day, was prayed to.

For immediate practical help the best-known expert on childbirth was Soranus of Ephesus, the first to discover how a displaced fetus could be turned in the womb – a discovery that was lost for the next 1,500 years. Soranus also recognized the signs of maturity in a fetus and advised on how the umbilical cord should be cut.

Soranus said that a newborn baby's eyes should be bathed in oil, and it should be fed on boiled honey, not milk, for the first two days of its life. Then mother's milk was best. Not only, said Soranus, was it more healthy, but it built up a closer bond between mother and child. Breastfeeding could continue for up to two years and provided a more sterile source of food than any alternative.

A bronze mask of Lucina, more fearsome than sympathetic.

Surviving the surgery

In one famous scene from Virgil's *Aeneid*, Aeneas is wounded in battle against Turnus, the champion of the Italians. One of Aeneas's companions from Troy struggles vainly to pull out the arrow with forceps, but it is too deeply embedded. Aeneas is saved only when the goddess Venus arrives bearing some dittany, a herb from Crete, which she mixes with Tiber water to release the arrow.

The Romans were used to dealing with wounds. The physician Galen was said to have learned his skills from patching up wounded gladiators, and every legion had its own skilled medical team accustomed to dealing with the various injuries suffered in army life. They knew how to assess the seriousness of each wound; when to leave a weapon embedded and when to try pulling it out. Each legion had its own hospital and these were well designed. At

one, on the German border, a hearth was found which was believed to have been used to sterilize instruments.

The fullest picture of the work of the Roman surgeon comes from Cornelius Celsus who compiled a treatise on medical practice in the 1st century AD. A surgeon, he recommends, should be young and have a strong and steady hand, able to use both left and right hands, and with sharp vision and an undaunted spirit. He must have enough sympathy to want to cure his patients but at the same time sufficient detachment not to be moved by their cries of pain. Otherwise he might be pressurized into working too fast or not cutting deeply enough.

There were some anesthetics: henbane and the opium poppy

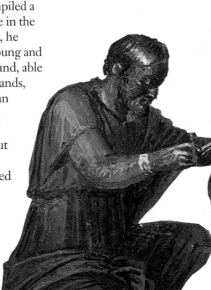

This 1st-century AD painting depicts the wounded Aeneas comforting his son while receiving treatment.

There were surgical instruments for almost any operation.

were two recommended herbs, but speed of operation was of the essence if the patient was not to suffer too much. It was also very important for a doctor to have strong assistants – they might be needed on occasion to hold a struggling patient down.

Celsus mentions over a hundred different medical instruments used in his time; many of these have survived. There are scalpels and catheters, probes and forceps, special instruments with hooks to pull out spearheads, and iron forceps for pulling out teeth. These precision tools were all carefully designed with a particular task in mind, from the removal of hemorrhoids to the breaking up of cataracts. Some of these instruments – the catheter for example, have lasted in the same form until today. Galen

recommended steel from the province of Noricum as being the best metal for surgical instruments, though many that have been found are made of bronze .

Celsus describes one amputation in gory detail: "A scalpel is used to cut the flesh to the bone, but not at a joint. When the bone is reached, the flesh is pulled back from it and undercut from around it so that part of the bone is made bare. The bone is now cut with a little saw as close as possible to the flesh. Then the end of the bone is smoothed and the skin drawn over it."

Some operations were quite delicate and complicated: top surgeons could insert a needle into an eye to push down or break up a cataract. Other operations seldom succeeded. Many skeletons have been found with unhealed holes in the skull where attempts to relieve pain by cutting through the bone ended instead in death.

PUBLIC AND PRIVATE FACES

Romans loved to be commemorated by portraits. They were a way of spreading one's influence, to contemporaries and posterity. Many were made only after death to be added to the collection of ancestors kept by the older families of Rome. Others were designed as a public memorial of benefaction or military achievement. The center of Rome was crammed with statues honoring real and mythical Romans of the past. The most interesting of the portraits are those on funerary monuments, portraying the deceased with the tools of their trade or at home with their families.

The emperors were adept at using their portraits for propaganda purposes. Statues were carefully designed to show off the virtues an emperor championed: piety, military valor or serene good government. The most prestigious public portrait was a statue cast in bronze; most of these have long since been melted down and marble statues are more common survivors. On a more intimate level, some of the finest portraits are those on engraved gems, the work of such gifted craftsmen as the Greek Dioskourides and his sons.

Death masks

When Drusus, son of the emperor Tiberius, died in AD 23, a long procession of portrait busts of his ancestors, stretching back even to Aeneas – claimed by the Julian family as their founder – slowly made its way through the streets of Rome.

Portrait busts were the treasured possessions of any aristocratic family. As soon as an important member of the family had died his features were immediately saved on wax. A death mask would be made and carried in his funeral procession. These masks were kept and paraded again at later funerals to show off the antiquity and achievements of the family.

This Roman noble is carrying busts of two of his ancestors.

Unsentimental portrayals

This bust is one of the finest portraits of the age of imperial sculpture. It is totally unsentimental in its portrayal of an aging woman who feels no need to flatter her looks. This realistic approach reflects a long tradition in Roman portraiture that has its roots in early Italian art. Subjects are portrayed as they are, not as they would like to be seen.

The tradition was created by sculptors of the republic who worked direct from death masks to produce some of the finest pieces of Roman art. Some of the best are of unknown Romans who had no concern with their public image. Wrinkles, sagging skin and dour expressions give an intimate picture of the typical middle class Italian of the period. Romans were not ashamed to be depicted as old. Age implied maturity, experience and

This bust of a woman dates from the end of the 1st century AD.

achievement and these were valued more highly than good looks.

In imperial times, portraits of the emperors went to the opposite extreme and idealized the subjects. Augustus was the master of the new approach. His statues were meticulously designed for the maximum propaganda effect. Many others followed the pattern set by Augustus. In one statue, the bow-legged and shambling Claudius was presented as the god Jupiter.

By the 3rd century, however, the older tradition of realism had reasserted itself. With its enemies closing in, the state desperately needed strong men, ruthless in their defense of the empire. The emperors are portrayed as tough but troubled men, their faces tormented with the strain of office.

One man and his wife

Less wealthy Romans could have their likenesses painted on wood or as frescoes on the walls of their houses. Some homes contained whole galleries of them but nearly all of them have now disappeared. Romans believed that a portrait carried with it many of the attributes of its subject. After the death of Faustina, wife of the emperor Marcus Aurelius, a gold statue of her was carried into the theater to set alongside her husband whenever he went there. When a person was discredited his or her portrait could be defaced, as Caracalla did with a portrait of his brother Geta and himself.

The most accomplished survivals come from Egypt where hundreds of portraits, painted on wood and then attached to the coffins of the deceased, have been preserved in the dry desert air. They are intensely realistic and detailed works of art. This example of a man and his wife comes from Pompeii where it was found on the wall of a house with a baker's shop attached. The name Paquius Proculus, also on the wall, was long assumed to be the man's name. In fact, it was part of an electioneering poster.

This painting is very similar in style to those found in Egypt. The woman's hair is styled in a fashion popular in the 1st century AD and she is wearing a tunic with a mantle over it. As was common at the time, she is portrayed with a pen and a writing tablet. The husband wears a toga, a sign of citizenship. He is carrying a papyrus scroll fastened with a red seal, and it may be that he was a law student.

Even an unknown Roman and his wife could be immortalized in a fresco on the wall of their house.

The secret of Roman portraiture

When a sculptor began to carve a marble bust, he used a geometrical technique which can be seen by looking at a popular bust of the emperor Hadrian.

The first likeness of the subject was probably modeled in clay; the task of translating the image into stone in a manner economical of material and effort involved a great challenge to the artist's skill.

The bust was initially carved as a relatively simple shape, with a cube for the head above a larger block for the shoulders. The head was planned to sit diagonally within this cube, so that the bust can be seen looking half-left.

Within this cube, the sculptor carved out the general shape of the head in the form of an oval, and several key points, such as the tip of the chin, the earlobe, and the longest curl of the beard, were all marked on its surface, each one measured with callipers to be equidistant from the curl in the center of the forehead.

The main planes of the face, such as the temples, the cheeks and the side of the nose, were then cut away, producing a portrait which is powerfully expressive and – equally important – capable of being copied by other sculptors in order to replicate the emperor's image as necessary. Over 30 copies of this bust of Hadrian have been found.

By the mid 2nd century sculptors had discovered how to reproduce the texture of skin and exploit contrasts of rough and smooth. This achieved an illusionistic effect, bringing much more life to the subject that had been previously known.

Drills were used to make the hair, mouth and ears. Drilling out the pupils was a technique developed in Hadrian's reign, or shortly after, to portray expressions, and later the eyelids were gouged.

The size of the torso also grew through the imperial era. At first, portraits were cut off at the collarbone; by the 2nd century they included the upper chest and arms; by the 3rd century the entire chest was depicted.

CULTS OF THE EAST

By the 1st century AD cults from the east had been brought in by traders, imported slaves and through the authorities themselves over a period of 300 years and Romans were used to them. These cults were highly mystical in comparison to the traditional ones of Rome. They abounded in secret ceremonies with complex rites often involving a final ecstatic experience in which the believer could find a personal and more direct relationship with his or her chosen deity. Promises of an afterlife in union with the god were common.

Christianity was to prove the most important of these mystery religions of the east. Although Christians insisted that theirs was an exclusive religion involving the rejection of all other cults, the popularity of Christianity cannot be understood if viewed in isolation from them. The idea of the death of a young man and his resurrection into new life was found in the legends of Attis and Osiris and the initiation into new life through the drinking of the blood of a savior was part of Mithraism. Most mystery cults involved shared meals similar to the Last Supper while portrayals of the Egyptian mother-goddess Isis with her son Horus are little different from those later made of the Virgin Mary and the child Jesus.

Sabazios, a god of creation

Sabazios's origins were in Thrace but his cult spread from his homeland first to Greece and then throughout the empire. Some equated him with Bacchus, others with Jupiter. His symbol was a serpent and one would be drawn across the breast of an initiate during ceremonies of initiation into his cult.

The most common symbol of Sabazios is a hand with two fingers and the thumb raised, a gesture adopted by the Christian church as a sign of benediction. The hands are sometimes bare but often contain figures: of Sabazios himself, a serpent or a cavern containing a mother and child.

Roman devotees saw Sabazios as a universal god of creation.

The men-only Mithras cult

Mithra, known as Mithras by the Romans, was originally the Iranian god of the sun. At the beginning of time Mithras had sacrificed a great bull. As its body was torn apart its blood brought to life grain and grapes and its scattered sperm fertilized all living things.

By the 2nd and 3rd century his worship had permeated the Roman empire from the east. As the cult traveled westward it took on new elements. Mithras became the god of kings, justice and

This gruesomely realistic statue shows blood flowing from the great bull which Mithras has just slain.

contracts, attractive to all those such as soldiers bound in complete loyalty to their rulers.

Women were excluded from the worship of Mithras but all men, whether they were freeborn or slaves, could participate equally in the long initiation ceremonies.

These involved complex rituals of purification as well as the simulated death and resurrection of the initiates.

Mithraeums, the underground chambers where the worship of Mithras took place were located throughout the empire, particularly where legions were stationed. The mithraeums were small – none could take more than 100 worshipers – and they were approached by subterranean passages where the initiation rites took place. There was always a relief of Mithras and the bull at one end and occasionally a bull sacrifice actually took place during the ceremonies.

"I approached the borders of death…"

And then, at the time deemed appropriate by the priest, he led me to the nearest public baths, accompanied by a crowd of priests. After I had been allowed my ordinary bath, he himself washed me and poured holy water over me and prayed to the gods for my purification. Then we returned to the temple in the afternoon, and he placed me at the feet of Isis and privately entrusted to me certain secrets which are too sacred to be revealed. But openly, with everyone else serving as a witness, he ordered me to abstain from the pleasure of food for ten consecutive days, to eat no meat, and to drink no wine. I maintained this fast with admirable self-restraint, and finally that day arrived which had been set for my appearance before the goddess. The setting sun made way for the evening star. At dusk, throngs of initiates poured in from all directions, each one honoring me with various gifts…Then, when all the laymen had been ordered to leave, the priest dressed me in a garment of new linen, took my

ABOVE **Every afternoon devotees of Isis took part in the water purification ceremony.**

RIGHT **Palm trees played a large part in the processions of Isis.**

ABOVE **The goddess Isis, here depicted with cow horns and a disk representing the sun.**

hand, and led me into the most sacred recess of the holy sanctuary…I approached the borders of death, I stepped upon the threshold of Proserpina, I was borne along through all the elements…I came into the presence of the gods who dwell above the earth and those who dwell below, and I paid them honor… When it was morning and the solemn rites had been concluded, I came out of the sanctuary as an ordained priest…I was splendidly garbed in a vestment of finest linen embroidered with flowers. Around

my shoulders was a priceless shawl which hung down my back right to my ankles. All over it were embroidered animals in different colors, Indian dragons, for example, and Hyperborean griffins…In my right hand I carried a blazing torch and around my head was a garland of white palm leaves, which projected outward like the rays of the sun, and I stood there like a statue.

In this autobiographical passage from *The Golden Ass*, Apuleius describes an initiation to Isis.

THE ARTS OF LIVING

Entering a wealthy Roman home in the 1st century AD would have been a colorful experience. The richness of the wall paintings of the public rooms and the ornate furniture covered with gaily colored cushions would have created an atmosphere of opulent – and perhaps even ostentatious – comfort.

Public rooms in the homes of well-off Romans were designed to impress. Marble was the most prestigious material for decoration and was brought in from every corner of the empire. At the Roman palace at Fishbourne in southern England, for instance, the white and colored marbles came from as far afield as the Pyrenees, the Greek islands and Asia. Wall paintings of Greek or Egyptian scenes were chosen to give an atmosphere of culture. Proud owners would commission extravagant pieces of gold or silver plate and boast – as did Trimalchio – of how many ounces they weighed. Huge numbers of statues from the east, often imported in mass, would line the walls.

These were only the richer homes; smaller villas – in Britain for example – normally had only one fully decorated reception room. The less wealthy had little in the way of furniture, usually wood, but every homeowner, no matter how poor, wanted to own at least one or two pieces of silver tableware.

Extravagant styles

In their desire to impress, wealthy Romans of the 1st century AD would fill their homes with furniture in the most extravagant of styles. Tables of bronze, marble or fine grained wood could be graced with legs carved in the shape of animals' paws and then topped by the head of a panther or lion. After Augustus's conquest of Egypt set off a new craze, some tables were supported by sphinxes or other animals from Egypt's rich mythology.

Fine statuary in marble or bronze would be shown off on elegant tripods and there would be ornate lamp stands with four or five bronze oil lamps hanging from a central column. The mosaic floors were often covered with furs – of deer, wolf, bear, leopard or lion – or with brightly decorated rugs from Asia Minor or Egypt.

Couches, on which guests would recline during a meal, were mostly of wood, but some might be inlaid with ivory, tortoise shell or even gold. This fine example of a *fulcrum*, the head rest of the couch, is in bronze. At one end is a mule's head with eyes inset in silver, at the other a satyr's head. Scenes from a vine harvest are inlaid in silver in the bronze. The couch dates from the 1st century AD and was found in a grave at Amiternum, modern Rimini, in northern Italy.

Everyday items, luxury materials

The richer households of imperial Rome were crowded with *objets d'art*, many of them specially commissioned. The Romans of imperial times had a passion for silver, sparked off by treasures brought back from the east by victorious generals.

By the 1st century blown glass was becoming increasingly common, and some blowers produced fine works of art. One glass masterpiece, known as the Portland Vase, was rediscovered in Rome in the 16th century. It was made of two layers of glass, one dark blue and one opaque white. The white was chipped away to create a cameo of the marriage between Peleus

and Thetis, the parents of Achilles.

Semiprecious stones were also popular. Large nodules of sardonyx (silica from Sardis in the province of Asia) were carved out into bowls and other vessels.

RIGHT **Objects of silver and pottery and a priceless fluorite cup (above right).**

Designs for the whole interior

"Room of the masks" from the palace of Augustus in Rome.

ABOVE **This detail from an unusual mosaic shows what is left after the banquet is over.**

LEFT This cameo glass plate was probably made by the same method as the Portland Vase.

By the 1st century AD patrons had an enormous variety of sources to draw on for the decoration of their rooms. Some would copy famous Greek paintings or show the cycle of a Greek legend such as the travels of Odysseus. Others would choose a theme, love or fertility, and portray the gods and goddesses of love.

Landscapes were particularly popular. Many were of idealized and exotic locations, such as the Nile. Others found in Pompeii were of local scenes, villas from along the coast, or woodland and hills. Rich garden themes were another favorite. When one owner in Pompeii lost part of a garden to a new room, he recreated the lost garden on the walls of the room.

Wall painting was only one part of internal decoration and rooms were designed as a whole. The floor was normally mosaic, another fashion imported from the east. In a richly painted room the fashion was to have a fairly plain design, often a black and white geometrical pattern. By the 1st century AD mosaic was also found on walls, particularly in rounded recesses where the colored glass used could best reflect light. Stucco reliefs on walls or ceilings were also common.

The colors used in decoration were strong. Black and red were popular in the early empire but at Pompeii hazy blues and greens are often used to give a more peaceful and less opulent look to rooms.

This detail from a stone relief shows the elaborate designs used on objects of any size.

Chapter 5

PILLARS OF THE EMPIRE

"Others, no doubt, will better mold the bronze
To the semblance of soft breathing, draw from marble
The living countenance; and others plead
With greater eloquence, or learn to measure
Better than we, the pathways of the heaven,
The risings of the stars; remember, Roman,
To rule the people under law, to establish
The way of peace, to battle down the haughty,
To spare the meek. Our fine arts, these, forever."
- Virgil's *Aeneid*

The self-appointed destiny of Rome was to bring peace and the rule of law to the subject peoples of the empire, and Romans had supreme confidence in their ability to reach this goal. Roman rule was often imposed brutally, but once peace had been secured the new rulers were relatively tolerant. Local customs and religious beliefs were respected – so long as they did not threaten the state – and many major cities survived with their governments and traditions intact. In the less-developed west, Roman culture spread through new patterns of town life and the granting of Roman citizenship to those who accepted Roman rule. This combination of tolerance and harshness ensured the empire's existence for more than four centuries. Many of the institutions that upheld it – the roads, the towns, the law, the language – survived the eventual collapse of the empire itself, making its ultimate impact on western history and culture a profound one.

Even in ruins, this 1st-century theater at Leptis Magna in north Africa displays the former wealth and splendor of the Roman world.

The **people** of the empire were equally diverse. By the 3rd century AD only 40 percent of the senators were Italians by origin: about 30 percent came from the east, another 15 percent from Africa.

At the height of its power, the Roman empire was one of extraordinary diversity, encompassing the damp hills and woodlands of northern Britain and Germany, the mountain ranges of northern Italy and Spain, the scorching deserts of Africa and Syria. Within this vast area there were over 100 million people under Roman rule.

Among the subject peoples of the empire were the heirs of ancient civilizations, such as Greece and Egypt, whose traditions were so deeply rooted that they were hardly affected by the culture of Rome. Greek, for example, remained the unchallenged first language of the eastern empire with Latin used only for official business. The Jews also had a strong national and religious identity which they were determined to preserve against Roman control.

In the north and west of the empire the Romans had gained control of most of Celtic Europe. The Celts were a warrior people who had offered impressive resistance to Roman rule over four centuries. Although their leaders were to adopt Roman manners in the years that followed, local customs and religious beliefs survived and were often absorbed by the Romans. In Africa, the Punic civilization, established by the Phoenicians, persisted under Roman rule.

The Roman empire was a cosmopolitan one: a loose collection of peoples whose only common link was that they had once been conquered by the Romans. There had been other, similar, empires before, but what was remarkable about the Roman empire was that it was able to maintain effective control of such an enormous area for so long with relatively little opposition.

Ultimately much of Roman rule relied on the use of force. A great deal of the empire was acquired by direct conquest and on some occasions, such as the pacification of inland Spain under Augustus, this was carried out with great cruelty. If revolts occurred the Roman response was ruthless. A million lives were lost in the Jewish revolt of 66–70; in AD 61 when Boudicca, queen of the Iceni in Britain, led her people against the Romans, retribution was terrible.

In the long term, however, an empire as large and widespread as Rome could not be maintained by force alone. The Romans were a pragmatic and practical people and their achievement as administrators was to design a system which would work without unnecessary stress.

The emperor himself has direct control of many provinces

The structure of the administration was simple. The empire was divided into provinces – between 30 and 40 in the 1st and 2nd centuries. As part of the "restored republic", the Senate retained nominal responsibility for the older and more settled provinces of the empire and selected a governor, proconsul, for each by lot. Governors were normally experienced senators who served for a year.

Any province which was vulnerable to unrest or invasion was placed under the direct control of the emperor. This was the result of the settlement made between Augustus and the Senate in 27 BC. All 11 provinces along the Rhine and Danube borders, and Syria and Britain, were imperial provinces. The governors in these provinces were directly appointed by the emperor himself and tended to serve for longer than the senatorial

After the **Iceni** king Prasutagus died, the Romans brutally annexed the kingdom. His widow Boudicca led her people into battle and caused the death of thousands of Romans.

RIGHT **This beautiful 1st-century BC Nile mosaic depicts Egypt, one of Rome's most exotic provinces and a great financial asset. Augustus considered it so much his private property that senators could not go there without permission.**

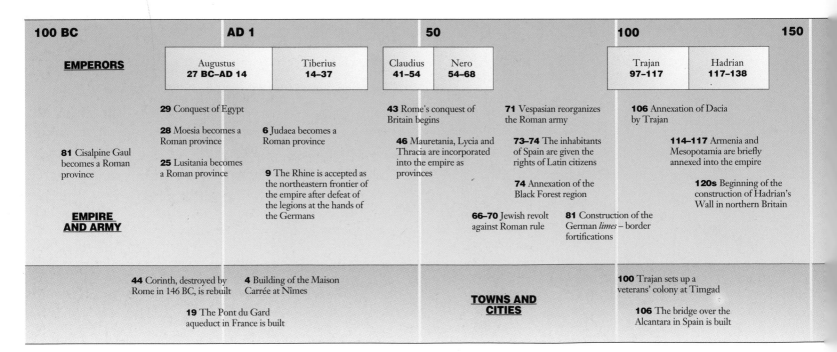

100 BC		AD 1		50			100		150

EMPERORS

Augustus 27 BC–AD 14	Tiberius 14–37	Claudius 41–54	Nero 54–68		Trajan 97–117	Hadrian 117–138

EMPIRE AND ARMY

81 Cisalpine Gaul becomes a Roman province

29 Conquest of Egypt

28 Moesia becomes a Roman province

25 Lusitania becomes a Roman province

6 Judaea becomes a Roman province

9 The Rhine is accepted as the northeastern frontier of the empire after defeat of the legions at the hands of the Germans

43 Rome's conquest of Britain begins

46 Mauretania, Lycia and Thracia are incorporated into the empire as provinces

71 Vespasian reorganizes the Roman army

73–74 The inhabitants of Spain are given the rights of Latin citizens

74 Annexation of the Black Forest region

66–70 Jewish revolt against Roman rule

81 Construction of the German *limes* – border fortifications

106 Annexation of Dacia by Trajan

114–117 Armenia and Mesopotamia are briefly annexed into the empire

120s Beginning of the construction of Hadrian's Wall in northern Britain

44 Corinth, destroyed by Rome in 146 BC, is rebuilt

4 Building of the Maison Carrée at Nîmes

19 The Pont du Gard aqueduct in France is built

TOWNS AND CITIES

100 Trajan sets up a veterans' colony at Timgad

106 The bridge over the Alcantara in Spain is built

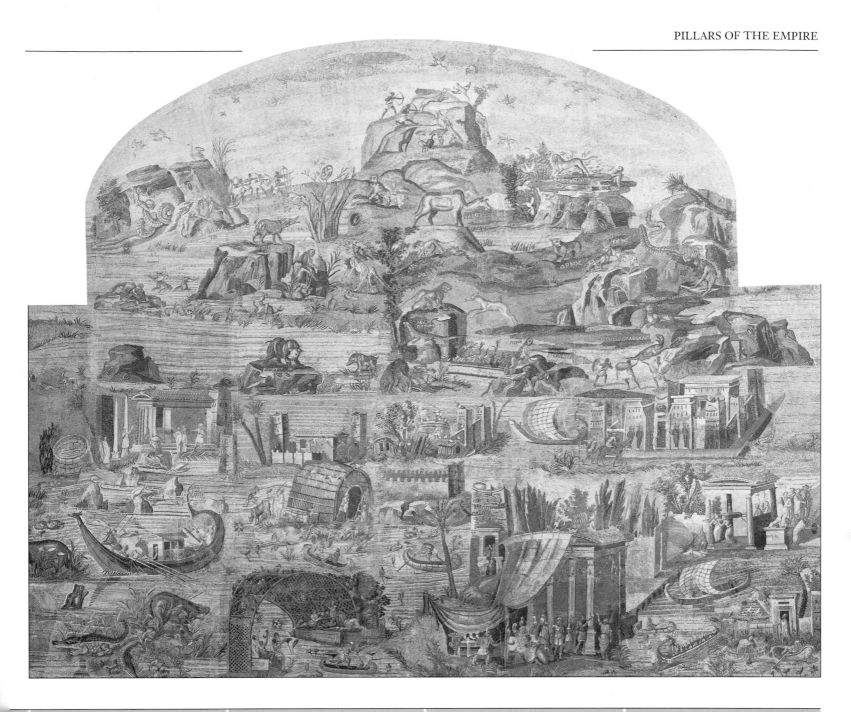

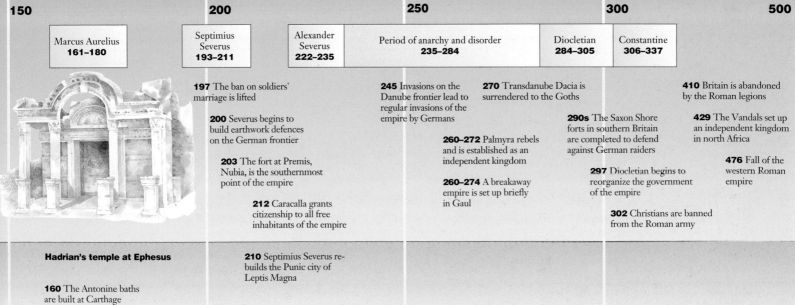

150		200		250		300		500

| Marcus Aurelius 161–180 | Septimius Severus 193–211 | Alexander Severus 222–235 | Period of anarchy and disorder 235–284 | Diocletian 284–305 | Constantine 306–337 |

197 The ban on soldiers' marriage is lifted

200 Severus begins to build earthwork defences on the German frontier

203 The fort at Premis, Nubia, is the southernmost point of the empire

212 Caracalla grants citizenship to all free inhabitants of the empire

245 Invasions on the Danube frontier lead to regular invasions of the empire by Germans

260–272 Palmyra rebels and is established as an independent kingdom

260–274 A breakaway empire is set up briefly in Gaul

270 Transdanube Dacia is surrendered to the Goths

290s The Saxon Shore forts in southern Britain are completed to defend against German raiders

297 Diocletian begins to reorganize the government of the empire

302 Christians are banned from the Roman army

410 Britain is abandoned by the Roman legions

429 The Vandals set up an independent kingdom in north Africa

476 Fall of the western Roman empire

Hadrian's temple at Ephesus

160 The Antonine baths are built at Carthage

210 Septimius Severus rebuilds the Punic city of Leptis Magna

governors – normally terms of between three and five years. However, despite the formal distinction between senatorial and imperial provinces, it was still the emperor who had ultimate responsibility for the whole of the empire, and he would be quite ready to send an imperial governor into a senatorial province if it proved to be necessary.

What was extraordinary about the administration of the empire were the small numbers involved: there were perhaps 150 key officials in the whole of the empire. The Romans' secret of successful control was to be found in the smallest unit of administration, the *polis* or *civitas*. This was a community with some measure of independence, normally based on a town or city but including the territory around it.

It was the job of the provincial administrators to collaborate with the local elite of each *polis* or *civitas*. Normally these elites were represented in

CITIES AND ROADS OF THE EMPIRE
The romanization of towns was a vital element in spreading the Roman way of life throughout the empire. By the early 4th century, the Romans had built a road network of 85,000 kilometers throughout the empire, linking Rome with the most distant provinces. The empire embraced people of many different races and traditions.

BELOW **This life-sized statue from southern France depicts a noble Gallic warrior in full battle dress.**

RIGHT **2nd-century farmers from the Rhineland, dressed like modern monks.**

LEFT **Juba, the king of Numidia, was a friend of Augustus and married the daughter of Antony and Cleopatra.**

LEFT **This funerary portrait of an Egyptian woman is in the Christian Coptic style, created in the 3rd century AD.**

the councils of each city, so it was vital to ensure that these councillors remained loyal to Rome. The first approach was to leave them the responsibility for law and order and the everyday running of city life. Councillors competed with one another in beautifying their cities with fine buildings. This gained them local status and access to Roman citizenship; a few with the required wealth could also achieve equestrian status and then progress to a seat in the Senate.

One particular task delegated to local councillors was the collection of tax. For the empire this delegation cut the cost of administration. For the councillors it kept unwanted officials away from them and allowed them to determine, at least in part, how the burden of tax should be distributed.

The main direct tax, from which Italy was exempt, was the tribute, which was raised partly on property and partly on citizenship. Each

provincial area had to produce a census of its citizens and wealth on which the assessment would be made. Once the councillors had collected what was due, money and goods (some tax was paid in grain or other produce) were given to the central government in Rome which made the decisions about how they should be allocated.

"Quickly he calculates what the Roman armies beneath every sky demand, how much the tribes and the temples, how much the lofty aqueducts, the fortresses by the coasts or the far-flung lines of roads require," is one description of an imperial accountant. The more wealthy provinces – particularly those of the east which provided 60 percent of the taxes of the empire – subsidized the defense and the administration of the poorer provinces, such as Britain. One of Rome's greatest successes was convincing taxpayers of the benefits of paying taxes for the maintenance of defense and order.

Taxation included an indemnity, a fine exacted from a nation's people in compensation for the Romans' costs of fighting and defeating them. A poll tax covered the cost of keeping a governor and army in a province.

A network of roads helps spread Roman civilization throughout the empire

However, there were weaknesses in the tax system: it was too rigid, and for centuries there was no proper budgeting system. New money could not be raised quickly and there were seldom any reserves. When war broke out, the strain was felt immediately, and at one time Marcus Aurelius even had to auction some of the furniture of the imperial household to make ends meet.

As soon as a new part of the empire had been absorbed, a network of roads was planned. The roads were, at first, instruments of control; the best were built with surfaces of crushed limestone or stone slabs set above gravel from which water would drain into side ditches. Armies and administrators moved along them, the official couriers covering at least 80 kilometers a day. Although the armies could not move quite as fast, they were still able to reach trouble relatively quickly, snuffing out revolts before they spread. Roads also provided a link between the urban centers, vital to the spread of Roman administration.

The Romans, like the Greeks, valued towns as transmitters of civilization. Their fine public buildings acted as a backdrop to all the social and political activities which made up civilized living. In the newly conquered territories of the west, towns were used to turn warlike tribes into peaceful citizens.

Once town leaders had demonstrated their loyalty to Rome, they could be offered citizenship. Citizenship was a reward for cooperation and it was restricted at first to the more influential local leaders. "You have divided all the people of

Roads were marked every Roman mile (1,000 paces) by cylindrical milestones with details of the current emperor and the distance from the nearest town. This information was either engraved or added later in paint. Many emperors paid for the repair of badly damaged roads.

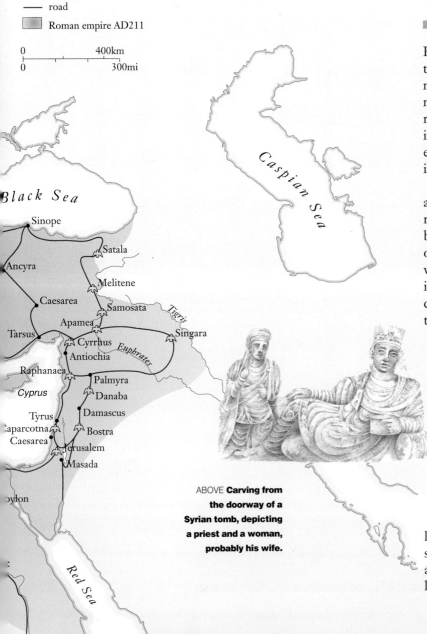

legionary camp
— road
Roman empire AD211

0   400km
0   300mi

Caspian Sea

Black Sea

Sinope

Satala

Ancyra

Melitene

Caesarea

Samosata

Apamea

Tigris

Tarsus

Cyrrhus *Euphrates* Singara

Antiochia

Raphanaea

Palmyra

Cyprus

Danaba

Tyrus

Damascus

aparcotna Bostra

Caesarea

erusalem

Masada

Red Sea

ylon

ABOVE **Carving from the doorway of a Syrian tomb, depicting a priest and a woman, probably his wife.**

the empire in two classes: the more cultured, better born and more influential everywhere you have declared Roman citizens…the rest vassals and subjects," proclaimed Aelius Aristides.

Citizenship gave some protection. The original rights of citizens, under the republic, included a vote in the popular assembly and a right of appeal to the assembly against sentence for criminal charges. In the early empire, a right of appeal to the emperor was particularly cherished. The Acts of the Apostles tell how Paul's citizenship saved him from being flogged.

Not even the emperor can hold himself above the law of the land

On the other hand, citizenship could bring liability to certain taxes from which others were exempt, such as the inheritance tax instituted by Augustus in 6 BC specifically to pay for the discharge settlements of the legionaries. Caracalla, short of money, doubled the rate of inheritance tax in 212 shortly before he proclaimed citizenship for all free inhabitants of the empire. Despite any disadvantages of citizenship, however, this extension to everyone was a remarkable occurrence, welcome to those who benefited from it, and an indication of the existence of a true world-state.

The concept of citizenship suggests a legal system in which rights were recognized and protected. This legal system was central to Roman rule. "Law is the bond which secures our privileges in the commonwealth, the foundation of our new liberty and the fountain head of justice…the state without law would be like the human body without mind," as Cicero wrote.

The Romans grasped the essential features of an effective legal system. The law was supreme and everyone, even an emperor, had to operate within its rule. Once a law had been passed by a competent authority it had to be obeyed, however cruel its operation. With the decline of republican institutions the emperor became increasingly the fount of law but he always had to abide by it.

Two principles of Roman law were that it should be publicly known and new cases should be decided by rational argument proceeding from earlier decisions. By the 2nd and 3rd centuries AD the laws of the state and the principles for deciding new cases had become so developed that it was possible for jurists, such as Gaius and Ulpian, to compile codifications of the law, a process which was followed under Diocletian and which resulted finally in the great *Codes and Digests* of Justinian issued in 529 and 533.

It is difficult to assess the cultural impact of all these influences on the ordinary subjects of the empire. A Jewish document of the 2nd century records the conversation of two rabbis. "How fine are the works of these people," says one. "They have made streets, they have made bridges, they have erected baths." The other replies, "All that they have made they have made for themselves, they have built marketplaces to put harlots in, baths to rejuvenate themselves, bridges to levy tolls for themselves."

Over 90 percent of the subjects of the empire continued to live in the countryside, often remote from the main institutions of Roman control. Although they remained vulnerable to local exploitation and to an economy which remained undeveloped, all benefited from the *pax Romana*, the long years of peace in which fields could be cultivated without fear. Once internal order had been achieved, the *pax Romana* depended on the maintenance of stable frontiers. There was no way this could be done easily or cheaply. There were thousands of kilometers of frontier to defend, passing through a variety of landscapes. In most cases little more could be done than to define the limits to be held against outsiders. Sometimes these ran along natural boundaries – rivers and mountains – and when no such boundaries existed, walls, roads or palisades were built across open areas.

The length of the empire's border makes the army's job of defense harder

On the frontiers, auxiliary troops were stationed to watch the movements of unconquered tribes and respond to attacks from raiders. The main strength of the Roman army, the legions, were stationed back from the borders and were on call to deal with more serious invasions. By the 2nd century each was allocated a permanent place in one of the more vulnerable areas of the empire.

These arrangements could never be strong enough to ward off a concerted attack. The best hope of security, as the Romans were aware, came from keeping the frontier tribes split among themselves. As the historian Tacitus remarked, "May the tribes ever retain, if not love for us, at least hatred for each other." Some tribes were bought off by regular payments, but if real trouble

Cornelius **Tacitus** was trained in rhetoric. He was a public orator, a government official and one of the most famous writers of Roman history. His historical books were appreciated for their style as much as for their facts.

threatened, force would have to be used. A common tactic was to launch preemptive strikes across the borders in order to break up enemy tribes.

In the north, a frontier line had been drawn along the Rhine and the Danube (with a 2nd-century expansion northward into Dacia). Here there were 4,000 kilometers to guard, mostly along river banks but overland between the sources of the two rivers. The rivers on their own did not offer much of a barrier so during the 1st and 2nd centuries a complex of forts and watchtowers were erected along the more vulnerable stretches.

It was the Danube frontier which was most exposed to the pressures of northern tribes and it was here that the bulk of the frontier legions were stationed. In AD 138 there were 10 legions – with auxiliaries, a total of about 100,000 men – along the Danube, compared with four on the Rhine.

Another unsettled frontier in the north of the empire was that of Britain. Successive emperors had debated whether to try and subdue the whole island or whether to accept that the north was unconquerable. Under Hadrian, a formal boundary was established between the Tyne and the Solway — Hadrian's Wall.

It was at the eastern end of the empire that Rome faced its strongest enemy, Parthia. Augustus had resisted the temptation to attack the Parthians: their territory was inhospitable and difficult to hold while their horsemen were more than a match for the cumbersome Roman infantry. Rome and Parthia used Armenia as a buffer state between them; to the west of Armenia, client states were gradually absorbed by Rome and a frontier stabilized. It was of formidable length, running along the Euphrates and then breaking south across the Syrian desert to the Red Sea. The shortest marching route between the Black Sea and the Red Sea was 3,000 kilometers. An extensive system of roads was built to support the frontier, with eight legions stationed well back in Roman territory but able to move forward to deal with any threats.

The southern frontier of the empire across northern Africa – 4,000 kilometers in a straight line – proved the easiest to defend. Once the power of Carthage had been broken at the end of the 3rd century BC, there were few major military threats to Roman control. It was the climate, the desert and the mountains which hindered expansion. In the 2nd century only 45,000 troops (including legionaries and auxiliaries) were allocated for the entire frontier. Ditches and watchtowers were built along parts of the border. Their main purpose was to protect from raiders the richer

ABOVE **This 2nd-century bronze sestertius shows the Danube, the frontier which at one time required more legions than any other for its defense.**

RIGHT **Romanization often had its violent and brutal side: in this stone relief a defiant barbarian fights back against a legionary.**

LEFT **Trier was an ancient capital of the Treveri, a mixed Celto-Germanic people. The** *Porta Nigra* **(black gate) was part of the defensive walls. In the 3rd century the gate reflected the city's status as an imperial capital.**

agricultural areas where both native and Roman settlers produced grain and olives.

Augustus had judged that 150,000 men, divided into 28 legions, represented the smallest number of soldiers which could keep order without offering a political threat to the state. It was vital that the army should never become the tool of ambitious generals; to make sure that it remained loyal to the emperor, Augustus insisted on adequate pay and conditions. The yearly pay for a legionary was 900 sesterces a year, over double that of a laborer in 1st-century Rome.

The legions were scattered throughout the empire. This was mainly for reasons of defense, but offered the added advantage that a sizable force would have difficulty in combining to offer a political threat to any emperor. The soldiers were also bound by oath to the emperor and they were not allowed to forget their loyalty. A 3rd-century military calendar of feast days was dominated by the commemoration of anniversaries of emperors.

As pressures on the frontiers grew in the 2nd and 3rd centuries, many senior commanders proved inept. Marcus Aurelius reversed the standard practice by appointing the most able officers he could find and then making them senators.

Armenia was strategically crucial as it offered the best access from the empire into the fertile plains of Mesopotamia, the main source of food for the Parthian kingdom.

The **Zealots** were a Jewish sect totally opposed to the authorities and pagan gods of Rome. Many turned to terrorism, and these extremists were known as *sikarioi* or dagger men.

Septimius Severus took the process a stage further by appointing equestrians direct to army commands and making promotion easier from below. The emperor Gallienus excluded senators from command altogether.

Generals had to be prudent – particularly when, by the 2nd century, the role of the army had become essentially one of defense rather than expansion. The siege of the Zealot stronghold of Masada in the Jewish revolt of AD 66–70 is a good example of professional caution. Nothing was left to chance: an enormous assault embankment surmounted by a stone platform, in all over 100 meters high, was painstakingly built for the final attack. It was this steady and systematic approach – engineering warfare – which was the hallmark of Roman fighting tactics.

During the long years of peace there were problems in maintaining good discipline and high morale. Troops in Syria, where the Eastern High Command was based, were particularly susceptible to temptation. "The army you took over," one 2nd-century senator was told, "was demoralized by luxury and immorality and prolonged idleness. The soldiers at Antioch used to spend their time applauding actors and were more often found in the nearest tavern garden than in the ranks… gambling was rife in the camps, sleep night-long, or, if a watch was kept, it was over the wine cups."

The riches of the empire make it an irresistible target for attack

Although the Roman troops were the backbone of the empire, by the 3rd century they had lost mobility and become anchored to their permanent forts across the empire. What they could not do was to respond quickly to a mass of invaders who could choose when and where to breach the extended frontiers of the empire.

The wealth of the Roman empire made it attractive to outsiders and the length of its frontiers made it vulnerable to attack. From the 2nd century the German tribes were becoming better organized to face the legions and grouped in larger units. In the 3rd century the revived Persian empire of the Sasanids posed a dangerous threat to Mesopotamia, Armenia and Syria. It was the combination of these two enemies that proved catastrophic. As soon as the frontiers were broken the invaders could swarm along the road network hundreds of miles into Roman territory.

The structure of administration was shattered in the 3rd century with invasions continuing year after year and reaching a climax in the latter part of the century. The collection of taxes became

LEFT **A wild boar, the symbol for the 20th legion which invaded Britain with Claudius.**

RIGHT **Masada, once the stronghold of King Herod, was captured in AD 66 by Jewish Zealots who fiercely defended their position until AD 70 when they were finally overcome by the Roman army after a siege of several months.**

RIGHT **The peace-loving Antoninus Pius preferred to settle disputes with diplomacy rather than war. However, he could not avoid all conflict and this relief, carved in his honor, shows soldiers preparing for battle.**

impossible just when enormous resources were needed to pay the armies. Soldiers and officials resorted to the direct seizure of whatever they needed, forcing local populations to flee. As one petitioner to the emperor Philip the Arab put it in 245, "Soldiers, powerful men from the cities, your own officials, leave the highways, descend on us, take us from our work, seize our plough and oxen and illegally extort what is not due to them."

Throughout the empire, city life was seriously dislocated. Systems of law and order broke down, and deserters and bandits roamed the countryside. Many independent kingdoms sprang up: in 260 the army commander Postumus declared an independent state in Gaul, which lasted until 274. In the east another state, around the trading city of Palmyra, maintained its independent status from 260 until 272.

What was remarkable, however, was that, despite all the setbacks, the empire survived. The mass of its people remained loyal, a tribute to the success with which the Romans had integrated subjects into their own world. There were always new leaders ready to keep the Roman world politically united, and many of these came from outlying provinces.

HADRIAN'S WALL

Hadrian's Wall, built between 122 and 128, is the most celebrated Roman remains in Britain and the most impressive surviving frontier of the empire. It runs for 80 Roman miles – 117 kilometers – from the Tyne river to the Solway Firth, and was built on the orders of the emperor Hadrian. The wall was not designed to be a major military barrier and would not have been able to withstand a major invasion. It was, instead, intended to mark the frontier of the empire and to provide a base from which the tribes to the north could be watched and controlled. There were gates at regular intervals along the wall and "barbarians" were free to go through to trade in the empire, so long as they were unarmed.

MAIN IMAGE **Hadrian's Wall followed the natural contours of the rugged landscape. It was a bleak winter posting for the 11,500 soldiers manning the wall and its forts.**

The wall, of rubble and concrete faced with stone, was built by the soldiers of the legions stationed in Britain. They were men who were highly skilled in surveying and stonework and would have needed no outside help. When the wall was finished it was manned by auxiliaries drawn from northern Europe. Germans and Gauls served alongside locally recruited British. The most troublesome time was the 4th century when a new enemy, the Picts, menaced the frontier from the north. No fewer than three Roman emperors came to Britain to confront them. By the early 5th century, however, all was over. Britain ceased to be part of the empire and the wall was gradually abandoned.

ABOVE **There were forts built at relatively equal distances along the wall. They could each accommodate up to 1,000 soldiers.**

RIGHT **The wall was a typical *limes*, or complex with roads, forts and frontier posts to dominate border regions.**

RIGHT **Security was provided by a deep, steep-sided ditch in front and a broader ditch, the *vallum*, behind. A sloped north bank gave sentries a clear view.**

Ditch   Wall   Road   Vallum   North mound   South mound

111

CRADLES OF CIVILIZATION

To the Roman way of thinking, civilized life depended almost entirely on the city. In newly conquered territories, particularly in the west, the first settlements would be the *coloniae*, settlements of retired soldiers, which were laid out on a uniform plan in provincial territory. The typical Roman town had a grid pattern of streets, a colonnaded forum, temples, a basilica and perhaps a theater and baths.

Gradually, provincials copied the design of the Roman city in the development of their own cities. The expensive building program which each of these towns demanded was sustained by rents from city land, the sale of offices and, most important of all, local benefactions – in some cases, that of the emperor.

In Greece, and along the north African coast, there were old traditions of city life to build on, but in the northwestern provinces of the empire, city life was much less developed and the spread of the Roman colonies and administrative centers brought a new way of living with them. The way in which the empire induced provincial leaders to take on the culture of Rome was a great success, and it was achieved above all through their adoption of the culture of the city.

A day at the theater

The art of the theater came to Rome from Greece. Comedy and tragedy were at first the most popular but by the 2nd century AD the preference had shifted toward mime and farce, with music and dance an essential part of every performance. Later many theaters staged wild beast fights as well.

The seating arrangements were very formal with heavy fines for anyone who occupied the wrong row. This emphasis on rank was not so strongly enforced in any other public setting, and was an inducement to provincials to conform.

Masks were used in every kind of play.

Exercise, relaxation and cleanliness

In one of his letters the Stoic philosopher, Seneca, described what it was like to live over a bath-house. The noise was appalling: there were the groans of those exercising with weights, the splashes of those jumping into the pools, the shouts of those whose armpits were being plucked by the professional arm pluckers. The baths were far more than just places to wash in: they were leisure centers where one could exercise (an idea imported from Greece), meet friends, or even retire to a library to read.

Stallholders thronged the passageways, prostitutes lingered looking for custom. An apt Roman saying was, "Baths, wine and sex ruin our bodies. But what makes life worth living except baths, wine and sex?" The bath-house spread throughout the empire. In Greece baths were added to the gymnasiums and often

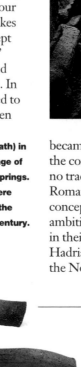

Bathing implements: strigils, for scraping the skin clean, and an oil flask.

Baths at Aquae Sulis (Bath) in Britain took advantage of the natural hot springs. The baths were rebuilt in the 18th century.

became the dominant building of the complex. In the west there was no tradition of bathing and the Roman bath-house was a new concept, eagerly adopted by ambitious locals in their towns and in their villas. In some cases – the Hadrianic baths at Leptis Magna or the North Baths at Timgad in Numidia – provincial bath-houses rivaled the great imperial baths of Rome. Normally, however, they were much smaller establishments, run privately. All baths offered people from all walks of life the chance to relax and enjoy the luxury of hot water – a luxury which, once lost, did not reappear for centuries.

The heart of the city

The Roman temple derived from both Greek and Etruscan models. Greek columns were used increasingly from the 2nd century BC, but normally they were placed only along the front of the temple – not on all four sides as was in the practice in Greece.

Temples were imposing buildings and formed a striking feature of any Roman town. They were raised on a high platform to dominate the area around them and were approached up a flight of steps. Temples were not built to house congregations, but to be used by priests and certain officials for the set rituals of Roman religion.

The temple was, however, much more than just an imposing building: it brought the cults of Rome to the provinces, aiding the process of romanization. During the time of Augustus, a dedication to the three gods of the Capitol – Jupiter, Juno and Minerva – was common and was adopted by many of the cities of north Africa.

Later temples were dedicated to deified emperors or their families. Augustus was often coupled in the dedication with the city of Rome. There was a monumental temple to Domitian in Ephesus and another to Hadrian, in addition to the city's ancient temple to Diana – one of the seven wonders of the ancient world. Claudius allowed a temple to be dedicated to himself in Britain while he was still alive, in the hope of fostering loyalty in a newly acquired province.

The Romans were prepared to accept provincial cults – so long as

A temple to Jupiter, Juno and Minerva at Thugga (Dougga in Libya); Diana depicted as a mother-goddess at Ephesus.

they did not threaten the power of Rome – and these were often adapted within Roman culture. In Gaul, statues of the Celtic god, Cernunnos, have been found alongside those of Apollo. The Romano-Celtic temples were generally decorated with Corinthian columns.

Roman temples were not designed for large gatherings; as Christianity became the official religion of the empire they slowly lost their religious significance. The Christians preferred to adopt another form of Roman building – the basilica – for their worship.

COMFORTS OF HOME

The spread of Roman civilization, especially through the western provinces, was highly successful and the villa, like the town, was introduced throughout the empire. Villas took many forms, according to the demands of the local environment and the social position of their owners. Not all were based directly on Italian models, but they all incorporated many features of Roman culture: the mosaic, the bath-house and the colonnaded courtyard were the most common.

The villa, with its ostentatious decorations and furnishings, provided a certain status for its owner. The public rooms were invariably the best furnished and sometimes a portico was added to the front of the villa to give it a sense of grandeur. However, villas also gave their owners a chance to escape the damp, cold and drafts of earlier buildings. Above all, they also provided the privacy of separate bedrooms and bath-houses. The Roman villas were probably the first comfortable homes in the history of western Europe.

"A fountain plays…"

From the end of the colonnade projects a dining room: through its folding doors it looks on to the end of the terrace, the adjacent meadow and the stretch of open country beyond…

Almost opposite the middle of the colonnade is a suite of rooms set slightly back and round a small court shaded by plane trees. In the center a fountain plays in a marble basin, watering the plane trees round it and the ground beneath them with its light spray…

At the corner of the colonnade is a large bedroom facing the dining room. Some windows look out on to the terrace, others on to the meadow, while just below the windows in front is an ornamental pool. A pleasure both to see and to hear with its water falling from a height and foaming white when it strikes the marble. This room is very warm in winter when it is bathed in sunshine and on a cloudy day hot steam from the adjacent furnace room serves instead.

Then you pass through a large and cheerful dressing room belonging to the bath, to the cooling room, which contains a good-sized shady swimming

bath. If you want more space to swim or warmer water, there is a pool in the courtyard and a well near to it to tone you up with cold water when you have had enough of the warm.

I can enjoy a profounder peace there, more comfort and fewer cares. I need never wear a formal toga and there are no neighbors to disturb me, everywhere there is peace and quiet which adds as much to the healthiness of the place as the clear sky and pure air.

In one of his letters, Pliny lovingly describes the joys of his villa in the hills of Tuscany.

A private water supply was a luxury even for rich Romans.

A desirable residence

The typical villa, with its plaster work, mosaic floors and colonnades, brought new elegance to the countryside.

Mosaics were common in the grandest rooms, and the finest mosaics were found in the villas of north Africa. One popular theme was villa life itself; many people also had mosaics of dogs, warning would-be intruders to beware of the dog, or *cave canem*.

In the richer villas throughout the empire the walls had painted plaster and for hotter days there was a courtyard adorned with columns and a fountain or ornamental pool.

Except in the homes of the very rich, furniture was limited. Most furnishings – chairs, stools and beds, for instance – were made of wood and were in quite simple designs. Woven cloth was used as bed and floor coverings and for hangings on the walls. Colors were bright – even garish – as were many of the colors used on the painted wall plaster.

Many villa owners tried to be as self-sufficient as possible, and employed their own weavers,

Agriculture was an important part of life in any Roman villa and the four seasons were a popular motif for mosaics.

fullers, dyers, smiths and carpenters. The furniture in a villa was often made on the premises.

The very status-conscious provincials imported goods from Italy or even farther afield. Roman lamps were popular: they used olive oil and were more pleasant to use – though far more expensive – than the commonly used candles that had an unsavory smell.

Samian ware – the rich red pottery from Arretium (modern Arezzo) in central Italy, with its reliefs of Roman mythology or daily life – also spread throughout the empire. Glass drinking cups spread northward from centers such as Aquileia. These would all be kept stored in cupboards or displayed on tables along the sides of the room. A few homes even used silverware. By the end of the 1st century most of these goods were being made locally, a sign of how strong the market had become for such everyday objects.

Impressing the neighbors

For the Roman aristocrat the villa provided a civilized retreat away from the noise and bustle of Rome. By building their homes facing away from the farm yard and labor quarters the wealthy could show off their cultured status as aristocrats rather than farmers.

Roman civilization brought to the provinces new standards of physical comfort. Effective heating was one of the most welcome, particularly in the northern provinces, and most villas had a hypocaust (underfloor central heating) system for at least one reception room. Hot air from a furnace was fed under a floor and then left to escape up flues in the walls. Though simple, hypocausts were fairly efficient.

Painting of a villa near Augusta Treverorum (Trier in Germany) showing farm hands at work.

Fixtures and fittings

In the towns, running water was brought into homes by clay, lead or wooden pipes or collected from the local fountain. In the countryside, though, villa owners had to find their own sources, using rainwater, wells or neighboring rivers. Not every villa had its own running water supply and slaves or domestic staff were used to carry and store what the household needed.

Water was required to service the bath-house – an essential part of most villas. The grander ones had three main rooms, one to change in and then a hot and a cold plunge. Their

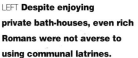

LEFT **Despite enjoying private bath-houses, even rich Romans were not averse to using communal latrines.**

ABOVE **Oil lamps were expensive, so days often ended at sunset; locks were used for doors as well as chests and boxes.**

floors were also heated so that the bathers were insulated as far as possible from the cold. Sometimes drainage was built in and often surplus water was used to flush down the waste pipes leading from the latrines.

Romans combined the pursuit of personal hygiene with their social life. Both the bath-houses and the latrines were places to relax and talk. Inhibitions on nakedness, which had been strong in republican times, were now more relaxed and people enjoyed communal facilities.

However, a great comfort for many well-to-do Romans was also the new opportunities for privacy. In particular this was provided by the small bedrooms in their homes – a revolution in social life.

BUILDING SKILLS

Roman architecture was surprisingly uniform. The basic building types of the empire – the arches, the baths, the theaters and temples – were spread through the provinces in instantly recognizable forms. Often a complex with temple, basilica and forum was planned together as a single unit. In a new town the streets were planned on a rectangular grid.

People with the necessary skills for building works were invaluable. There were independent surveyors and architects – such as an architect whose name plate was found at Pompeii – but the main source of skills was the men of the army, and most soldiers carried construction equipment with them.

In the 2nd century, once the legions had gained permanent bases their engineers and surveyors became available to local towns. By the end of the 3rd century the army was building bridges, temples, colonnades and other public buildings. However, the army, with its needs for roads and bridges, also took priority on engineering and building. The specific command of the emperor was necessary to divert surveyors to other work.

Army surveyors

In one letter to the emperor Trajan (in about AD112), Pliny the Younger asked for a land surveyor to be sent out to Bithynia to help plan a canal between a lake and the sea: "It only remains for you to send, if you deem proper, a civil engineer or an architect to examine carefully whether the lake lies above sea level." Although Trajan was concerned that the lake would simply drain into the sea, he did give Pliny the necessary authority to ask the nearest military leader for a surveyor to plot the lie of the land.

Sculpted head of a builder, a job suitable for men of the lower classes.

Arches, vaults and aqueducts

In the development of their architectural styles the Romans' greatest achievement was to combine the use of the arch with the vault. With the help of concrete this enabled them to construct high domes such as were seen for the first time in Nero's Golden House in

Concrete: the great building breakthrough

Stone was the most important Roman building material; fortunately, the nearest quarries to Rome were of soft volcanic rock. By the time more durable stone was needed, stonemasons were highly skilled. Many Roman buildings were constructed of dry stone without any mortar or cement, and later faced with brick.

A great breakthrough came with the discovery of lime mortar (concrete). In the north, deposits of volcanic sand were found which, when combined with lime, formed a very hard and adaptable building material. At first it was used, mixed with rubble, to form the inside of walls but gradually became used alone. It was cheaper and much stronger than stone, particularly when large open spaces had to be bridged.

BELOW LEFT **Bricklayers hard at work, as depicted in this frieze from a vault which contained the urns of cremated bodies.**

BELOW **Some rulers could be folded for carrying; dividers allowed for scales of half natural size.**

Rome. Trajan took the process of vaulting further in his market, and in Hadrian's villa, the vaulting was designed to show off light and so became beautiful as well as functional.

It was in the aqueduct that Roman engineering skills were most impressive. All large cities needed to import water: for drinking, for bathing, to supply decorative public fountains. In Italy the coolness and cleanliness of water brought direct from the neighboring hills was particularly appreciated and the requirements of Rome were voracious.

The technical problem was how to ensure a steady flow using only gravity. The Aqua Claudia, an aqueduct built in 47 and supplying Rome with water from a source 70 kilometers away, had a fall of 250 meters. This meant that the aqueduct had to drop no more than one meter in height for every 280 meters in length.

Most Roman aqueducts ran underground: the Aqua Claudia, for instance, was above ground for only 15 of its 70 kilometers.

This system of building meant that the water was less easily contaminated and safer from enemies. Often the ducts were concealed as soon as they were completed. The great Pont du Gard in France was constructed to keep the water at a height for a short distance so that it could then run underground for the remaining 50 kilometers of its length.

LEFT **The aqueduct feeding Carthage was nearly 80km long.**

ABOVE **The 1st-century Pont de Gard aqueduct near Nîmes.**

LIFE IN THE ARMY

The years of the republic had been, almost without exception, years of war, but much of the first two centuries of the empire saw long stretches of internal peace. By the 2nd century the legions had permanent bases along the frontiers.

Life in the army could be monotonous but the troops built up close links with the region and often recruited from the villages. Although soldiers were not allowed to marry, many had families with local women. Civilian settlements grew up alongside the legionary forts and all profited from the army's constant needs for supplies. However, there were still complaints of soldiers being aggressive to the locals and beating them if they caused offense.

The soldiers spent much of their time on tasks in the local community. Often more than half of the men would be away from the camp: training, guarding mines or saltworks, fetching supplies, going on recruiting missions or carrying the mail. A list preserved on a sheet of oak from about AD 90 suggests that 470 of the 751 men of a cohort were away from their base at Vindolanda in Britain. From the 2nd century onward the army was also used for local construction work in the towns.

With these diversions it was difficult to maintain effective discipline and train the army as a fighting force. When a campaign was planned commanders often had to spend some time getting the men fully fit for action again.

Auxiliary and legionary

An important distinction in the Roman armies was between the legionaries, recruited only from Roman citizens, and the auxiliaries, recruited from provincials. At first auxiliaries had their own leaders and local equipment. Many were specialist units: the Gauls provided cavalry, others provided archers. Later they were organized by Roman leaders and with standard equipment. Infantrymen wore a mail cuirass, leather trousers and a helmet and carried a sword.

Although auxiliaries never achieved the status of legionaries and were paid less, in numbers and significance they were at least as important. The auxiliary service was yet another crucial element of romanization. Auxiliaries also provided military flexibility: they could be sent ahead of an advancing legion to reconnoiter and deal with skirmishers. Later they were the troops who guarded the borders.

A centurion was actually in charge of about 80 men, not 100.

Pay and reward

"Military service itself is harsh and unprofitable. Your body and soul are valued at a few pence a day, and from that pittance, clothing, weapons and tents have to be paid for, as well as bribes to buy off the cruel centurion and escape onerous tasks."

This was the complaint of Percennius, leader of a mutiny against Tiberius in AD 14. Certainly life in the legions was tough – discipline was harsh and until the time of Septimius Severus a legionary could not enter into a legal marriage. In fact, legal marriages were actually dissolved once a man joined the army.

There were some advantages: pay was regular and considerably above that of a laborer, and the medical service was among the best in the empire. There was the chance to learn skills, and victory in war might also bring the

Bronze purses like this were designed to be worn on the wrist, giving security against theft.

Bronze citizenship plaques dating from the time of the emperor Claudius.

opportunity of plunder.

Apart from the pay, there were other financial rewards: Augustus left each legionary 75 sesterces while Claudius instituted the custom of paying a cash donation at the beginning of an emperor's reign. Augustus also ensured that legionaries were treated well on

their discharge (after 20 or 25 years of service) with either land or, later, a cash gift equal to 12 years' pay.

For an auxiliary the main reward was citizenship, given at the end of service, which could be passed on to the man's family. Marriage was allowed once more; relationships and families started during military

service were now recognized.

The grant of citizenship was kept in Rome but copies of the decree, inscribed on two thin tables of bronze bound together, were given to the new citizen. This was known as a *diploma* – literally, a doubling, as when the two leaves were bound together.

Training and discipline

A legionary on the march with his belongings and food.

Many provincial auxiliaries were specialists, such as this archer.

The Jewish writer Josephus, writing at the end of the 1st century AD, tried to explain why the Romans had defeated the Jews so decisively in the revolt of 66 to 70. One important reason was thorough military training. Josephus recorded how the Roman armies went through their drills continually, rather than training only when a war broke out.

"If you study carefully the organization of the Roman army, you will realize that they possess their great empire as a reward for valor, not as a gift of fortune."

Even practice battles were as demanding as the real thing. Every activity was carried out according to a meticulous routine, whether in the building of camps, on the march or in battle. The centurions were the officers responsible for obedience and discipline.

"Absolute obedience to the officers creates an army which is well behaved in peacetime and which moves as a single body when in battle – so cohesive are the ranks, so correct are the turns, so quick are the soldiers' ears for orders, eyes for signals, and hands for action," according to Josephus.

With the army spread too widely, these rigid standards of training could easily fall. Often a new commander, such as Corbulo, taking over troops in the east in 55, had to retrain the men and get things back into good order before he could advance in battle.

The emperor Hadrian, in particular, believed that his policy of consolidating rather than expanding the empire was bound to affect discipline. He made it his task to visit the army in the frontiers. He would order the troops out on maneuver and once they had finished would give them a critical report on their standard.

Soldiers often wore bronze masks during parades.

Social life

A remarkable document found in the waterlogged ditches of the 1st century Roman fort of Vindolanda shows that it was not just the soldiers who were able to enjoy a social life. The document, an invitation to a birthday party, came from Claudia Severa and was addressed to Sulpicia Lepidina, wife of the prefect of a cohort of auxiliary troops.

The two women were 35 miles apart and this document provides an amazing early glimpse of social life among army families in the early empire in an area only recently subdued. Sulpicia Lepidina would certainly have needed a military escort to travel that distance to a party.

The main local centers for relaxation were the military bath-houses built outside the forts. Excavations in northern Britain show that the troops relaxed here with mugs of wine or local beer and played games such as dice, backgammon or checkers.

There was even the opportunity to enjoy delicacies – pastries, sweets, oysters, mussels – which were certainly not part of an everyday diet. By the 2nd century the armies were more settled and their social life spread even farther afield.

Dice playing was a favorite pastime of Claudius, who even wrote a book on the subject.

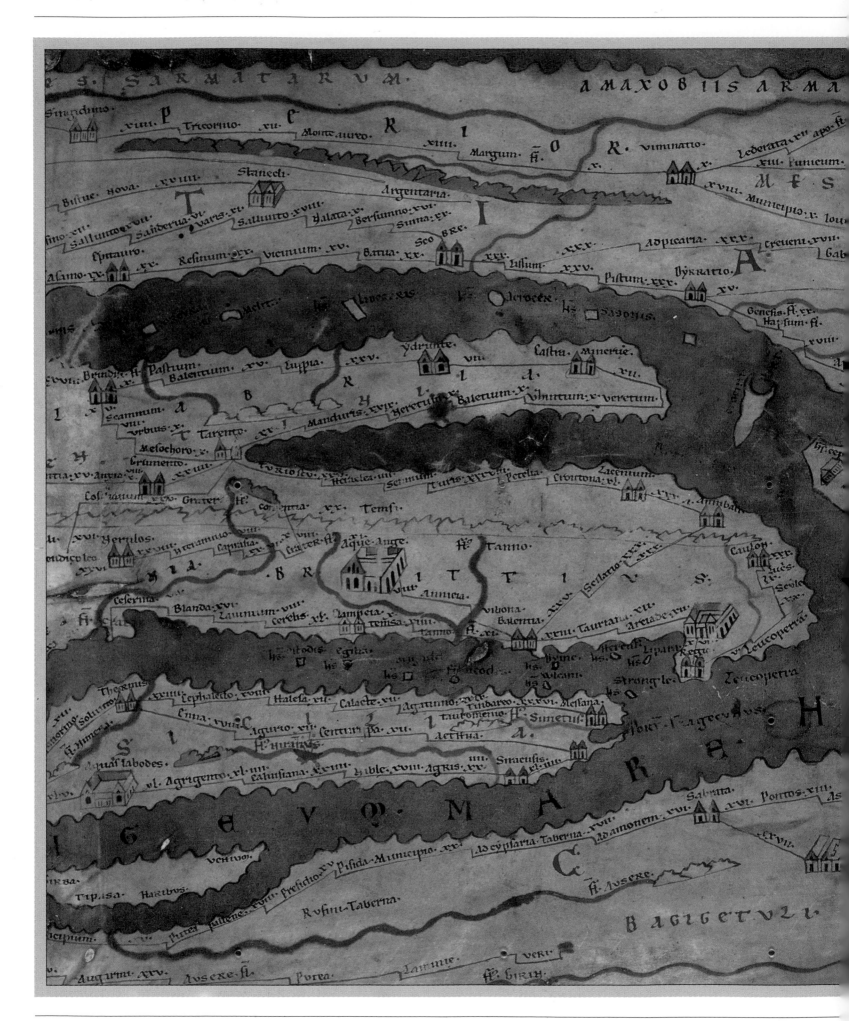

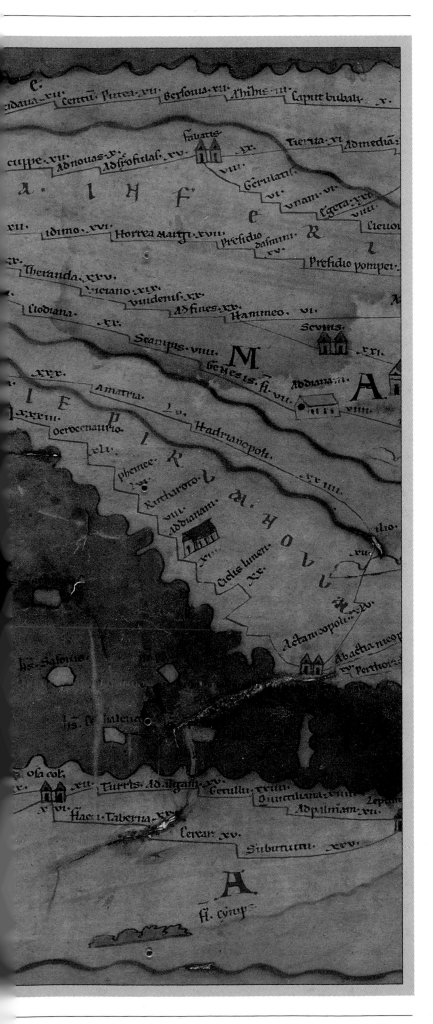

Chapter 6

WEALTH AND POVERTY IN THE EMPIRE

All roads led to Rome, administrative hub of the empire and voracious consumer of goods from its fields and workshops. The vast network of paved highways along which the legions marched and imperial couriers passed underpinned the *pax Romana* – the "Roman peace" – that guaranteed stable conditions in which commerce could flourish. The strict internal security was of great benefit to traders, though much trade remained local and the regional currencies remained in use for centuries.

Important as these roads were, they played little part in long-distance trade: ox carts were too slow and expensive to be used for more than local journeys. The real arteries of trade were the sea and river routes, along which merchant ships carried the bulk cargoes of grain, oil, pottery and wine as well as luxury items. A testament to the volume of this trade can still be seen in Rome today, in a mountain of shards from 40 million amphorae used to bring olive oil from Spain and Africa.

No city, least of all the capital, ever became a self-sustaining industrial center, as there was no technology for mass production. Land was the main focus for investment, and most of the empire's population were country-dwellers. Rich landowners sold the produce of their farms to the cities, and with the proceeds could afford the luxuries – amber, silk, exotic spices – imported from beyond the empire's borders. Less privileged citizens, freedmen and slaves provided low-cost labor and supporting services. Only a minority of people could earn enough to lift themselves out of grinding poverty.

The Peutinger Map, a medieval copy of a late Roman map of the empire, shows southern Italy, Sicily and north Africa in the foreground.

From Augustus's time and for the next two centuries as the empire grew in strength, Rome was the main home of the emperors, with their grand residences built on the Palatine Hill overlooking the Forum.

It was the proud boast of Augustus that he found Rome a city of brick and left it a city of marble. He launched a massive building program, partly to boost his own popularity, but also to stress the continuity of his rule with the past. The first public building was a temple dedicated to the memory of his adoptive father, Julius Caesar. Augustus also completed a forum and hall – the Basilica Julia – which had been left unfinished by Caesar. Only then did Augustus add a grand new forum of his own, the Forum Augusti, alongside it. A host of other buildings followed, and with them Augustus brought a new confidence and sense of grandeur to the city.

For most people, life in the "city of marble" is bare survival

Not so easily transformed were the vast, over-crowded blocks of apartments – the *insulae* – where most of Rome's inhabitants lived. Outside the great ceremonial areas of the city they dominated Rome and there were 25 insulae for every grand, privately owned house. Overcrowding in the city was bad and speculators succumbed to the temptation to increase profits by constructing their buildings as high as possible and with scant regard for safety. Some of the rickety structures were six storeys high and entire blocks sometimes collapsed under the weight of their numerous inhabitants. Rents were exorbitant and conditions for the poorest people were appalling.

The poet Juvenal, in a memorable picture of life in an insula, wrote: "We live in a city which is, to a great extent, propped up by flimsy boards. The manager of your building stands in front of the collapsing structure and, while he conceals a gaping crack…he tells you to 'Sleep well' – even though a total cave-in is imminent." The very poor had to live up under the eaves where pigeons nested and escape from fire was impossible.

Rome may have been a grand city, but it lacked sufficient trade or industry to support itself. The richer classes lived off the rents of their country estates, and much of public and private life was subsidized by the taxation raised in the provinces. In Ephesus, for instance, city council charges included a licence fee of one denarius for selling salt and parsley, the same cost as for the registration of a birth; it cost six denarii, however, for a proclamation announcing a victor at the games.

At least 200,000 men and their families – three-quarters of the total population of a million – depended on free handouts of grain. If the harvest was inadequate or the grain ships from Egypt were delayed the poor would become restless. On one occasion, Augustus paid for grain with his own money in order to relieve a famine. On another occasion, Claudius was nearly mobbed by an angry crowd and had to be saved by soldiers.

There were, however, some benefits to city life not available in the country, such as the aqueducts which supplied water day and night to public fountains and baths. Some people, with special permission, could even pipe water to their own

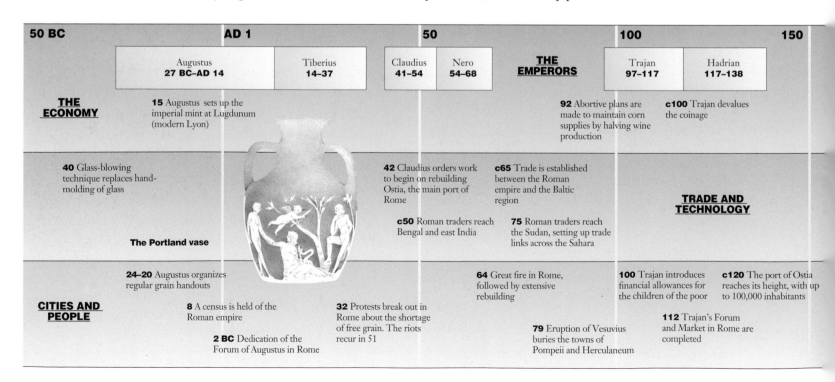

50 BC		AD 1		50		100		150

| | Augustus 27 BC–AD 14 | Tiberius 14–37 | Claudius 41–54 | Nero 54–68 | **THE EMPERORS** | Trajan 97–117 | Hadrian 117–138 |

THE ECONOMY

15 Augustus sets up the imperial mint at Lugdunum (modern Lyon)

92 Abortive plans are made to maintain corn supplies by halving wine production

c100 Trajan devalues the coinage

40 Glass-blowing technique replaces hand-molding of glass

The Portland vase

42 Claudius orders work to begin on rebuilding Ostia, the main port of Rome

c65 Trade is established between the Roman empire and the Baltic region

c50 Roman traders reach Bengal and east India

75 Roman traders reach the Sudan, setting up trade links across the Sahara

TRADE AND TECHNOLOGY

CITIES AND PEOPLE

24–20 Augustus organizes regular grain handouts

8 A census is held of the Roman empire

2 BC Dedication of the Forum of Augustus in Rome

32 Protests break out in Rome about the shortage of free grain. The riots recur in 51

64 Great fire in Rome, followed by extensive rebuilding

79 Eruption of Vesuvius buries the towns of Pompeii and Herculaneum

100 Trajan introduces financial allowances for the children of the poor

112 Trajan's Forum and Market in Rome are completed

c120 The port of Ostia reaches its height, with up to 100,000 inhabitants

LEFT **Trajan's Market in the center of Rome, a multi-storey group of 150 shops set into the hillside. Trajan encouraged and financed wasteland reclamation and building projects throughout the Roman empire.**

150	200	250	300	350

| Marcus Aurelius 161–180 | Septimius Severus 193–211 | Alexander Severus 222–235 | Period of anarchy and disorder 235–284 | Diocletian 284–305 | Constantine 306–337 |

c170 Marcus Aurelius devalues the coinage

215 The Antoninianus, a high denomination silver coin, is issued

250 A period of great inflation begins, leading to economic crisis

274 Aurelian attempts to restore the value of the coinage

301 Diocletian issues his edict on prices, attempting to end the inflation

166 Greek merchants reach India, bringing back silk and other precious goods

c200 The road system is virtually complete throughout the empire

c200 The glass industry is now centered on the region around modern Cologne

Marble cutters at work

165–7 Plague spreads throughout the empire

212 Roman citizenship is granted to all inhabitants of the empire, allowing more taxes to be raised

217 The Baths of Caracalla at Rome are completed

251 Franks and Germans invade but are defeated in northern Italy, near modern Milan, in 258

293 The division of the empire into east and west leads to higher taxes for all

Water commissioners controlled the use of Rome's water. Frontinus, a 1st-century commissioner, estimated that, every 24 hours, aqueducts supplied 1,000 million liters of water to Rome.

homes. Because any breakdown of water supply could not be risked, a permanent staff of 240 slaves was employed to maintain aqueducts and keep water flowing from beyond the city.

The Roman crowd was always ready to criticize a Roman emperor to his face when he appeared in public, and no emperor could afford to risk political unrest in his own capital. Augustus realized the need for efficient management of the city if he were to maintain his popularity and his control. From his time onward, the running of the city became an imperial responsibility. He created a new government post: prefect of the

city. Among the responsibilities of the post, which was directly accountable to the emperor, was ensuring that meat was sold at a fair price and that proper discipline was maintained at the games.

Many of Rome's impressive public buildings are in the tradition of imperial patronage set by Augustus. They were public relations exercises on a grand scale, usually financed either from the personal wealth of an emperor or from the plunder of the empire's wars.

The revived magnificence and prestige of Rome attracted visitors from all over the empire and the city became crowded with different races

and cultures. The Greeks came as philosophers, doctors and rhetoric teachers, the peoples of Asia Minor as traders, entertainers and slaves. Richer provincials from the west, having mastered the Latin language, came to make their fortunes.

For only a few with luck and skills were there sufficient opportunities. Rome had 150 trade corporations, from bakers to goldsmiths and mirror-sellers, with a host of carriers, warehousemen and watermen to keep goods on the move. Some people did make fortunes, but it was a hectic, unstable existence and most people did no more than survive, dependent on the handouts of grain.

Augustus makes the seas of the empire safe for shippers and traders

Many writers of the empire, such as Martial, describe the appalling noise of the city, the impossibility of fighting a way through the streets and the brutality of everyday life mirrored by the blood sports of the public shows. In the words of Martial, "there is no place in the city where a poor man may have a quiet moment for thought…before dawn bakers disturb you; and the whole day the hammers of coppersmiths jar your nerves. Over here the moneychanger idly jangles Neronian coins on his filthy table; over there a man hammering Spanish gold dust pounds his well-worn stone with a shiny mallet."

There was little streetlighting in the city and only rudimentary policing by the watchmen. In the last resort there were large numbers of troops, stationed in or near the city, to keep the peace.

In contrast, conditions throughout the empire had generally become safer. Near the end of his life Augustus made a journey to the island of Capri, and on his way he passed by a merchant ship from the great Egyptian port of Alexandria. The traders aboard it praised him for the peace he had brought that enabled them to sail the seas in freedom and make their fortunes. Their praise was justified. Not only had Augustus brought peace throughout the empire, he had stabilized an enormous area within which trading could flourish with few bureaucratic restrictions.

This does not mean that trading within the empire was easy. Transport by land largely remained slow and expensive and almost all heavy goods had to be sold locally or moved by water. An ox cart – with six men and six boys to drive the oxen – could take as long as 12 days to transport an olive press 80 kilometers by road. Moving wheat in this way would have doubled its price every 500 kilometers.

The need to provision garrison troops led to frontiers being established along rivers such as the Rhine and Danube; new urban centers such as Londinium, Lugdunum and Colonia (modern London, Lyons and Cologne) were also on rivers. In fact, the main trading routes of the Roman empire can be mapped entirely on rivers and the sea.

One legacy of these trading activities is the waterfront where goods could be unloaded for transport inland. At the emperor Septimius Severus's home town of Leptis Magna (in what is now

LEFT This painting shows an elaborate and prosperous Italian harbor. Heavy goods traveled by sea, and Ostia, on the estuary of the Tiber river, became a major port in the 1st century AD. Claudius rebuilt the port at Ostia, digging a new channel and cutting a large new basin nearly 3km away with break-waters reaching out to sea. A lighthouse was set in the harbor mouth by sinking a huge ship there.

Protection against marine hazards had existed since 280 BC when the first known lighthouse, Pharos of Alexandria, was built. The Romans had erected around 30 lighthouses by AD 400.

BELOW Grain was so vital to the people of Rome that the mere rumor of delays in the regular shipments could cause riots. This led some cynics to say that Romans were interested only in bread and circuses.

BELOW LEFT Weekly markets in a town, a carefully guarded privilege, needed permission from the emperor or Senate.

Libya), there are remains of a quay 1,200 meters long. Roman wharves have also been found along the Thames river in London. Ostia, the port of Rome and the best documented of these waterfronts, developed into an important city in its own right. Goods were stored here in vast warehouses before being moved upriver by barge.

Merchants who face the dangers of the sea gain special privileges

Most of the goods moving through the Roman world were those required by the empire for its own survival, and grain was by far the most important. The demands of Rome were voracious: 400,000 tonnes were shipped into the city yearly, and another 100,000 tonnes were required every year by the army. This was only the first of the army's needs: for its tents alone, one legion would require about 54,000 calf hides.

Some of the army's demands could be met locally and many frontier areas became prosperous as local producers profited from the army's needs. Even the less productive areas, such as northern Britain or Syria, benefited from the carriage of imported goods. Networks of private trade also exist though a great deal of capital was needed to

build ships and load them. One ship of 400 tonnes would have cost between 250,000 and 400,000 sesterces to build and 185,000 sesterces to load with wheat. A whole legion – over 5,000 men – could have been fed for a month with this money.

There were high risks involved in trading: shipwrecks were common and some piracy still existed. Because of all these problems, the emperors gave special privileges, such as freedom from local city duties, to merchants and shipowners who transported the empire's grain.

The empire had no great bankers to take in

TRADING ROUTES OF THE EMPIRE
Trading routes of the empire encompassed water routes by sea and river. The road network, virtually complete by AD 200, was used for military and administrative purposes rather than moving heavy goods.

ABOVE **Roman merchant ships were generally heavy and slow, and many of them had only one square sail.**

MAP KEY:

- ◆ copper
- ◇ gold
- ✦ iron
- ◆ lead
- ◇ silver
- ✦ tin
- ◐ grain
- ▽ olive oil
- ▼ wine
- ✝ slaves
- ◖ brass and bronze
- ◗ glass
- ◡ pottery
- ✛ timber
- ✤ marble
- # textiles
- ◓ purple dye
- — trade route
- ▨ Roman empire AD200

0 — 600 km
0 — 400 mi

Gades - Ostia 9 days

Ostia - Carthage 3-5 days

and lend out capital for commercial expansion. The wealthy commercial class remained small and when merchants had made their fortunes many preferred to invest in land. The new city elites and more successful landowners were eager to show off their sophistication and merchants rushed to satisfy their demands. In among the grain, oil and wine which formed the staple goods of the empire's trade, there were also the luxuries: good quality pottery, lamps, glass and metalware.

Gradually the manufacturers found it paid to move closer to these growing, profitable markets. As demand grew in the western provinces, for instance, the fine pottery from Arezzo in central Italy was reproduced in Gaul, and glass production spread throughout the empire.

The risks of trade meant that only highly profitable luxury goods were sought outside the empire. There was ivory from East Africa, incense and myrrh from southern Arabia, amber from the Baltic, pepper from India and damask silk from China. Wild animals for the shows — the more exotic the better — came across the African and Asian frontiers of the empire.

ABOVE **Rome was the heart of the empire; all roads led to it as shown on a detail of the Peutinger map.**

Rich citizens of the empire aspire to be landowners

For goods produced within the empire, production centers were relatively small and involved very little technology. The vast majority of the empire's inhabitants were so poor that there was no market to support an extensive manufacturing industry. This is one of the most remarkable things about the Romans: their failure to develop more efficient ways of producing goods. When demand grew the response was to set up more

LEFT **Horses were vital to the empire's communications and carried a special courier service.**

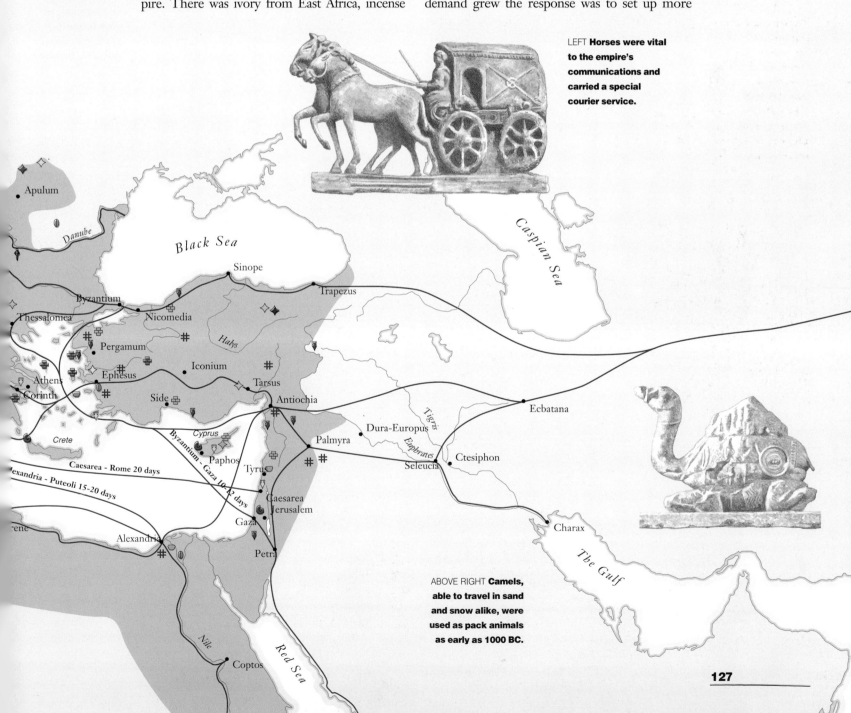

ABOVE RIGHT **Camels, able to travel in sand and snow alike, were used as pack animals as early as 1000 BC.**

workshops on the same model as before rather than devise new methods of manufacture.

Investment in land remained important in the Roman empire. For those who managed their estates with care it earned a steady and stable income and provided a social status unequaled by any other form of wealth. The emperor was the largest landowner of the empire. His estates were swelled by land either inherited from well-wishers or confiscated from political enemies.

Provincial senators are ordered to invest in Italian land

By the late 2nd century AD there were imperial possessions in almost every province; in some cases these landholdings constituted nearly 20 percent of the land. These estates increasingly came to be seen as part of the empire's resources rather than the personal possessions of the emperor alone. In the 3rd century AD, Septimius Severus provided free oil for Rome from his African estates.

No one could begin to rival the emperor for landholdings, but rich men often owned land in several provinces. Trajan even ordered provincial senators to hold one-third of their fortune in Italian land. The rest would normally have been kept in their home province. A common pattern for a wealthy landowner was to own scattered blocks of land in one area, built up through inheritance, marriage or purchase.

In Italy even the biggest estates were run as a series of smaller farm units. This was in contrast to the *latifundia*, or vast estates worked as single entities, which were common under the republic. Some of these units were rented out to tenants, providing the landowner with an income from the rents. Others were run by teams of slaves or free laborers under the supervision of a bailiff.

The Romans, despite their expertise as civil engineers, were not interested in innovation. They used traditional donkey wheels to drive their mills rather than the more efficient water-powered wheels. Technologically, the Romans tended to borrow what they needed. The arch and vault came from Mesopotamia and concrete from the Etruscans.

BELOW **This mosaic of a Roman villa in Tunisia highlights the dual nature of the villa. Even luxury residences could be working farms, as much "home" to slaves and domestic animals as to owners.**

Vespasian tried to improve the empire's finances by introducing new taxes. One was a tax on the urine used in fulling cloth.

Glass-blowing, a technique widely adopted in the 1st century AD, was a Phoenician invention, and the greatest commercial enterprises of the empire – the Spanish mines – were drained by Egyptian screw pumps. The emperor Vespasian actually refused to use a new building device in Rome on the grounds that it would put laborers out of work.

Technology remained as primitive in farming as in other areas and Roman never developed harness for horses or windmills. One of the few Roman inventions was a harvesting machine that was pulled by oxen and cut the corn at mid-stalk with iron teeth. The main reason for its invention was probably the need to bring in the grain harvest of northern Gaul quickly before winter set in.

Slave labor is considered the best option for a wealthy farm owner

With such primitive equipment, the most practicable farm was one centered on a single team of workers who could easily reach every corner of the land. The ideal for an Italian farm was described by a 1st-century writer on agriculture, Columella, who considered between 60 and 100 hectares to be the most suitable size. Such a farm would also have both grazing and arable land and sustain a crop of grain, olives and vines as well as copses for timber and pasture. It would be near a road or have good access to the sea.

The most productive labor was that of slaves closely supervised by their owner. Failing direct management by the owner, local tenants often proved conscientious and hard-working. The worst option of all, according to Columella, was the unsupervised slave manager — and if you had one, it was best to provide him with a female companion to keep him in line and to help him out with the work that had to be done.

Practices varied widely across the empire. In some cases the pre-Roman patterns of farming continued. Asia Minor remained a large wool-producing area, as it had been before the Romans. In other areas the pull of markets encouraged new crops, such as vines in Gaul and olives in Spain and North Africa. Grain, wool, olives and wine were the staples of the empire; crops in Britain included peas, cabbages, parsnips and mustard; and figs, dates and plums were grown in Syria.

About 90 percent of the inhabitants of the empire worked on the land for themselves or for other landowners. The empire relied on their labors for the bulk of its taxes, which were increasingly paid in kind rather than money. Very little is known about these small farmers: they are hardly ever mentioned in records and most of their activities have left little mark in the soil. Still, the settled conditions of the empire before the 3rd century must have brought a modest prosperity for many inhabitants.

RIGHT **Wine was the most common drink of the empire and grapes were an important crop for any farm other than in Britain and northern Gaul. A wide range of different grapes were grown throughout the empire.**

LEFT **Many farms had heated rooms for wine presses. This detail of a stone relief shows slaves treading the grapes to make wine.**

The most celebrated buildings of the Roman countryside are the villas – a word describing a wide range of residences. At one extreme these were luxurious homes on the coast where the owner retired to relax: the Bay of Naples was especially popular with rich Romans. When prosperity and the influence of Roman culture spread through the western provinces the villa spread too, as one of the main symbols of Roman life. Much more common throughout the empire, however, was the working villa.

The working villa often developed on one site over a number of years, and the increasing success of a farmer was reflected in the growth of his villa. As a farmer became more successful, he would segregate himself first from his animals and then from his workers so that he could have a separate house. He would gradually make various addition and improvements to his home.

An important moment in the rising status of the owner came when the front of the villa was built facing away from the working areas. At the top end of the scale were villas built around a courtyard and adorned with mosaics and painted wall plaster. But no amount of elaborate adornment could divorce these working villas from the estates that sustained them and the local economies that provided the markets for their surplus produce.

The larger landowners of the empire were extremely wealthy. A laborer's daily wage was four sesterces – enough, at normal prices, to buy grain for a family of four for three days. To qualify as a senator, the pinnacle of social status, capital of one million sesterces was required and many senators comfortably exceeded this. Pliny was estimated to be worth 20 million sesterces and the philosopher Seneca a staggering 300 million. With careful management of land these sums were relatively secure, though there is a record of one of Augustus's admirals losing 100 million sesterces through choosing the wrong crops for his estates.

Some freed slaves manage to become millionaires

Men of this wealth did not need to concentrate on making more. Publicly they claimed to despise the commercial classes though privately many did dabble in trade, using agents or freedmen to hold their investments for them. Their main source of status was to be found in success in public life, in the administrative and military commands which were always available for ambitious senators. They could also gain prestige by financing games

Lucius Annaeus Seneca (c 4BC–AD65) was also tutor to the future emperor Nero and wrote Nero's first speech. Seneca was later accused of conspiracy and ordered to take his own life.

LEFT **Not all slaves were owned by individuals; these slaves working a treadwheel crane belonged to the city and worked on building projects.**

BELOW **This painting shows the lavish indulgence of Roman banquets. With no incentive to invest in industry, the rich had little to do with their money but spend it on luxuries while poorer people served them.**

or providing a temple, bath-house or other public building in their local town.

In the 1st century AD the senators were not alone in enjoying great riches: a new wealthy class grew as a result of the opportunities available in imperial service and in commerce. Narcissus, a freedman, secretary to Claudius, collected 400 million sesterces from payments for favors and the sale of offices. The satirist Petronius lampooned the extravagant vulgarity of these new rich.

Inflation and invasion destroy the Roman economy

Few people outside the aristocracy attained this level of wealth but there were enough to sustain a small class of skilled craftsmen such as sculptors, ivory workers or jewelry makers. Below them on the social scale were more basic trades such as bakers and clothmakers supported by semiskilled workers, many of them slaves. The stability of the Roman empire and the demands of the richer classes gave this class a modest prosperity.

Artisans predominated in the cities, but in city and countryside there was a mass of laborers, many of whom relied almost entirely on seasonal work. A laborer needed to earn 400 sesterces a year to keep at subsistence level. With no guarantee of work, and probably no access to land, it was a constant struggle.

The free poor in town and country had to compete for work with slaves. Although the number of new slaves coming into the empire declined from the 1st century AD with the slowing of Roman conquests, slavery remained fundamental to the Roman economy. In many areas, such as household work, mining and farming, slaves formed the majority of the work force. They were property – bought, sold or bequeathed – and completely dependent on the whims of their masters. Some slaves were also rented out for fixed periods; they often had to keep up some jobs for their owner as well as their temporary master, and could sometimes be made to work nearly 24 hours a day.

The strongest asset of slaves was their commercial value: between 2,000 and 8,000 sesterces on the open market. The worst conditions for slaves were mainly in the country where owners were often absent and did not inquire too closely about how farms were run – so long as they were profitable. The very worst placement of all was in the Spanish mines with their work force of 40,000. Profits were large and so the commercial value of slaves was lower. Conditions in private homes were usually better

than in the country or the mines, where many of the slaves died young.

In the 3rd century AD the empire's internal security, established by Augustus, was shattered by invasions from German tribes to the north and a reborn Persian empire to the east. The invaders disrupted trade routes and market centers. The demands of defense brought increased taxation and inflation. The empire was weakened further by battles between rival Roman generals and became even more vulnerable to attack.

The downward spiral of economic collapse was only halted at the end of the century, when Diocletian restored order. The local economies in many parts of the empire had remained intact and were revived when stability was achieved. What Diocletian could not prevent was inflation: despite his attempts to introduce a new currency and control costs throughout the empire, prices continued to rise. Only under Diocletian's successor in the early 4th century, Constantine, was a more permanent economic stability achieved.

ABOVE **This portrait of a young 2nd-century Roman woman from Egypt shows the self-confidence of wealthy citizens. Many Roman women had elaborate hairstyles and, like this one, wore a great deal of jewelry made from gold and precious stones.**

RIGHT **Glass objects were popular luxury items with the rich, and glass objects were often used as funeral offerings and some graves had up to a dozen items. Jugs with handles were used as cinerary urns as well as wine jugs.**

Household slaves were often treated better than country slaves because they had more personal contact with their owners. Some were given a *peculium*, or small gift of money, from time to time and could sometimes save enough to buy their freedom.

POMPEII · ROMAN TOWN LIFE

Pompeii, a small but prosperous town in the resort area of the Bay of Naples, was a bustling place. Its wealth came from wine, olives and the fine wool of sheep which grazed on the rich inland plains. From Pompeii's port wool and finished cloth were shipped north to Rome and Gaul and eastward to the Greek world. Many inhabitants grew rich from the trade.

The homes of the wealthy were built round courtyards into which the main rooms opened. These houses had enclosed gardens and private water supply, and elegant paintings decorated the walls. Innkeepers, dyers, bakers, barbers, mat-makers and fullers all made their living in the same areas of town. People could enjoy their leisure in the local baths and brothels and on feast days the town's amphitheater was packed for games and gladiator shows.

One day in August, AD 79, the sky over the Bay of Naples was suddenly overshadowed by a huge cloud spreading upward for several thousand meters. Without warning, Mount Vesuvius – a volcano assumed to be extinct – had erupted. Thousands of tonnes of lava and ash were thrown upward, then drifted south and slowly settled over the rich countryside along the coast. Pompeii was directly in their path. The weight of ash and the toxic fumes meant certain death for those unable to escape. However, the ash also preserved what it destroyed: homes, shops, uneaten food and the cavities left by bodies provide an unrivaled picture of everyday life.

LEFT **This pet dog belonged to a man called Vesonius Primus. The poor animal, tied in the atrium of the house, could not escape and suffocated at the end of its chain .**

RIGHT **When Vesuvius erupted, Pompeii was buried under volcanic ash four meters thick. Herculaneum, to the west, was buried under a mud flow. Pliny graphically described the eruption in which his uncle died after going too close to study it.**

Neapolis

Misenum

Herculaneum

Mt Vesuvius

Sarno

Oplontis

Pompeii

Nuceria

Bay of Naples

Stabiae

→ route of Pliny the Elder

⬭ lava deposit

depth of ash (cm)

200
100
50

Surrentum

0   15 km

0   10 mi

MAIN IMAGE **Many wealthy homeowners rented out the front space of their houses to shopkeepers, and the residential blocks of the town were a mixture of workshops, shops and homes in close proximity.**

WAREHOUSE
OF THE WORLD

"Everything that is grown or manufactured by each people is not only always present here, but is present in abundance. So many merchant men arrive here with cargoes from all over, at every season, and with each return of the harvest, that the city of Rome seems like a common warehouse of the world…The arrival and departure of ships never cease," marveled Aelius Aristides. "And consequently it is quite amazing that there is enough room in the sea, much less the harbor, for the ships."

Rome, with its vast needs for grain, oil and wine, as well as the luxury goods demanded by its rich elite, was the center of the vast trading empire that flourished during the long years of peace which began during the rule of Augustus.

The Amber Road

The electrostatic properties of amber may have given it a special magic for its owners.

Amber, the fossilized resin of an extinct species of pine, was one of the most prized gemstones of early Europe. The richest deposits in the world were found along the coast of the Baltic Sea. Roman traders reached the Baltic in the 1st century AD and for 150 years amber was carried southward on the Amber Road to Aquileia in northern Italy, where craftsmen worked it into boxes, small figures and pendants.

Finished amber was expensive, and a single figurine could cost more than a number of slaves. Many delightful small figures have survived: a troupe of actors in cloaks from Pompeii, a figure of the god Bacchus from Gaul, a knife handle in the shape of a sleeping hound from the German border.

Most common were small jars, pots and rings. Rings were often carved with lucky motifs to ward off evil and the forces of darkness, and smart women carried small balls of amber which they could rub and smell to combat the stink of the city. Also valuable were pieces of amber in which insects or small bits of plant had been trapped.

By the end of the 2nd century Baltic sources had been exhausted and from then on the trade in amber began to decline.

The hazards of the sea

Shipwrecks help to construct the patterns of Roman trade.

The empire centered on the Mediterranean and, when times were good, the sea was dotted with sails as ships, large and small, made their way between the main ports. Travel ranged from trips along rivers and coastlines to voyages across the open seas. It normally took 15 to 20 days for grain ships to reach Italy from Egypt and 9 days to reach southern Spain from Ostia.

Shipping was risky: the Mediterranean is subject to sudden storms and it is dangerous to cross, especially between the months of November and March. In the New Testament, St Paul gives a dramatic account of his ship running aground on the coast of Malta and beginning to break up. Shipwrecks like this were common, and thousands of wrecks from Roman times have been located around the shores of the Mediterranean.

The wildlife trade

Luxuries from afar

In the 1st century fashion dictated, complained Seneca, that Egyptian marbles should be set alongside mosiacs from Numidia, swimming pools had to be faced with marble and water must flow from silver faucets. The exotic tastes of the wealthy few drove merchants to scour the world in search of luxuries and novelties. Adventurous traders traveled down the Red Sea and crossed the ocean as far as southern India; from here local traders might bring in the produce of south-east Asia. By the end of the 1st century pepper was the main commodity brought in from this region; later the trade included perfumes, spices and fine cloths. The Romans also used the overland route across Asia to China. The route passed through the hostile regions of Persia and direct contact between the Romans and the Han empire was never established, though a few Greeks and Syrians braved the journey. Nevertheless Chinese silk was not unknown in Rome, and Mediterranean textiles have been found in China.

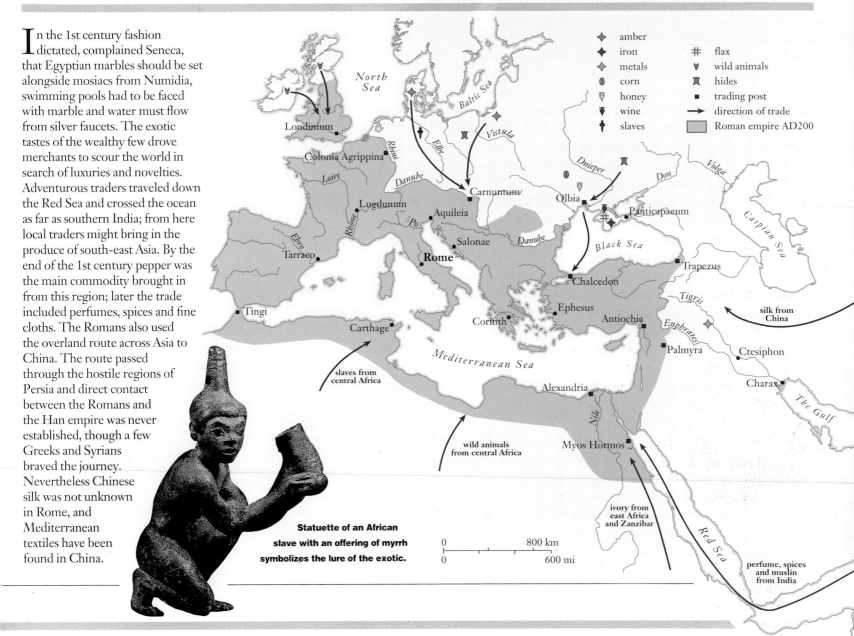

Statuette of an African slave with an offering of myrrh symbolizes the lure of the exotic.

African animals en route to a cruel death.

When the Roman statesman and orator Cicero was governor of Cilicia in the 1st century BC, one of the strangest requests he received was to search the mountains for wild panthers to send to the arena at Rome. A new source of profit for traders had been opened up. In the century that followed, the clamor of the Roman people for the public slaughter of animals increased and emperors responded to this demand. Augustus had 3,500 African animals killed in 26 wild-beast baitings and during the 100 days of events when the Colosseum was opened, 9,000 animals were killed. In just one set of games, sponsored by Trajan in AD 107, 11,000 beasts were slaughtered. The whole empire was scoured for these beasts. Lions and tigers came in from the Asian provinces; rhinoceroses, camels and crocodiles from north Africa; wolves from Ireland and bears from Scotland. The more exotic creatures were sometimes trained and put on exhibition before they were killed in brutal matchings of rhinoceros against elephant or bear against bull. Substantial areas of the empire were deprived of their larger native wildlife.

LIFE ON THE LAND

Nearly all imperial subjects earned their living from the land. Some had vast landholdings – it was rumored in Nero's time that six men owned half of Africa – but had little involvement in the day-to-day running of the estates. These were left in the hands of supervisors or rented out to tenants. Most people lived on and worked their own lands with free and slave labor. Slave labor, so prominent under the republic, was now in decline as owners realized the benefits of employing seasonal labor. In this Italy was now becoming very similar to the rest of the empire.

Success for the smaller farmer depended on experience, skill and careful management. In few parts of the empire was land rich enough to guarantee a profitable surplus. However, the needs of the cities, improved communications and a long period of peace meant that any surplus could be sold and so the small landowner gradually prospered under Roman rule. The thousands of villas built throughout the western provinces reflect the new-found prosperity of agriculture in the 1st century AD. Most remained as the centers of working farms.

Crops and land conditions varied widely: from vegetables in wetter northern provinces to cereal and olives in the hotter, drier southern provinces. Cattle ranching became increasingly important in Italy, as the demand for meat grew, and many breeds were imported from the east.

FAR RIGHT **Some of today's beautiful, tranquil Tuscan countryside is still farmed using old Roman methods.**

Tillers of the fields

The farmer's life

"Happy is the man who remains far from business and who cultivates the family farm with his own oxen," was the poet Horace's romantic picture of life in the country. Many Romans believed that life on the farm was simple and relaxing, in contrast to the hectic life of city dwellers.

Life for such a farmer, though, was very tough and unromantic: his chores were never-ending and he had to worry about bad weather or failed crops. A farmer's tools were primitive: simple rakes, hoes, sickles and scythes which made working on the land an incessant and backbreaking task.

Oxen were the main draft animals on Roman farms.

Over much of Italy, rainfall was so low that a crop of grain could only be produced every two years. It was vital for the farmer to retain what moisture there was in the soil and much of the tilling of the land revolved round this.

Normally, there had to be constant weeding so that water would not be lost through evaporation. Then the cleared soil would have to be plowed continually – some writers advised nine or ten times in a year – so that a fine tilth would be formed which would allow the winter rains to sink in. The plowing was done by oxen pulling an ard, a simple plow which broke through the soil but did not turn it.

In Egypt, the irrigation system using Nile water was so efficient that crops could be produced every year. With so much cheap grain coming into Italy from overseas, cereal cultivation was on the decline by the 1st century AD and the olive had become more popular. This needed attention for a number of years before it bore its crop. Often cereal crops were sown between the trees while they were maturing.

3rd-century mosaic with fruit pickers.

BELOW **A special plow (top) developed by the Gauls. Unlike the simple ard (bottom), it could dig and turn the heavy soils of the north.**

Far from glamorous

Roman writers often romanticized the life of a shepherd, but it was far from glamorous: the job was considered so undesirable that it was usually given to slaves. Pasture for the flocks was often in remote upland areas and the shepherd had to be a tough, self-sufficient man, able to endure loneliness and the worst of the weather. During lambing a shepherd might not have a proper night's sleep for weeks. Mountain thieves would try to carry off the sheep and there was also a serious threat from wild animals.

In a letter to his tutor Fronto, the future emperor Marcus Aurelius admits to being another kind of worry for shepherds:

"One shepherd spotted our little group of horsemen and said to the other shepherd, 'Keep your eyes on those horsemen, for they often steal and cause very great damage.' When I heard this, I jabbed my spurs into my horse and galloped him into the middle of the flock. The terrified sheep quickly scattered. They ran off in all directions, bleating loudly. The shepherd hurled his staff at me…the shepherd, who feared to lose his sheep, lost his staff."

Ideally, a shepherd should be nimble and fleet of foot.

"Advice to new farmers"

The threshing floor is to be placed so that it can be viewed from above by the master. Such a floor is best paved with hard stone since the winnowed grain is cleaner and is free from small stones and earth which a dirt floor nearly always casts up during the threshing…the orchards and the gardens should be securely fenced and should lie close to where the manure may flow from the barnyard and baths and the watery lees squeezed from the olives, for both vegetables and trees thrive on nourishment of this kind.

Columella, *On Agriculture*, 1st century AD.

EARNING A LIVING

In the countryside most unskilled laborers could earn a living only with seasonal work, but in the cities there was a wide variety of more stable occupations. There could be more than a hundred kinds of small traders, skilled craftsmen and sellers of services and although such people were scorned by the landed classes, they were proud of their occupations. They organized themselves into self-help societies – *collegia*, with social and religious functions – and they formed an essential part of the empire's economy. One of the services these groups provided was a "burial club": for a subscription, members would have decent funerals and suitable memorials.

There were many who sold their skills on a more personal basis: teachers, doctors and professional entertainers. Teachers of rhetoric enjoyed high status and could become very wealthy while other teachers were poorly paid and despised by the cultured classes who expected them to force basic skills into their children. Prostitution flourished in the cities and troupes of dancing girls or acrobats entertained at banquets.

An important part of commerce. This abacus has grooves, not string, for the counters.

The color of money

Under Augustus a full range of imperial coins was produced. The smallest denomination was the copper *quadrans* and four of these made up an *as*, also in copper. Four asses made a brass *sestertius* while four sesterces made up one silver *denarius*; the gold *aureus* was valued at 25 denarii.

At first these mingled with an enormous variety of local coinage and it was not until the 3rd century that imperial coinage became the dominant currency of the empire. Meanwhile, there was thriving business for money changers who would bargain between different currencies. The state purchased goods with its coins and accepted taxes either in coin or in kind and Roman rulers realized the superb propaganda value of coin faces. A special issue publicized Augustus's generosity to the cities of Asia after an earthquake.

An assortment of bronze, silver and gold coins from Nero's reign.

Vespasian struck a large issue of coins to celebrate his subjugation of Judaea. The claims of Nero and Commodus to the imperial throne were boosted by coinage while a condemned emperor such as

Shameful occupations

"The most shameful occupations are those which cater to our sensual pleasures, fish sellers, butchers, cooks, poultry raisers and fishermen," Cicero reflected the upper classes' disdain for those who had to work. Yet every city had to have its providers of bread, meat and clothing. These were often freed slaves who would rent premises and perhaps employ their own slaves to do the manual work. Others traded in timber for building or furniture or retailed the vast range of pottery in even the poorest home. Many died rich and erected impressive stone tombs for themselves and their families on which the main activities of their trade would be carved.

Many women, such as the poulterer shown in this funerary monument, worked for a living.

RIGHT **Coins commemorating Claudius (top) and Augustus.**

The craftsmen of the empire

A shoemaker and cordmaker at work; detail from a sarcophagus.

Roman coinage was originally created as a way to pay armies.

Caligula would be dishonored by having his coinage defaced or even completely withdrawn.

Emperors had total control over the mint and some issued too much coin or changed the content to raise short-term funds. Under Septimius Severus the silver content of the denarius was reduced to 50 percent. In the 3rd century emperors, desperate to pay their troops, issued vast quantities of debased coinage. The currency was not stabilized again until the reign of Constantine in the 4th century.

The cost of living

Poor laborers in 1st-century Rome might expect to earn 400 sesterces a year, a legionary 900 sesterces, and a schoolmaster in a provincial Italian town would charge two sesterces a pupil per month – 1,200 sesterces a year if he had 50 pupils. A senior civil servant, on the other hand, had an annual salary of about 200,000 sesterces.

What could poorer people buy with their money? The price of grain – crucial for those not entitled to a free ration – fluctuated wildly. A *modius*, or enough to keep one person for eight days, varied from just over one as in a glut to 20 sesterces during a famine.

A modius of salt, on the other hand, could cost as much as 25 sesterces. Sea salt was one of Rome's most vital commodities. It was the only available food preservative and was used as a condiment and in the treatment of leather. Soldiers were given an allowance of salt: a *salarium*, from which the word "salary" derives.

Visitors to an inn in the early empire were charged one as for their bread and two asses for the extra relishes which went with it. Hay for a visitor's mule would be another two asses and the favors of a local girl would cost eight asses.

The rich lived far beyond this. A single peach, for instance, retailed at 30 sesterces in Rome. Lollia Paulina, the third wife of the emperor Caligula, was seen at a banquet covered in 40 million sesterces worth of jewels. A moderate-sized country estate was on sale in the early 2nd century for three million sesterces, reduced from five million.

The peoples of the Mediterranean, absorbed by the expanding Roman empire, often had cultures more sophisticated than that of their conquerors. In the east, Rome was heir to great traditions in sculpture and building. Greek craftsmen carved the friezes of Augustus's Altar of Peace, and the architect of Trajan's great forum was from Damascus. Even in the Celtic west, native metalworkers were often at least as skilled as were their Roman counterparts. The craftsmen of the empire were cosmopolitan, the more skilled traveling wherever they could find work, such as the Syrians who introduced blown glass across the empire.

Much of the craftwork of the empire was local and involved semiskilled work. Potters, clothmakers and metalworkers responded to the basic needs of every community, producing goods in small workshops.

Probably the largest and most labor-intensive of industries was that of making cloth. A wide variety of skills had to be mastered and coordinated so the raw wool could be cleaned, spun, woven into cloth and then finished and dyed. In Pompeii the fullers and dyers dominated the industry of the city. Wool from Campania would then be sent northward to Rome.

Some cities became renowned for their sophisticated crafts which were often exported throughout the empire. Aquileia, on the northern Adriatic coast, exploited its position as a port close to the high-quality iron mines of Noricum and at the end of the Amber Road. It was also a major center for silverware and glassmaking.

Shoes and boots for women were essentially the same style as those for men.

FEAST AND FAMINE

Augustus prided himself on his simple way of life, and was quite happy to live on bread and fish with a piece of hand-pressed cheese or some fruit. "I had a snack of bread and dates while out for my drive today," he writes in a letter. These were actually the staples of the Roman diet and many Romans would have eaten little else. For the poorest people, though, such a diet would have seemed like a great luxury.

Richer Romans were tempted by the growing range of delicacies produced in Italy or imported from abroad and banquets became increasingly lavish as hosts competed with each other to show off their favorite dishes. Many items were so exotic and expensive that there was even legislation against buying and eating them.

Breakfast and lunch were usually light meals with the main meal eaten early in the evening. This would often be a formal occasion, with guests invited and entertainment provided. However exotic the food, drinking was generally light with the wine being mixed with water. At only the most unrestrained of parties was wine drunk undiluted.

Food of the poor

Among the mass of poor in the large cities there was little to eat other than a porridge (*puls*) made of wheat ground up and mixed with water. In the country greater variety was possible. The poorer peasants would grind up a sauce of herbs and vegetables with oil, adding cheese if they were lucky enough to have any. People who owned a little land might grow cabbages or leeks, and a few might keep a pig and smoke its meat inside their homes.

In the case of slaves, their diet depended largely on the disposition of their masters. Seneca believed that slaves should be allowed to dine with their masters, but Cato, in the 2nd century BC, was less generous and thought they should be fed on bread, discarded olives and the dregs of fish sauce.

Pepper was the most widely used spice. For his country sauce (*moretaria*) Apicius ground it with herbs and honey.

Daily bread

The poorest Romans would not eat bread at all – even the cost of baking it would be beyond them – and their grain ration would be used for puls. People lucky enough to have their own home and oven would bake their own bread. They would grind their grain daily, mix it with salt and water and then bake it in the oven or by a fire. It was a tedious business, especially when it was yet another part of a hard day's work. From the 2nd century BC professional bakers appeared in Rome, with primitive methods that were little different from those of Egyptian bakers of 2,000 years before. It was a Roman baker, a freed slave from Greece, who introduced the first mechanical dough mixer.

TOP **This bakery would have sold bread like the centuries-old loaf found preserved in Pompeii.**

Dough, leaven and water were placed in a stone basin and wooden paddles, powered by horses or donkeys, kneaded the mixture.

The typical loaf weighed about half a kilogram. Loaves found at Pompeii were marked with a cross before baking so that they could be broken up more easily.

The bread ovens of professional bakers were fired by wood and different varieties of bread were produced. Some were cooked directly on a spit and others were baked in an earthen vessel.

"From the egg to the apples"

For the wealthier Roman, the most important social occasion was the banquet when friends, clients and acquaintances would be formally invited to share the evening meal. "You will dine well at my house, Julius Cerialis. If you have no better invitation, come on over," wrote the poet Martial to a friend. He went on with tempting mention of lettuce and leeks to start with, followed by tuna garnished with eggs, then oysters, baked chicken and sow's udders. Eggs were the most common appetizers and fruit the most common dessert.

RIGHT **Few people owned ovens; they cooked over open fires.**

RIGHT **Edible dormice, raised in special enclosures, were more expensive than oysters.**

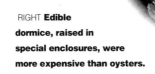

Instead of saying "from soup to nuts" Romans used the phrase *Ab ovo usque ad mala*, "("From the egg to the apples") for a full three-course meal.

Many meals were even more elaborate than those provided by Martial. Meat and fish were usually boiled and the Romans had a passion for rich sauces to pour over them. The most popular sauce was *garum*, a fish sauce, which the Romans introduced to every part of the empire. It could be bought ready made and often it would be mixed with honey and vinegar to create a sweet and sour sauce to be added to meat and fish.

Dormice were one of many delicacies, often served sprinkled with honey and poppyseed. They were considered so extravagant that

LEFT **Fish was an important element in the Roman diet.**

laws were even passed forbidding them to be eaten.

Few Romans took heed of such laws and the dinner parties of the 1st century AD became more and more extravagant. In the *Satyricon*, Petronius describes one of Trimalchio's banquets which included a wild boar stuffed with live thrushes and escorted into the dining room by hunting dogs while a golden hoop loaded with gifts was lowered from the ceiling.

Roman cooks took special delight in disguising their foods. Trimalchio's cook could make a fish out of a sow's womb or a dove out of a piece of ham. Quinces were decorated with thorns to make them look like sea urchins. The 1st-century gourmet, Apicius, describes how to make an anchovy delight without anchovies – a dish, he says, guaranteed to fool anyone.

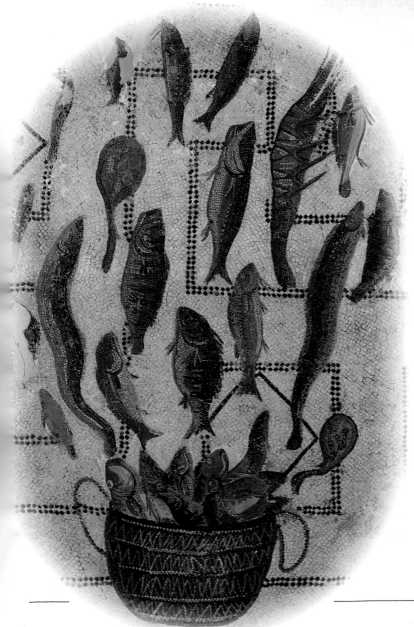

Chapter 7

THE CHRISTIAN EMPIRE

The year 285 marked a turning point in the history of the Roman empire. Faced with almost continual invasion for several decades and with increasing economic and political weaknesses at home the empire seemed on the verge of collapse. Yet in 285 an upstart general – Diocles – became emperor, ruled for 20 years as the emperor Diocletian and reorganized the empire so effectively that, in the west, it survived for another 170 years.

The 4th century was one of the most interesting in the history of the empire. The emperor Constantine's adoption of Christianity had enormous consequences for Roman society. With the public support of the emperor, Christians were now a privileged class; only a few years before, under Diocletian, they had been executed.

Although the aristocracy of Rome mounted a determined rearguard action against the new religion, by the beginning of the 5th century Christianity provided the framework within which politics, culture and even sexual ethics were created.

In the west the pressures on the empire from the Germanic tribes increased. These pressures brought desperate governmental demands for taxes and military men. Desperation led to brutality and brutality to a gradual alienation of the mass of citizens from their government. When collapse again threatened, there was no Dioc___ __ save the empire.

Christ depicted as the warrior fighting evil, an image easily understood by many beleaguered Romans who found their empire under attack.

The original Senate house, the Curia Hostilia, burned down in 52 BC during riots. Julius Caesar began a new one, the Curia Julia. It was completed by Augustus and later restored by Diocletian

LEFT **The interior of the Curia, the Senate house rebuilt in the Forum Romanorum by Diocletian to reassure the people of the empire that he was not neglecting the old capital of the Roman world.**

	250	300	310	320	330	340	350
THE EMPERORS		Diocletian 285–305		Constantine 312–337			

POLITICAL EVENTS

285 Diocletian becomes joint emperor with Maximian

301 Diocletian's edict on prices attempts to control inflation by regulating the prices of many commodities

305 Diocletian and Maximian abdicate, succeeded by Constantius and Galerius

306 On the death of Constantius, his son Constantine is declared emperor by the troops in Britain

312 Constantine defeats Maxentius, the son of Maximian, at the Milvian Bridge and claims inspiration from Christ

315 The Arch of Constantine is built in Rome

324 Constantine establishes his position as sole ruler of a reunited empire

324 Constantinople is founded by Constantine; it becomes his imperial residence in 330

326 Constantine's son Crispus is executed at Pola in Dalmatia; his wife Fausta dies soon afterwards

337 Constantine dies after being baptized on his deathbed; he is succeeded by his three sons

340 Constantine II is killed fighting his brother Constans at the battle of Aquileia

340 The empire is again split in two under Constans in the west and Constantius II in the east

RELIGION

297 Diocletian issues an edict against Manichaeans

303 Diocletian begins to persecute Christians at Nicomedia, then elsewhere

311 Galerius recognizes Christians at Nicomedia

313 The Edict of Milan grants toleration to Christians in the empire

325 The Council of Nicaea condemns Arianism as a heresy

330 The church of St Peter is erected in Rome

335 The church of the Holy Sepulcher is dedicated in Jerusalem

341 Ulfilas begins a mission to convert the Goths

The emperor Diocletian was one of the truly great men of Roman history. He was typical of the traditional Roman: a hardheaded, down-to-earth military man – but one with a vision that reached far beyond the army camps.

Diocletian's origins are obscure, but his early life was one of incessant campaigning along the Danube border, in Gaul and against the Persians. His experiences had shown him the scale of the threat to the empire from Rome's external enemies, and as he fought his way to power by defeating the legitimate emperor, Carinus, in 285, he also realized the instability of the post of emperor. One of Diocletian's first achievements was to transform the nature of the post itself.

Diocletian's reforms bring an end to years of crisis

The need to delegate authority was urgent: the empire was too far-flung for one emperor to rush from one crisis point to the next. Diocletian selected three trusted colleagues and created a rule of four: the Tetrarchy. One, Maximian, was to share power with Diocletian as an Augustus, an emperor. The other two of the four, Galerius and Constantius, were given the title of Caesar, designating them as lieutenants. Diocletian's plan was that they would succeed the two Augusti.

The first task of these colleagues was to restore order to the empire, and each was given a specific area to police and defend. Diocletian took the east, though it was Galerius, normally responsible for the Danube frontier, who achieved a great victory over Sasanian Persia in 298. Maximian kept guard in Italy and Africa while Constantius was responsible for Spain, Gaul and Britain. By 298 the empire was stabilized. The peace with Persia, Rome's most formidable enemy, was to last 40 years. The years of crisis of the 3rd century were over and what appeared to be a much more stable and effective government had been established.

Diocletian's next achievement was to break the link between emperor and army, which the invasions of the 3rd century had strengthened. Some other form of legitimacy had to be found and Diocletian sought it in religion. Earlier emperors had tried to harness the powers of the traditional gods of Rome in their support and Diocletian followed their example. He claimed that the gods of Rome had given their special protection to him and his colleagues. He presented himself as a son of Jupiter, father of the gods, while Maximian was proclaimed the son of Hercules.

Diocletian elevated the emperor to a form of divine monarch. The emperor was made increasingly inaccessible to the public; when he did appear it was with elaborate court ceremonial in the staged settings of imperial buildings. Supplicants were expected to prostrate themselves before him. In an age of tension and anxiety many people were reassured to think of their ruler as a superhuman being.

The consolidation of the emperor as a religious figure fused with the old gods put extra pressure on Christians who had now begun to permeate the army and civil service. Diocletian saw Christianity as a threat to the traditional relationship between the state and its protecting gods. In the great persecution which began in 303, Christians were forced

BELOW **This gold medallion asserts Diocletian's claim to the patronage of the victorious Jupiter. His claim to be the son of a god altered the post of emperor. Before, emperors were deified after death. Now Diocletian was claiming divinity as a living ruler.**

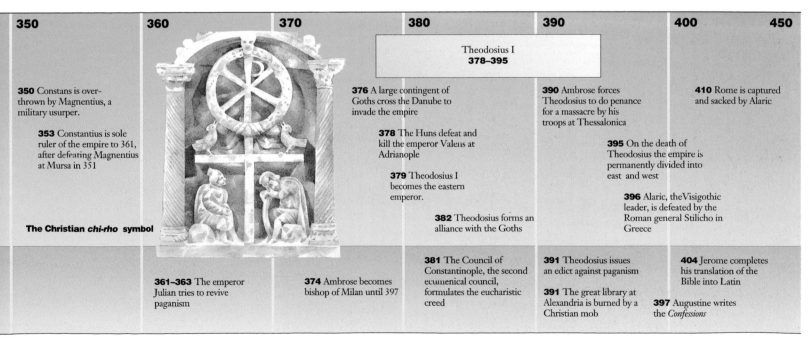

350	360	370	380	390	400	450

Theodosius I 378–395

350 Constans is overthrown by Magnentius, a military usurper.

353 Constantius is sole ruler of the empire to 361, after defeating Magnentius at Mursa in 351

The Christian *chi-rho* symbol

361–363 The emperor Julian tries to revive paganism

374 Ambrose becomes bishop of Milan until 397

376 A large contingent of Goths cross the Danube to invade the empire

378 The Huns defeat and kill the emperor Valens at Adrianople

379 Theodosius I becomes the eastern emperor.

382 Theodosius forms an alliance with the Goths

381 The Council of Constantinople, the second ecumenical council, formulates the eucharistic creed

390 Ambrose forces Theodosius to do penance for a massacre by his troops at Thessalonica

395 On the death of Theodosius the empire is permanently divided into east and west

396 Alaric, the Visigothic leader, is defeated by the Roman general Stilicho in Greece

391 Theodosius issues an edict against paganism

391 The great library at Alexandria is burned by a Christian mob

410 Rome is captured and sacked by Alaric

404 Jerome completes his translation of the Bible into Latin

397 Augustine writes the *Confessions*

to sacrifice to the gods of Rome. Those who refused were brutally punished.

As the emperor became transformed into a divine and remote figure, the Senate lost much of the little power it had retained. Diocletian did not ignore Rome completely – he built a new Senate building and a vast baths – but he visited the city for the first time only on the 20th anniversary of his accession. Rome retained immense symbolic importance for the empire but it was useless as a center for its defense. The centers of power had moved north, close to the attacks which might come across the Rhine, the Danube or the Euphrates. The cities of Trier, Milan, Sirmium, Nicomedia – Diocletian's own seat – and Antioch all became imperial bases.

Diocletian's approach to defense was conventional. He believed in holding the line against Rome's enemies by securing well-defended borders. Along the Rhine and the Danube and in the Syrian countryside he undertook a vigorous building program of fortifications. An enormous number of soldiers was required to police fortifications on such a large scale. Diocletian raised

ATLANTIC OCEAN

North Sea

Londinium

BRITANNIA

Rhine

Augusta Treverorum

GALLIA

Loire

VIENNENSIS

Rhine

Mediolanum

Ticinum

Arelate

Ravenna

PANNONIA

Aquileia

Po

Siscia

Sirmium

ITALIA

Corsica

Rome

HISPANIA

Ebro

Sardinia

Sicily

Catana

Carthage

AFRICA

Mediterranean

principal Roman mint
province boundary AD300
diocese boundary AD300

dioceses under command of
Diocletian
Maximian
Galerius
Constantius

0   600 km
0   400 mi

the size of the Roman army to 500,000 and then reformed the taxation system so that they could be supported. Each landowner's estate was assessed and a proportion of the produce demanded each year. These proportions could be varied according to the needs of the moment: Diocletian had succeeded in introducing the first budgeting system to the empire.

Inevitably, a more efficient administration was needed to collect the tax required, whether paid in coin or produce. Diocletian embarked on a major restructuring of the empire. The number of provinces was doubled to 100, grouped in 12 dioceses under the central control of the emperor and his Praetorian Prefect. The army was developed as an independent force directly under the control of the emperor. To prevent governors from challenging for power, each provincial governor was given closer control over cities than before, but could hold no military command.

Diocletian abdicated in 305. His health had been failing and he retired to a great palace he had built at Spalatum (modern Split). His achievements were extraordinary. Defense was better and the empire's resources were being used more effectively in the cause of its survival. The emperor had acquired a new status – that of a ruler appointed by the gods – and headed a bureaucracy which reached into every corner of the empire.

Diocletian's palace was laid out in grids like a Roman military camp, with main streets crossing at right angles. His private mausoleum later, ironically, became a Christian church.

Constantine becomes the Roman world's first Christian emperor

Only a year after Diocletian's abdication, his carefully constructed political system began to fall apart. At one point there were seven Augusti contending for power – precisely what Diocletian had hoped to avoid. The eventual winner of the struggle was Constantine, the son of Constantius, one of Diocletian's Caesars. Constantine was violent and temperamental, ambitious for power and confident of his ability to win it.

ABOVE **The Tetrarchy in battle dress show their unity by clasping shoulders. This statue was long thought to portray crusaders.**

The Battle of Milvian Bridge, in AD 312, was an especially decisive victory for Constantine as the followers of his rival, Maximinius, outnumbered his own by between two and four to one.

Constantine was also deeply religious. In 312 he claimed he had been told, in a dream vision, to put Christian symbols on the shields of his men in a crucial battle against one of his rivals for power. He did so and at the battle of the Milvian Bridge which followed, Constantine's armies triumphed, giving him control of the west. Absolute control of the whole empire followed in 324 when Constantine defeated his last rival, Licinius, who had been nominated as the successor of Galerius and had taken control of the east.

Constantine was deeply affected by what he believed to be the evidence of divine support. In 313, in the Edict of Milan issued jointly with Licinius, he announced full toleration for Christians and vigorously supported the scattered churches. Despite his intense devotion, Constantine may not have fully understood his adopted religion. At first he treated Christianity as yet another cult and he continued to hold the title *pontifex maximus*. He issued coins stamped with Mars, Jupiter and Hercules as late as 320, and was not baptized until he was on his death bed.

With Constantine's conversion, Christians were no longer subjected to the bitter persecution of Diocletian's reign. Christianity was associated with the military triumph of an emperor and the wealth of the whole empire was available to it. In Rome Constantine built a vast new cathedral, St John Lateran, and a number of churches on the burial sites of martyrs. The great basilica of St Peter, built on the Vatican Hill – the traditional site of the burial of the apostle – was the most imposing. A vast terrace had to be constructed on the hill and then the basilica built above it. The inside was decorated sumptuously with a pure gold cross weighing 60 kilograms and set on an earlier 2nd-century shrine to Peter.

Other churches and cathedrals rose across the empire. A great cathedral was built at Trier, the northern capital of the empire which Constantine had used as his base before the conquest of Rome. The holy places of the Christian tradition were honored with their own churches: the Church of the Holy Sepulcher in Jerusalem, over the tomb of Christ; another at the traditional site of the Nativity in Bethlehem; and another at the supposed site of the Ascension. This grandeur had a cost and was criticized by many including Jerome, the great theologian and scholar, who commented in the 5th century that the church had become richer in possessions

Baptism very late in life or even at the point of death was a common practice, undertaken in the hope of minimizing the chance of sinning between baptism and death.

BOTTOM **The Arch of Constantine in Rome. Much of the sculpture was taken from an earlier monument to the emperor Trajan.**

LEFT **Constantine was a religious man given to visions and varying beliefs. Before his conversion to Christianity, he was a believer in the old gods. He identified with the god Apollo and claimed to have been visited by him in a dream vision.**

and power but poorer by far in virtue.

Like Diocletian, Constantine could not ignore the threat to the empire posed by the Germanic tribes, continually pushed toward Roman frontiers by tribes farther north and east. Ambrose, bishop of Milan, later summed up the process: "The Huns throw themselves on the Alans, the Alans on the Goths, the Goths on the Taifali and the Sarmatians and the Goths, driven out of their homeland, have pushed us back in Illyricum."

Constantine's solution was to create more mobile forces, under the direct command of the emperor, which could be rushed to trouble spots. Inevitably, however, this meant drawing troops from the frontier posts. The empire's resources of manpower became increasingly overstretched.

After Christianity, the most significant contribution that Constantine made to the empire was to found the great city of Constantinople, planned as an equal to Rome. It was strategically placed, both for trade and defense, on the great routes that ran between the east and the west of the empire. The vulnerable borders of the Danube to the north and the Euphrates to the east could be reached with relative ease, and the city itself was virtually impregnable. It provided a base from which the eastern half of the empire was to survive and be defended for over 1,000 years.

The survival of the empire meant the survival of the romanized aristocracy. The most important feature of 4th-century society was the consolidation of wealth in the provinces in the hands of this landed elite. In Italy the old senatorial aristocracy

became wealthier than they had ever been before, as did the larger landowners in Britain. In Africa the fine mosaics of the 4th-century villas are a vivid testimony to an affluent, leisurely way of life where culture was increasingly enjoyed in the isolation of palaces or villas. City life in the west, in contrast, continued to decline.

Many landowners found posts as governors or high court officers in the expanding imperial administration. These jobs confirmed their status and increased their wealth. As *honestiores*, they formed a privileged caste, immune from certain taxes. The burden of taxation shifted toward the mass of the population, the *humiliores*. They were the most vulnerable to the tax collector and the army recruiter as the demands of government grew and became increasingly brutal. Constantine ordered those who accepted bribes to have their hand cut off, and torture was used as a punishment as well as a method of gaining confessions.

Taxation collection methods are so severe that some people are driven to suicide

In Illyricum, in the later reign of Valentinian, the government was so ruthless in its pursuit of taxation that people fled or committed suicide. The result was to force the poor to seek the protection of the richer landowners. Often they surrendered their land to the rich and worked it as serfs, a boon to landowners faced with a growing shortage of

Honestiores and *humiliores* were classes of people similar to the earlier distinctions between Italians and provincials or patricians and plebeians.

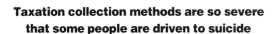

ABOVE **The cross became an important part of Christian symbolism during Constantine's reign.**

RIGHT **This 4th-century mosaic from the basilica of a consul, Junius Bassus, shows the changing art style of the Christian Roman empire. The traditional consul's triumphal procession is presented in a far more stylized manner than that of the lifelike art from earlier times.**

labor. There was thus little incentive for the rich to provide men for the armies.

In the eastern half of the empire city life and commerce showed more vigor. The centuries-old loyalties to the local town kept alive the tradition of public-spirited involvement in local affairs that was dying in the west. The towns provided a market for local farmers and so a free peasantry continued to exist in the countryside, able to pay their taxes from money received for their corn. In 4th-century Syria the peasants were rich enough to build new villages in stone. The eastern economy's strength was vital in the following century.

Many Christian writers argued that the Roman empire had been created by God specifically as a seedbed for Christianity. Its far-flung frontiers and easy communications were part of a divine plan to lead to the triumph of the faith and, following Constantine's conversion, the Christian church emerged for the first time as a major social and political force in the Roman empire. In eastern cities, such as Alexandria and Antioch, Christians already constituted a large part of the population. In other parts of the empire, especially in the west, Christians were still a tiny minority. Some aristocrats of Rome held their pagan beliefs until the late 4th century and were particularly outraged when a later Christian emperor boldly removed the ancient pagan altar of the goddess of Victory from the Senate house.

The church was still a loose grouping of communities, each under its own bishop. Bishops were now acquiring new status as respected and powerful local leaders. By the end of the 4th century such formidable individuals as Ambrose, Bishop of Milan, were telling emperors how to behave. The power of each bishop was, however, normally limited to his own diocese. If disputes on doctrine arose, a superior authority, the emperor, was called on to solve them.

The most prolonged dispute Constantine faced was the theological issue of the true nature of Christ. Arius, a senior priest from Alexandria, had preached that Christ was the son of God, created by God out of nothing and thus subordinated to him. This view particularly appealed to the intellectuals of the east but it was opposed by those who claimed that Christ was totally divine, and part of God from the beginning of time.

Christianity becomes a major political force in the empire

The dispute was a bitter and inherently insoluble one. The impatient Constantine dismissed it as a trivial argument between rival bishops and had to be persuaded that it was a matter of profound import and must be settled. Accordingly, in AD 325, Constantine

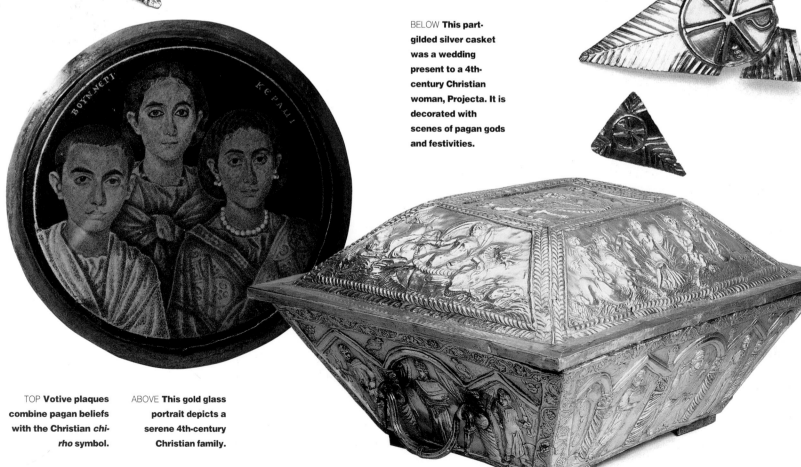

RIGHT **A late 4th-century mosaic of Ambrose, bishop of Milan, who was an unbaptized layman at the time he was elected bishop. He was the mentor of emperors and once imposed a public penance on the emperor Theodosius for massacring the citizens of one town after a riot.**

BELOW **This part-gilded silver casket was a wedding present to a 4th-century Christian woman, Projecta. It is decorated with scenes of pagan gods and festivities.**

TOP **Votive plaques combine pagan beliefs with the Christian *chi-rho* symbol.**

ABOVE **This gold glass portrait depicts a serene 4th-century Christian family.**

summoned all Christian bishops to Nicaea, a coastal town near Constantinople. The west was hardly represented: the bishop of Rome did not even attend and sent instead two priests as his delegates. Constantine, determined to resolve the issue, enforced a proclamation that Christ and God were one essence: a total rejection of Arius.

However, belief in Arianism remained strong throughout the east; Constantine's own son, the emperor Constantius, was a supporter. The pendulum swung back again under a later emperor, Theodosius who, in 381, backed the Council of Constantinople when it finally declared Arianism a heresy. Arians were then treated as harshly as any pagan believers.

By the end of the 4th century emperors such as Theodosius were the guardians of Christian orthodoxy, using state laws against those who were proclaimed heretics. For those who believed that the empire was an expression of God's plan, it was natural to assume that the emperor was the agent of God, building his kingdom on earth. However, with the emperor's backing it was becoming an intolerant kingdom, demanding a rigid, unquestioning interpretation of the nature of Christ.

The flourishing of Christianity had important effects on 4th-century society. The transformation of Christians from persecuted minority to privileged elite attracted many in search of new status. It was this, perhaps, which induced more devout Christians to reject the pleasures of society: asceticism swept the empire in the 4th century. Renouncing the desires of the flesh was felt to bring spiritual freedom at a time of oppressive control by the state.

Asceticism took many forms. In Syria men retreated alone to the mountains or lived for years at the tops of pillars. In Egypt, communities of monks formed and developed a relentless routine of prayer and hard labor. Egyptian monasticism was a mass movement which unleashed enormous, sometimes destructive, energies. By the end of the century bands of monks were spreading into the cities, burning down pagan temples and synagogues and wrecking the homes of unbelievers. In a much less aggressive form, monasticism had spread as far west as Gaul.

One important element of asceticism lay in a renunciation of sexuality. By 400 the superiority of virginity and sexual abstinence over marriage was widely accepted. One popular ascetic thinker, the Egyptian Hierakas, doubted whether married people would be admitted to heaven. Although this was an extreme view, many theologians did argue that sex – confined to married couples – was legitimate only in so far as it was designed to lead to the conception of children. Restrictions about

Arius (c AD 250–336) was born in Libya and preached in Egypt. Although he was due to be taken back into the church after his excommunication as a heretic, he collapsed and died in Constantinople before that could happen.

intercourse on Sundays, during Lent and at the times of the great Christian festivals underlined the Church's attempt to control this area of private life. A mistrust of sexuality in all its forms lingered on in the Catholic Church for centuries.

Soon after the death of Constantine in 337 the empire was once again disturbed by civil war as his three sons fought each other for power. The culmination came in September 351 when the surviving son, Constantius, confronted a usurping general, Magnentius, at the great battle of Mursa. It was bitterly fought with enormous casualties on both sides. "Thus perished large forces," wrote the historian Eutropius, "that could have conquered any enemy and assured the security of the empire." Within two years Magnentius had been destroyed and Constantius was the sole emperor.

Constantius was a solid, experienced ruler, dedicated to the empire and its defense; by hard fighting he succeeded in maintaining its borders. He followed the precedent of Diocletian in appointing two Caesars to support him and one of these, Julian (known as Julian the Apostate), succeeded him in 361. Julian attacked the pomp of the court at Constantinople and dismissed many of its supporters. He abandoned the Christianity to which he had been born and reopened pagan temples with a priesthood of his own choosing.

Despite a lack of military training, Julian was an excellent general: he effected many reverses against the Germans and made himself popular with his troops. In 363, while he was on campaign in Persia, he was wounded in a minor skirmish and killed by the unhealed injury.

With Julian's death Constantine's family was almost extinct; only a granddaughter survived. The next notable emperor was Valentinian I (364–375), the nominee of the armies and a Christian. He was a tough and effective emperor who pushed the encroaching German tribes back across the borders. These conflicts fueled the ever-increasing need for men and financial resources. Valentinian imposed a military discipline on the society, a move that aroused increasing

BELOW **The Corbridge *lanx*, a rectangular presentation dish which indicates the sophistication of pagan art in the Christian empire. The scenes depict the birth of the god Apollo and his sister Artemis on the Greek island of Delos.**

hostility and unrest in some areas of the empire.

From the start Valentinian shared the empire with his brother Valens. Valens fought competently along the Danube and against the Persians but, like all the empire's commanders, was desperately short of men. The only hope was to recruit more German mercenaries. Many had already proved surprisingly loyal, perhaps because they were, in effect, refugees, only too glad to have a living. Luck seemed to be on Valens's side.

The empire becomes unable to defend itself properly

Valens was a dedicated Arian Christian. He left pagans alone, but mercilessly persecuted non-Arian believers, exiling and executing many of them. Valens' enemies claimed that his defeat was divine retribution.

In 376 a vast horde of Goths driven from southern Russia by the advancing Huns begged Valens to allow them to settle in the empire. There was land in Thrace which had been ravaged and abandoned in earlier frontier campaigns and Valens allowed the Goths in, hoping that many would then join his army. Settling this great body of refugees would have been difficult at any time but the situation was badly handled. Not enough food was put aside and the local officers who met the Goths were corrupt: some traded the meat of dogs for starving Goths who were then sold as slaves.

The outraged Goths rose in revolt. Valens marched against them, confident of victory, but at the battle of Adrianople in 378 he was horribly beaten and died with two-thirds of his army. This humiliating defeat was a turning point in the history of the late empire. The resources with which the empire had to defend itself in the west were rapidly diminishing. In a new power struggle, the winner was Theodosius, the son of one of Valentinian's most successful generals.

It had long been accepted that Germans could fight as mercenaries and even find homes in the empire under the supervision of local landowners. Theodosius, in the desperation of the times, was forced to accept that the Goths should now be allowed to settle in the empire under their own leaders and laws and fight alongside the Romans as allies rather than as an integral part of the Roman army. The distinction was crucial. If they were not well treated the German leaders could easily turn their men against the empire.

The tensions in the western empire were becoming acute; the desperate attempts of the government to raise men and taxes had led to increasing alienation of the mass of its citizens. The rich were gradually withdrawing from government, intent on holding their own local power against the demands of the center. Corruption was growing and the continual pressures from invaders and government caused morale to decline.

However, all was not yet lost. In 395, at the death of Theodosius, the empire stood with its frontiers intact. In fact it was still holding borders that were more extended than those of Augustus. Overall the empire had shown astonishing resilience in face of the pressures upon it. The question was whether it could maintain its unity into the 5th century and come to a permanent accommodation with the Germanic tribes.

The Goths were a Germanic people divided into two tribes: the Ostrogoths, which probably meant "eastern Goths" and the Visigoths, which may have meant "valiant people".

ABOVE **Cameo of Julian, portrayed in Hellenic fashion. His love of Hellenistic culture increased his hatred of Christianity.**

RIGHT **A Byzantine calendar with the Sun God at the universe's center, unmoved, to many people, by Christianity.**

CONSTANTINOPLE · THE NEW ROME

Constantinople, officially inaugurated on May 11, AD 330, was a blend of Roman organization and Greek art. This new capital of the east, situated at the very heart of the empire, was accessible to every major route from east to west across the Roman world. The city of Constantine was modeled on Rome: it had seven hills and, like the old capital of the empire, was divided into 14 districts, and was adorned with thousands of statues plundered from the cities of the east. Constantinople had its own Senate and was allocated one of the empire's two consuls; there were financial benefits for settlers who built houses, and free bread for the poor.

Constantinople was, above all, planned by Constantine to be a Christian city; there were several churches and few pagan temples, though pagan beliefs were tolerated. In the center were three great churches dedicated to Holy Wisdom (Hagia Sophia), Holy Power (St Dynamis, now lost) and Holy Peace (St Eirene). A church of the Holy Apostles was built to house Constantine's body after his death and here, in 337, he was laid to rest in his own tomb, surrounded by 12 memorial stones to the apostles themselves.

MAIN PICTURE **The Bosphorus strait. This name means "ox ford", from a mythical maiden, Io, whom Jupiter turned into a heifer. Io wanderd the earth and crossed the water in her travels.**

6TH-CENTURY CONSTANTINOPLE **The city in the mid 5th century, with the new walls built by Theodosius to accommodate the rapidly-expanding population. A century later over one million people lived there.**

St Mary

Wall of Theodosius

Cistern of Aetius

Cistern of Aspar

Wall of Constantine

Acropolis

Holy Apostles

St Eirene

Forum of Constantine

Hagia Sophia

Aqueduct of Valens

Forum of Theodosius

Great Palace

Hippodrome

Forum Bovis

Palace of Justinian

Forum of Arcadius

Harbor of Theodosius

Cistern of Mocius

Constantinople

St Carpus and St Papylus

St Menas

St John the Baptist

N

Golden Gate

0   0.5 km

0   0.5 mi

RIGHT **One of four silver-gilt decorations, possibly for a ceremonial sedan chair. They are in the form of Tyches, the female personification of great cities. Constantinople is represented with a cornucopia as the provider of bounty.**

ABOVE **Theodosius II built walls around Constantinople that were impregnable for over 1,000 years.**

LEFT **The frontispiece from a medieval manuscript of the Notitia of Constantinople. Among the notable buildings are the Hagia Sophia, the beautiful cathedral to Holy Wisdom, and the Hippodrome.**

THE BUREAUCRACY

The late empire employed a massive and sophisticated bureaucracy. Diocletian's economic reforms meant a huge increase in the size and costs of the existing bureaucracy and large numbers of census officers, accountants and clerks were needed to manage the new system effectively.

The citizen's duty did not end with paying taxes. Many classes had to perform a wide range of services and legal limitations on social mobility were introduced to prevent people leaving occupations which the state deemed essential. Businessmen and craftsmen, such as shippers and bakers, were organized into hereditary guilds. Municipal council posts with responsibility for public works and tax collections were also made hereditary; peasant farmers were tied to the land by hereditary obligations, reducing them to the status of serfs.

The main burden of taxation and service fell on the urban middle classes and the peasantry as the upper classes enjoyed extensive immunities. The impoverishment of these classes in some areas adversely affected town life and agriculture, weakening the empire's economy and, in the long term, adding to its problems.

"Fear is the most effective regulator"

Who does not know that wherever the common safety requires our armies to be sent, the profiteers insolently and covertly attack the public welfare, not only in villages and towns, but on every road? They charge extortionate prices for merchandise, not just fourfold or eightfold, but on such a scale that human speech cannot find words to characterize their profit and their practices. Indeed, sometimes in a single retail sale a soldier is stripped of his pay. Moreover, the contributions of the whole world for the suppport of the armies fall as profits into the hands of these plunderers...the pillagers of the state itself seize day by day more than they know how to hold. Aroused justly and rightfully by all the facts set forth above, and in response to the needs of mankind itself, which appears to be praying for release, we have decided that maximum prices of articles for sale must be established...experience teaches that fear is the most effective regulator and guide for the performance of duty. Therefore it is our pleasure that anyone who resists the measures of this statute shall be subject to a capital penalty for daring to do so. And let no one consider the statute harsh...

Diocletian introduces his Edict of Maximum Prices in AD 301.

Controlling inflation

A spiralling need for cash to pay the armies had led 3rd-century emperors progressively to debase the coinage. However, as the real value of the coinage fell, prices rose and inflation began to run out of control, playing havoc with the public finances. Diocletian used two methods to try to bring the rate of inflation under control. First, he reformed the coinage, increasing the purity of gold and silver coinage and introducing a better quality copper coinage. However, gold and silver coins were in too short supply; they soon became worth more than their nominal value and effectively devalued copper coinage. Then, in 301, Diocletian issued his Edict of Maximum Prices. This laid down maximum legal prices for a wide range of products and services and detailed their relative values. Initially the edict, with a death penalty for offenders, was vigorously enforced but despite many executions it, too, failed to halt inflation and was a complete failure as a law. Goods simply vanished from the markets and the edict was allowed to lapse.

Diocletian also abolished the old land taxes and replaced them with the *annona*, a tax paid in kind – for example, food and clothing – and redistributed to soldiers or other state employees. Other taxes took the form of compulsory public services, such as providing draft animals for the post service, quarters for troops and officials, or labor for building and road works.

Diocletian's tax reforms proved a heavy burden on taxpayers, one often made worse by corrupt officials practicing extortion. Taxes were collected by the *curiales*, municipal councillors, who were personally liable for the full amount of their area's assessment. Any shortfall had to be paid from their own property, and many curiales were over-zealous when collecting. "Every curial is a tyrant," was the complaint of one writer.

LEFT **Tax demands could be so high that the collectors could not bring in what was required.**

BELOW **In Diocletian's edict, olive oil was valued more highly than the finest wines of central Italy.**

Administering the empire

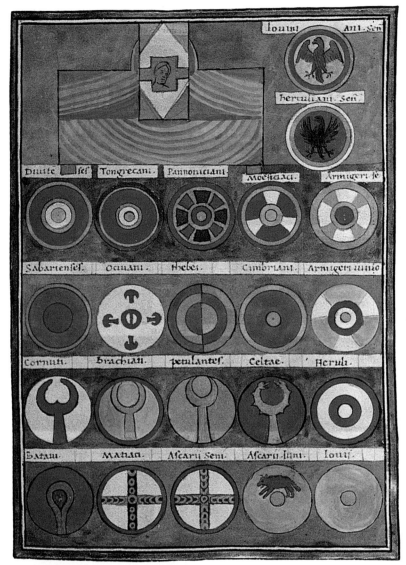

ABOVE **A quaestor's duties, shown by scrolls and a column.**

LEFT **The insignia of the western Master of the Infantry shown in a medieval copy of the Notitia.**

ABOVE **Provinces, such as Apulia and Calabria, were also depicted in the Notitia.**

A unique picture of the government and army of the late Roman empire is in the *Notitia Dignitatum*, the Register of Civil and Military Dignitaries. The Notitia, compiled about 395, contained ranks and insignia.

Military and civilian authorities were strictly divided. At the head of the military hierarchy were the Masters of Infantry of east and west and their subordinates, the Masters of Cavalry. Below them were the Counts who commanded the regional field armies and the Dukes in charge of the frontier armies.

The central civil administration was the *comitatus*: the emperor's personal household, his bodyguard, senior army officers, the council of imperial advisers, finance and legal ministries, and a secretariat.

The Praetorian Prefect was the senior official, with wide-ranging duties of supervision. The Prefect also ran the postal service and the state arms factories and could deputize for the emperor in the appeal courts.

Civil servants were classed as soldiers; they were organized into corps and wore uniforms. The administrative staff of all ministries were under the day-to-day control of the Master of the Offices, who also regulated audiences with the emperor. There were two finance ministries: one, under the Count of the Sacred Largess, was responsible for collection and expenditure of monetary taxes; the other, under the Count of the Private Estates, was responsible for the management of imperial property.

The Quaestor of the Sacred Palace drafted legislation and imperial communications. The Quaestor had no staff of his own and finished documents were drawn up in the secretariat – a corps, several hundred strong, of notaries, stenographers and accountants. Though the notaries were officials of low rank, their most important duty – keeping the minutes of meetings of the imperial council – kept them close to the center of power. The post was a popular first step in an civil career.

The orders of the comitatus were carried out by over 1,000 couriers who also acted as secret policemen, spying on the provincial governors and informing the emperor of corruption or sedition.

Below the comitatus were the provincial administrations under their governors. Diocletian had more than doubled the number of provinces, grouping them into dioceses under the supervision of a vicar who acted as deputy to the Praetorian Prefect. Both governors and vicars maintained staffs of several hundred clerks. The status of these clerks was much lower than those in the comitatus: most were freedmen or slaves.

BELOW **Officials used an ivory diptych, such as this consul's, to announce their new postings.**

BRITAIN: A LATE ROMAN PROVINCE

Britain was a typical outlying Roman province and, though vulnerable to pirate raids, was spared the worst effects of the barbarian invasions of the 3rd century. So, against the trend in most of Rome's western provinces, the early 4th century was a time of prosperity for Britain. Output from British industries, such as mining and pewter making, increased, while the growing demands of the Rhine legions for grain and woollen textiles meant that British agriculture flourished.

Richly decorated villas sprang up across the countryside, a sign of the wealth and confidence of the provincial aristocracy. By the second half of the century, however, increasingly severe barbarian raids meant that Britain began to experience the insecurity common in frontier provinces. Left increasingly defenseless as troops were withdrawn to the continent, the British provincials finally expelled the Roman administration in 410 and organized their own defense against the barbarians.

Christianity in late Roman Britain

Although the earliest reference to Christians in Britain dates back to about AD 200, Christianity was not widespread there before Constantine's reign. Unusually, Christianity in Britain seems to have been strongest in the countryside, not in the towns as elsewhere in the empire. Members of the British landed aristocracy may have adopted Christianity as a sign of loyalty to the imperial house. Much of the archeological evidence for Christianity in Britain comes from villa sites, such as the Christian mosaics from the villa at Hinton St Mary. Paganism remained strong and pagan shrines, such as a temple to Nodons in Gloucestershire, flourished.

One of the Hinton St Mary mosaics.

The defense of Roman Britain

The fact that Britain was an island was a disadvantage as well as an advantage to its defenders. The sea was a highway as well as a barrier and Britain's long coastline was very vulnerable to attack by pirates. By about 280 the Channel seas were increasingly dominated by Saxon and Frankish raiders. A host of coin hoards, burnt villas and abandoned villages from the coastal areas of Britain, Gaul and even Spain testify to their wide-ranging attacks.

The strength of barbarian pressure on the frontiers forced the Romans to increase greatly the resources devoted to defense. Troop numbers were increased and new fortifications were constructed. In Britain a chain of coastal forts was built to act as bases for coastguard troops and naval patrols. These forts were built to withstand a siege if necessary, with thick walls, strong gatehouses and external bastion towers to mount catapults. The Romans did not consider the defense of Britain in isolation from the rest of the empire and the coastal defenses on both sides of the Channel were organized into a single command area known, after the main enemy, as the Saxon Shore.

These defenses, though not impenetrable, brought Britain more security than most frontier provinces enjoyed. But the barbarians were becoming better organized and in 367 an alliance of

Barbarian raids, or the fear of them, particularly threatened Britain's agricultural economy. Some villas and farms met violent ends – decapitated skeletons have been discovered on a farm site at Sherston in Wiltshire – while many were abandoned or allowed to fall into disrepair. The towns, too, declined as their administrative functions were lost due to political instability. Late 4th-century Britain was a particularly fertile breeding ground for would-be emperors, and generals of frontier armies often used their troops to pursue imperial ambitions. Usurpers, such as Magnus Maximus in 383, weakened the garrison by withdrawing troops to fight futile civil wars on the continent, leaving the province even more exposed to attack. The last British mint had closed by 388 and and coins gradually went out of circulation. Britain was in a state of advanced decay by 410 when the province became independent.

LEFT **Roman resistance: a coastal fort at Portus Adurni (Portchester).**

RIGHT **German army belt fittings show the presence of barbarian mercenaries.**

ABOVE **Broken silver bullion was hidden by many Britons to avoid losing it to pirate looters.**

Saxons, Franks, Picts and Irish launched a devastating atttack on Britain, overwhelming the defenses. Although many towns, including London, held out, barbarian bands plundered the countryside at will. The invaders were driven out by the Gallic field army in 368 but security did not return. In a pattern which was to be repeated in other frontier provinces over the next century, the fabric of Roman Britain began to unravel.

Malton

Petuaria

Branodunum

BRITANNIA

Gariannonum

Walton

Othona
Regulbium
Dubris   Rutupiae
Portus Adurni   Lemanis
Anderita

English Channel

Grannona

GAUL

North Sea

Angles

Elbe

Frisians

Saxons

Trajectum

Noviomagus

Rhine

Franks

Oudenburg

GERMANIA

Colonia Agrippina

Marcis

Gesoriacum
Etaples
(naval base)

BELGICA

Moguntiacum

Schelde

Seine

Saxon Shore fort
other military site
road
invasion route

0   140 km
0   100 mi

THE GRAVEN IMAGE

When the early Christians first depicted Christ in glory in heaven they often added the figure of Caelus, a classical divinity of the sky, to make sure the theme was understood. This mingling of pagan and Christian images was common in early Christian art. Christ was often depicted looking like Apollo or Orpheus and pictures of the Egyptian goddess Isis, holding her son Horus, were very similar to later images of the Virgin Mary and the infant Jesus. A distinct and exclusive Christian art took many years to appear.

The earliest Christian art is that found on the walls of catacombs near Rome dating from about 200 AD. Decoration is simple and many of the pictures are no more than symbols. There are decorative pictures of the Good Shepherd and his flock and scenes from the Bible: Noah in the ark, the raising of Lazarus or the adoration of the Magi.

The earliest surviving Christian sarcophagi, found in Rome and Gaul, date from about 230 and are carved with the same themes as those in the catacombs. By the 4th century a rich, crowded style had developed. Christian art had moved onto the walls of churches; through mosaics and paintings believers were openly regaled with the stories and symbols of their faith.

The triumph of life over death

One aim of early Christian art was to proclaim the triumph of life over death. For Christians living under the continuous threat of persecution it was a powerful way of raising morale. The Old Testament was one of the most popular sources for inspirational examples. The scene of Isaac being saved from sacrifice by his father Abraham by the last minute intervention of God was common, as was the miraculous survival of Daniel in the lions' den. Very popular too was the story of Jonah, found in early catacomb art and on sarcophagi. The story is often told in a narrative series of pictures. First Jonah is seen falling from a ship into the jaws of a sea monster. Then he appears being vomited out alive and drifting to shore. Next he is found outside Nineveh under the plant provided by God for his shelter and finally with the plant withered around him as God rebukes him for his disobedience and lack of faith.

Gold glass painting, once the bottom of a vessel. It shows Jonah and the sea monster.

The life of Christ

Scenes from the life and death of Christ were chosen carefully for early Christian art. The most popular of the miracles was the raising of Lazarus from the dead, with Christ shown ushering the revived corpse up the steps of an underground tomb to the delight of a crowd gathered around him. Another favorite scene was the feeding of the five thousand, a reminder to the faithful of the perpetual generosity of God. Very rare in early Christian art is any reference to the Passion and Crucifixion of Christ and there is no direct reference in any catacomb art to the Resurrection. It was only in the 5th century that we begin to find detailed portrayals of the Crucifixion. Why there was this inhibition in the art of the period is not clear as the theme was treated fully by theologians of the time. It may have been felt that depicting Christ as dead detracted from his glory as the risen savior.

One of four ivory panels with scenes from Christ's Passion.

The faces of Christ

One of the most popular of the pictures found in catacombs is that of Christ as the Good Shepherd. He is often placed in a pastoral setting with trees and plants, sometimes carrying a sheep, at other times pasturing or milking a flock. This theme was not exclusive to Christianity. Representations of a man carrying a sheep go as far back as the Hittites and are common in classical art. Usually, however, the sheep are being carried to sacrifice. The Christians had a totally different perspective on these scenes. For them the sheep was being saved. It was a tradition that went back to the Old Testament where, in the Psalms, God is proclaimed as the shepherd of his people. Matthew and Luke tell the parable of the lost sheep and the rescuing shepherd

RIGHT **Christ portrayed as a youthful shepherd; sheep symbolize his faithful followers.**

while in John Christ is again the shepherd of his people, "he who lays down his life for his sheep". A traditional theme in art was given new form and meaning through Christianity. Sometimes the shepherd is portrayed carrying a pipe, another image from classical mythology. Here Christ is linked to Orpheus who, through his music, charmed the wildness of nature. Similarly, Christ will tame the hearts of wicked men.

In early Christian art Christ is often portrayed as a simple figure dressed in everyday clothes and with no aura of majesty. It is only in the early 5th century that he begins to be represented in art as the supreme judge enthroned in glory in heaven. One early example comes from the catacomb of Peter and Marcellinus outside Rome where Christ appears flanked by the apostles Peter and Paul.

Gradually the portrayal of Christ in majesty became a more dominant theme in Christian art. The impetus for the change came from the east. The emperor in Constantinople claimed to be God's agent on earth, and so Christ was increasingly portrayed as an emperor figure, removed from the common man and robed as a supreme ruler. From farther east, came the convention of depicting a ruler face on and this was adopted for the dominating figures of Christ in majesty that looked down from the domes of the great basilicas. Britain provides other representations of Christ on the fine mosaic floors, dating from the prosperous 4th century, found at many villa sites. In their vivid decoration Christian and pagan scenes are often intermingled. In

LEFT **Christ as judge, depicted in majesty in this painting from a catacomb in Rome.**

RIGHT **Bellerophon killing the Chimera; one image used to represent Christ as the fighter of evil.**

the mosaic from a villa at Hinton St Mary, the center is taken up with the head of a young, beardless man, set against the Christian symbol of the *chi-rho* surrounding the head as if it was a halo. It can only be Christ. Around the mosiac are more conventional pagan themes of dogs chasing deer and the four winds in the corner, possibly a representation of the evangelists.

Christ as the fighter of evil is represented in the same villa in the form of another traditional pagan classical figure on the floor: Bellerophon. Bellerophon was an ancient Corinthian hero, absorbed into Greek myth, who was set the task of killing the Chimera, a fire-breathing monster with the head of a lion and the tail of a snake. He is found in several British mosaics of the period and is often seen as a representation of good triumphing over evil. He fitted quite well into Christian art and may even have inspired later portrayals of St George and the Dragon.

THE HOUSE OF GOD

Early Christian communities were forced to meet in private houses, often using a dining room for their gatherings and water from wells or bath-houses for their baptisms. By the 3rd century, with numbers of converts growing, a whole house might be adapted as a church, with a large meeting room and separate rooms for baptism and clergy. These buildings were normally in the poorer areas of the cities and from the outside would look no different from any other house.

Once Constantine's Edict of Milan proclaimed toleration and support for Christianity throughout the empire this all changed. The emperor poured vast sums of money into his church building program and all over the empire new churches appeared, resplendent with their fine decoration. Many were built over the shrines of martyrs, places which had been venerated from the early days of the church. Others took over prime sites within the major cities – even the sites of earlier imperial palaces – while Constantinople was planned as a Christian city. Churches now became magnificent treasure houses, objects of awe and the inspiration of worship for the increasing number of converts to Christianity.

Benefactors of the church

The Christian churches built during and after the reign of Constantine were financed from the confiscated lands and palaces of defeated imperial rivals. The great church of St John Lateran in Rome rose on the site of the barracks of the Praetorian Guards, disbanded by Constantine for supporting the defeated Maxentius. St Peter's, built over an earlier shrine to St Peter, was financed from properties in Antioch, Egypt and along the Euphrates. St Paul's, appropriately, was financed from land taken by the emperor in Cicilia, Paul's birthplace. At Trier, the northern capital of the empire, a great cathedral rose from the ruins of the imperial palace while Diocletian's retirement palace at Split was converted to a church.

In the east of the empire the building program was equally ambitious. Constantinople, built as a Christian city, was largely financed from the revenues confiscated from pagan temples. In Palestine, Helena, the dowager empress and

Churches and basilicas

Under Constantine the church gained a new importance. With thousands of new converts, houses in the poorer parts of each city were no longer enough, and something grander had to be built. There was a pagan model to copy: the basilica, typically a long hall with a flat timber roof and aisles running along its length. For centuries the basilicas had been used as law courts, with magistrates enthroned at one end; as markets; homes of money lenders or places to meet and gossip.

Now they were to receive a new function. For the church the basilica model was ideal. The clergy or bishop could be installed at one end, as the magistrate had been, and large numbers of worshipers could fit inside. The greatest of the basilicas was St Peter's in Rome, constructed over the shrine which for generations was believed to be the resting place of St Peter's body. A vast terrace was levelled on the Vatican Hill and the basilica when built was 119 meters long and 64 meters wide. At the western end the building was crossed by a transept and it was at this end that worship over the shrine was conducted. The nave covered the old burial ground which was still used after

RIGHT **The nave of St Peter's had a mosaic of Constantine giving a model of his church to the saint.**

Tunnels under the city

mother of Constantine, initiated the building of fine churches on the holy places, including the supposed sites of the Nativity and the Ascension. The most fabulous of these was the Church of the Holy Sepulcher in Jerusalem which rivaled St Peter's in its grandeur.

The decorations of these great buildings were magnificent. A pure gold cross weighing over 60 kilograms was laid on the shrine of St Peter, and the altar was studded with gems. A visitor to one of these early churches described it "as a place of perfection, the heavenly Jerusalem, its walls and buildings made in heaven".

LEFT **Helena was the reputed discoverer of Christ's cross.**

the basilica was built so that the nave fulfilled the function of a great funeral hall. The inner aisles of the nave were marked off by 44 huge columns of marble taken from earlier Roman buildings and the whole building was decorated with beautiful objects of gold and silver.

TOP AND ABOVE **Christian catacomb and bread stamps with Christian messages.**

Early Christians did not carry out cremation, the Roman method of disposal for bodies of the poor. Often they could not afford to buy plots of land for cemeteries large enough to take their growing numbers. The solution adopted in Rome, in Naples, Sicily and and also in parts of north Africa, was to dig down into suitable rock. So appeared the catacombs, underground passages along which could be carved ledges and openings in which coffins or bodies shrouded in linen could be placed. In Rome, where the tufa rock was easy to dig, they ran for over 900 kilometers. The earliest catacombs around Rome date from about 150 AD and they were built for centuries. Before the 4th century they were vulnerable. In north Africa mobs attacked and plundered catacombs; in the persecution of the emperor Valerian (256-59) Christians were forbidden to visit them at all. The impulse to visit the burial places of the dead, particularly those of martyrs, was strong, even at these times of persecution. When persecutions ended the graves of martyrs in the catacombs could be openly marked by basilicas built above ground. Most catacomb sites in Rome became the cemeteries of city parishes and in the 4th century they reached their greatest extent.

Chapter 8

THE FALL OF THE WESTERN EMPIRE

The fall of the Roman empire has been attributed to everything from lax morals to lead poisoning. The truth is that the western empire – with its long frontiers and comparatively undeveloped economy – had always been vulnerable. What was remarkable, in face of incessant pressure from the Germanic tribes on its northern border for so many decades, was its ability to have survived as long as it did. Even in the 4th century the empire's frontiers remained intact and, under emperors such as Diocletian and Constantine, significant and successful reforms were achieved.

In the 5th century the pressure from hostile forces became too great. The west desperately needed to maintain access to the riches of the east – always the wealthiest part of the empire – and when the relationship between east and west began to break down at the beginning of the 5th century, the end was in sight. At the same time some accommodation had to be made with the Germans. Here the failure of Rome was a diplomatic, as much as military, weakness. If enough Germans had been successfully integrated into the empire they might have provided the manpower and tax resources to ensure resistance against later invaders from the north. The prejudices of Roman aristocrats, religious intolerance and the clash of cultures proved too much and when the Vandal leader, Gaiseric, set up his own independent kingdom in Africa in the 430s, the western empire moved past recovery.

The empire falls to hostile forces, as depicted in this 8th-century casket lid with Germanic warriors attacking a homestead.

Theodosius was the last emperor to rule over a united empire. When he died in 395 its frontiers were intact, but his successors, his sons, were still boys. Honorius, who took the west of the empire, was only 10; Arcadius, emperor of the east, was 18. Both proved to be weak characters, unable to meet the challenges that lay ahead.

The challenge for the western empire was the German tribes. There was a long tradition of using Germans as mercenaries; the Germans were happy to cooperate: without employment in the armies many of them were refugees, driven into the empire by more hostile tribes to the north. These mercenaries were surprisingly loyal: many valued Roman civilization and some even became supreme commanders of the Roman armies.

By the end of the 4th century the mercenaries were being joined by entire German tribes whom Theodosius had allowed to settle in the empire on the understanding that they would fight alongside the Romans as allies. These Germans were very willing to defend their land against later invaders.

Beyond the frontiers of the empire a mass of tribes still pushed down on the Rhine and Danube borders, largely as the result of the continued westward expansion of an Asiatic people – the Huns. The newcomers looked for land for themselves, fighting Roman armies and German tribes for it. Only the most gifted Roman leaders could enforce some kind of temporary stability in the hope of preserving the last stronghold of the western empire – Italy itself – from the turmoil.

The eastern empire was safer from imminent attack. Those Germans who broke through the Danube border and headed east were soon confronted by Constantinople's impregnable walls and it was almost impossible for them to cross the Bosphorus into Asia Minor. The most formidable enemy of the east was the Sasanian empire in Persia but this was a stable state, itself vulnerable to invaders from the east, so both sides were ready to maintain peace through diplomacy.

It was essential for the western empire to keep on good terms with the east. The east had always provided a large proportion of the wealth of the empire and its economy was much more vital than that of the west. Egypt produced three times as much grain as did the west's richest province, Africa, and its peasants enjoyed a prosperity completely unknown to the poorer classes of the west.

Stilicho strengthens the division between east and west

The division between the two parts of the empire was consolidated in the early 5th century by the ambitions of the west's supreme military commander, Stilicho. Stilicho was Theodosius's leading general and the emperor, on his deathbed, had asked him to be protector of both his sons and thus of the entire empire. In the east Stilicho was met with intense resistance which hardened when he tried to recruit men from land in the Balkans, an area the east claimed as its own.

The dispute came just as the west was facing new challenges. The first came from Alaric, an ambitious general of the Goths who had served in the Roman armies. Alaric, settled in Illyricum, had no desire to overthrow the empire: what he wanted was fertile land for his followers, and a leading role in the Roman armies for himself. At the end of the 4th century he and his men started

The **Huns**, or Hunni, were exceptional horsemen and fierce warriors, striking fear across Europe. They acquired huge sums of gold from the sale of prisoners back to the Romans.

Alaric (c370–410) was a nobleman by birth. Before he and his tribe attacked Rome, they invaded Greece, sacking the Piraeus, Athens' port, and several cities including Corinth and Sparta.

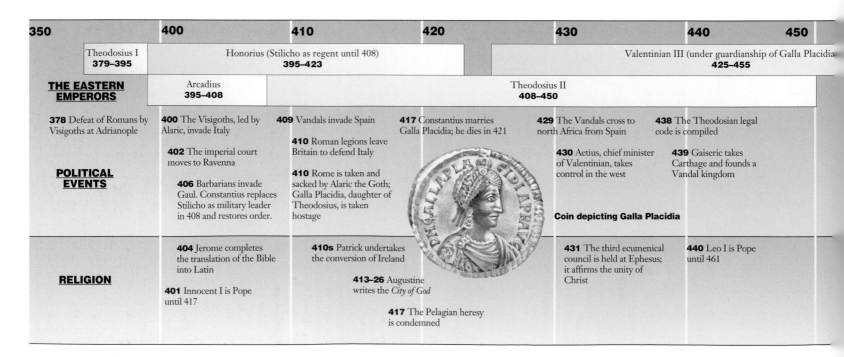

350	400	410	420	430	440	450
	Theodosius I **379–395**	Honorius (Stilicho as regent until 408) **395–423**		Valentinian III (under guardianship of Galla Placidia) **425–455**		
THE EASTERN EMPERORS	Arcadius **395–408**	Theodosius II **408–450**				
POLITICAL EVENTS	**378** Defeat of Romans by Visigoths at Adrianople	**400** The Visigoths, led by Alaric, invade Italy / **402** The imperial court moves to Ravenna / **406** Barbarians invade Gaul. Constantius replaces Stilicho as military leader in 408 and restores order.	**409** Vandals invade Spain / **410** Roman legions leave Britain to defend Italy / **410** Rome is taken and sacked by Alaric the Goth; Galla Placidia, daughter of Theodosius, is taken hostage	**417** Constantius marries Galla Placidia; he dies in 421	**429** The Vandals cross to north Africa from Spain / **430** Aetius, chief minister of Valentinian, takes control in the west / **Coin depicting Galla Placidia**	**438** The Theodosian legal code is compiled / **439** Gaiseric takes Carthage and founds a Vandal kingdom	
RELIGION		**404** Jerome completes the translation of the Bible into Latin / **401** Innocent I is Pope until 417	**410s** Patrick undertakes the conversion of Ireland / **413–26** Augustine writes the *City of God* / **417** The Pelagian heresy is condemned		**431** The third ecumenical council is held at Ephesus; it affirms the unity of Christ	**440** Leo I is Pope until 461	

LEFT **Silver plate, made to celebrate 10 years of Theodosius's reign. It shows marks where someone tried to break it up, probably for a hoard.**

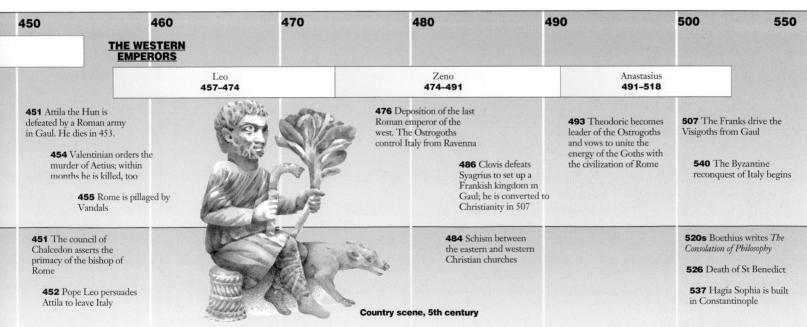

450	460	470	480	490	500	550

THE WESTERN EMPERORS

Leo 457–474	Zeno 474–491	Anastasius 491–518

451 Attila the Hun is defeated by a Roman army in Gaul. He dies in 453.

454 Valentinian orders the murder of Aetius; within months he is killed, too

455 Rome is pillaged by Vandals

476 Deposition of the last Roman emperor of the west. The Ostrogoths control Italy from Ravenna

486 Clovis defeats Syagrius to set up a Frankish kingdom in Gaul; he is converted to Christianity in 507

493 Theodoric becomes leader of the Ostrogoths and vows to unite the energy of the Goths with the civilization of Rome

507 The Franks drive the Visigoths from Gaul

540 The Byzantine reconquest of Italy begins

451 The council of Chalcedon asserts the primacy of the bishop of Rome

452 Pope Leo persuades Attila to leave Italy

484 Schism between the eastern and western Christian churches

520s Boethius writes *The Consolation of Philosophy*

526 Death of St Benedict

537 Hagia Sophia is built in Constantinople

Country scene, 5th century

plundering, first in Greece and then westward into Italy. By 401 the Goths were besieging Milan, now the base for the western emperors. The city was only narrowly saved from capture.

Honorius, the western emperor, took fright, fled Milan and found refuge in the remote city of Ravenna on the east coast of Italy. This failure of nerve on the part of the emperor was fatal for morale. It was a vivid contrast with Valentinian I (364–75) who lived his life at the head of his troops. As the emperor became more civilian, power in the west shifted toward the generals.

Ravenna was the last capital of the west. Court life, in the pampered seclusion provided by the marshland around the city, continued its elaborate ceremonials and flattery of the emperor. The emperor's advisers were rich Italian aristocrats, deeply prejudiced against Germans, who believed it beneath their dignity even to negotiate with Alaric. By 410 Alaric's patience had worn thin; he finally forced his way into Rome itself and for three days his men sacked the city.

Although the city was far from destroyed the sack of the old capital was a shock for the Roman world: "The human race is included in the ruins," wrote Jerome. The mystique of Rome, as the city destined to bring justice and ordered rule to mankind, had for centuries been an indelible part of the consciousness of the Mediterranean world.

From the north the news was just as bad. At the end of 406 there had been a massive series of invasions across the Rhine. By now the frontier posts were starved of troops and soon gave way. The invaders swept southward. By 409 Vandals, Sueves and Alans had crossed over the Pyrenees into the rich lands of Spain. In Gaul there was chaos: Burgundians freely settled in the north and Brittany was in open revolt against the empire. Britain was abandoned to invaders from northern Germany.

Some form of order was finally restored in Gaul by Constantius, a Roman from the Danube, who emerged as the leading military commander in the west after the death of Stilicho. Constantius concentrated on using the Germans as allies. The vulnerable Rhine border was stabilized by settling Burgundians there and the Visigoths were given land in southwest Gaul, partly to keep control of the Bagaudae, local insur-

THE INVADERS OF THE EMPIRE UP TO 420

The early 5th century saw the first invasions of Goths reaching deep into Italy and the heart of the empire. The Ostrogoths and Visigoths were settled as federates, maintaining a fragile Roman control over their movements.

Map

North Sea
Jutes
409
Angles
Britons
Saxons
Vistula
Franks
Rhine
Elbe
Sueves
Vandals
Alans
406
Augusta Treverorum
c400
ATLANTIC OCEAN
Loire
Aureliani
Alamanni
401
Burgundians
Rhine
Mediolanum
Po
Dnieper
Burdigala
Arelate
Visigoths
Sueves
411
409
418
414
Ravenna
401-402
Danube
Black Sea
Toletum
429
Barcino
Corsica
Rome
408
395-397
Adrianople
378
Constantinople
Alans
Sardinia
410
Vandals
Sicily
Gades
Hippo Regius
Carthage
Rhegium
Athens
Corinth
Sparta
Crete
Cyprus
Mediterranean Sea
Nile
Red Sea

Legend

✕ battle, with date

invasion routes of barbarians, with dates
→ Angles, Saxons and Jutes
→ Vandals, Alans and Suevi
→ Visigoths

Ostrogothic federate settlement 420
Visigothic federate settlement 420
Western Roman empire 395
Eastern Roman empire 395

0   600 km
0   400 mi

ABOVE Stilicho, in a detail from an ivory diptych. One of the empire's most competent military men, he was beheaded at Ravenna by Honorius in 408.

gents. This was an impressive recovery but Constantius died in 421, a few months after being made a fellow Augustus by Honorius. Honorius himself died in 423.

In 417 Constantius had married one of the most remarkable women of the late empire: Galla Placidia, a daughter of the emperor Theodosius and Honorius's half sister. When Rome was sacked in 410 she was carried off and married to Athaulf, the Visigoth chief. After his death in 415 she was returned to the Romans and forced by Honorius to marry Constantius. They had one son – Valentinian, who, under his mother's care, eventually succeeded as Valentinian III in 425.

Galla was determined that her son would grow up to be master of his empire. She concentrated on playing off one general against another so that none would have as much power as Stilicho. This left the empire weak and German tribes moved once more against it. The most successful were the Vandals, a nomadic German tribe with a history of migration. Since the invasion of 406-7 the Vandals had spread through Gaul, across the Pyrenees and into Spain. For 20 years they remained there, fighting the Romans and other German tribes. In 429, taking advantage of Roman civil war, they moved across the straits of Gibraltar into Africa.

The Vandal leader, Gaiseric, was probably one of the most formidable German leaders the Romans had ever faced. He had the unquestioning loyalty of his people and he was single-minded in his aims: a rich home for his people with complete inde-

pendence from Rome. Once he was in north Africa the Romans were forced to deal with him and give him land in Mauretania. Gaiseric was not satisfied. He moved eastward into the rich lands around Carthage, capturing the city in 439 and depriving Rome of vital corn supplies. He created the first independent kingdom within the empire, thus dealing one of the most humiliating and costly blows the Roman empire had ever suffered.

The Huns provide a great threat to the western empire

Despite Galla Placidia's efforts to prevent the domination of the generals, by 430 there was a new supreme commander of the west, Aetius. As a boy Aetius had been taken off as a hostage by the Goths; he had also spent time in the court of the Huns, Asiatic people who were extending their empire westward toward Europe. Aetius used Huns as mercenary soldiers to restore some order among the German peoples in Gaul. This was now the crucial area to defend if Italy itself was to be kept free of invasion. Aetius's policy was to play off one group against another: settling some, resisting others and letting rivals fight among themselves. By these means he succeeded in keeping a precarious peace and Italy remained unmolested.

However, in 450 a further disaster struck the empire. The Huns, whom Aetius had used so carefully as allies, had a new leader – Attila. His empire already stretched from the Baltic to the Danube and eastward into southern Russia but he

Flavius Aetius was consul for three years, unusual for someone who was not an aristocrat. He was so powerful that envoys from the provinces were sent to him rather than the emperor.

ABOVE **Differing metalwork styles of the empire. Germanic silver: spurs, brooch and arrow heads from the grave of a 3rd-century man; the bow-brooch and belt buckles of semi-precious stone are Vandal items from the 5th century.**

RIGHT **Mosaic scene of the harbor of Classis in Ravenna, showing the lighthouse towers and sailing vessels. Many emperors had contributed to the building of the city: Claudius had provided an encircling wall and Trajan erected an aqueduct.**

Attila became king of the Huns by murdering his brother, joint leader with him. Attila died on his wedding night; to keep his grave secret, the people who buried his body and treasure were executed.

now began ravaging along the border of the eastern Roman empire. When he met with resistance he turned westward in search of easier plunder.

Aetius had to draw on the Germans as allies to confront Attila. In 451, at the Catalaunian Plains near Troyes in northern France, Germans and Romans fought alongside each other in a great battle which forced Attila to withdraw. The next year, however, he was back, strong enough to sack the northern cities of Italy, including Milan. It was lucky for Rome that he died in 453 and that his empire collapsed with him.

Aetius's credibility was severely damaged when the Huns turned against the empire and in 454 Valentinian had Aetius killed, striking the first blow himself. "You have cut off your right hand with your left," one disillusioned adviser told the emperor. Within a few months Valentinian was himself murdered. The debility of the empire was shown in 455 when Gaiseric the Vandal sailed a fleet unopposed to Ostia, landed and sacked Rome for 12 days. Valentinian's widow and his two daughters were carried off as hostages.

The central government of the west began to break down. Nine emperors, each from different families, followed in 21 years. Power was shifting to the German commanders in a Roman army made up almost entirely of German conscripts and allies. The last strong man of the western empire was Ricimer, a German. He could control the Germans and he was shrewd enough to win the support of Leo, the eastern emperor. As supreme commander, Ricimer controlled a succession of western emperors between 457 and 472.

The western empire draws to an end almost unnoticed

The support of the east was essential for the west's survival, especially as the east had the empire's only navy with which to challenge Gaiseric. Eastern emperors were not indifferent to the defense of the west, and could conceive of the empire only as the Mediterranean one it had been for 600 years. They particularly feared the expansion of Gaiseric's Vandals farther along the north African coast to the rich cornfields of Egypt. However, an expedition of the forces of east and west against the Vandals in 468 was a disaster. Its failure allowed Gaiseric to capture Sicily – the oldest of all Rome's provinces, and a loss that symbolized the decline of the western empire.

The end came quickly. When Ricimer died in 472 the eastern emperor Leo imposed his own nominee – Julius Nepos, a general from Dalmatia

Flavius Ricimer was the son of a Germanic chief and a Visigothic princess. As a barbarian he was not permitted to be emperor himself, but he was able to rule through a series of "puppet emperors".

LEFT **Theodoric's mausoleum, built outside the walls of Ravenna. It was built on two levels. The 10-sided ground floor housed a crypt and the cupola, cut from one piece of stone from Istria, weighed over 300 tonnes.**

RIGHT **This mosaic, from the church of St Apollinare Nuovo in Ravenna, shows the grand palace of Theodoric. It originally contained figures of Theodoric and his court, but they were later removed.**

– as emperor of the west. Nepos was overthrown by his own military commander, Orestes, in 475. Orestes then declared his own son, Romulus Augustulus, emperor. Romulus was given no support in the east, where Nepos was recognized as the emperor, but Orestes had some support from the Italian aristocracy who were relieved not to have another eastern emperor imposed on them.

The problem was the encroaching Germans. Italy was now virtually the only part of the empire not controlled by them. Africa had long been lost. Euric, the king of the Visigoths, was the strongest ruler in the west. He carved a kingdom out of the old provinces of Gaul and Spain, and declared himself independent of the empire in 475. Other German peoples were now settled among the native Roman citizens in the north of the empire but none had been given land in Italy itself, as the Italian aristocracy resisted any compromise.

German troops under Roman control were dissatisfied. Their pay had become irregular as the tax base of the empire contracted. In 476, when their demands for land in Italy continued to be refused they revolted, electing as their leader a German from the Scirian tribe, Odoacer. Orestes was killed, and Romulus Augustulus was spared but exiled to a castle in the Bay of Naples.

Odoacer did not want to become emperor. He wanted supreme military command, like other German leaders before him, and was prepared to accept the authority of the new eastern emperor, Zeno. As a sign of goodwill he sent the imperial insignia from Italy to Constantinople. Zeno did not want to disavow Julius Nepos, who was still alive, but he did not want to spend money restoring him. In the end he did nothing. Odoacer was leader of a kingdom covering Italy and the remnants of the old provinces of Raetia and Noricum to the north. Almost without the world realizing it, the western empire had ceased to exist.

An evocative account of the end of the empire in the provinces comes from Noricum, alongside the Danube. By the 450s the border had been abandoned. The Roman governor and his staff had disappeared, and towns relied on protection

THE INVADERS OF THE EMPIRE AROUND 450

The northern borders of the western empire were swamped by Franks pouring over the Rhine, and the various tribes moving into the abandoned province of Britain. The Huns posed a violent threat from the east, while the Vandals set up an independent kingdom in north Africa.

BELOW **Attila the Hun may have had a skull like the one shown with his portrait. This deformity was a result of the Huns' practice of binding heads. An emissary from the eastern empire described Atilla as a short, squat man with a large head, deep-set eyes, flat nose and a thin beard.**

territories at 450

- Burgundian federate settlement
- Visigothic federate settlement
- empire of Attila
- Vandal kingdom
- Western Roman empire
- Eastern Roman empire

× battle, with date

invasion routes of barbarians, with dates

→ Angles, Saxons and Jutes
→ Britons
→ Huns
→ Vandals

0		600 km
0		400 mi

Noricum (in modern Austria) was annexed in 15 BC; Claudius made five of its communities into *municipia*. Many of its men became Praetorian Guards.

from the Germans settled among them. A few Roman troops remained in Noricum but they were poorly equipped and demoralized and there was little they could do to stop the breakdown of order. One unit sent to Italy for their pay but their envoys were killed in an ambush. In the 480s there is mention of one soldier, Avitianus, surviving, and in 487, Odoacer moved the surviving Roman population south to Italy.

The church survives and gives Rome new strength

The year 476 is traditionally accepted as the date of the fall of the western empire. This does not mean that the culture of Rome vanished completely as central power collapsed. In some areas – Africa and Spain, for example – it was severely disrupted by the German invaders. In Gaul, on the other hand, Roman aristocrats continued to live alongside the newcomers. Through the letters of Sidonius Apollinaris, a wealthy landed aristocrat – proud that he was still officially a senator of Rome

– a picture of compromise emerges. Sidonius visits the Visigoth court to play backgammon, while some of his fellow aristocrats learn Burgundian and one commands the Visigothic navy. These aristocrats realized that the survival of their lifestyle depended on accepting the new rulers.

The German rulers themselves were prepared to learn from the Romans. The Visigoth king Euric had the laws of his kingdom drawn up by Roman jurists and issued in Latin. Their form was heavily influenced by Roman law, as were the codes of most of the successor states. In Italy, the Ostrogoth Theodoric, who overthrew and murdered Odoacer in 493, proclaimed that it was his mission to unite the energy of the Goths with the civilization of Rome. By this time the magnificent buildings of Rome had begun to crumble. Great blocks of stone had fallen across the streets and thieves carried off the bronze statues that had crowded the city. Theodoric ordered the repair of monuments and cities. Cultured Roman intellectuals such as the philosopher Boethius and the scholar Cassiodorus acted as his advisers.

As the western empire collapsed the church survived and was to prove the bearer of classical

THE INVADERS OF THE EMPIRE UP TO 476
In 476 the western empire ceased to exist, apart from a rump on the eastern coast of the Adriatic. Even this became incorporated in the Ostrogothic kingdom which was set up by Theodoric when he overthrew Odoacer. The eastern empire remained intact.

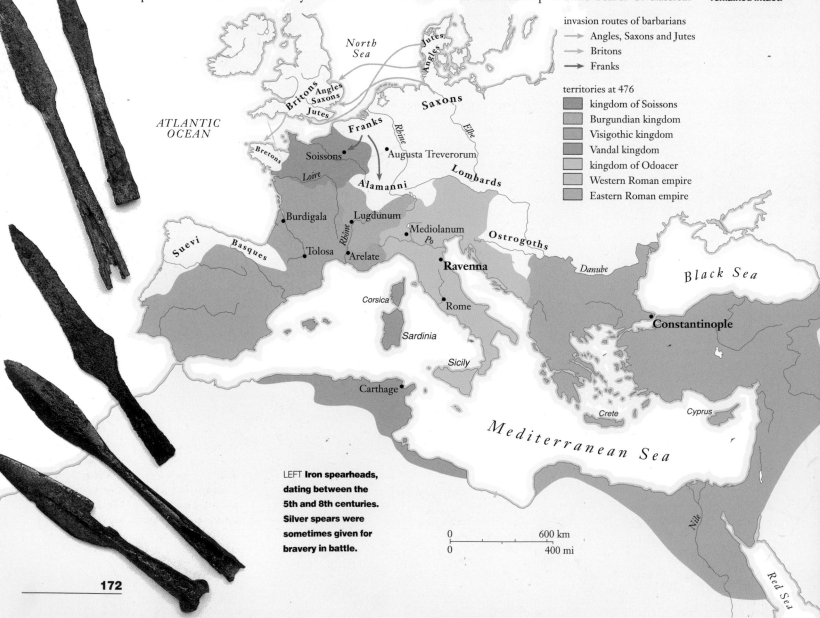

invasion routes of barbarians
→ Angles, Saxons and Jutes
→ Britons
→ Franks

territories at 476
kingdom of Soissons
Burgundian kingdom
Visigothic kingdom
Vandal kingdom
kingdom of Odoacer
Western Roman empire
Eastern Roman empire

LEFT **Iron spearheads, dating between the 5th and 8th centuries. Silver spears were sometimes given for bravery in battle.**

civilization into later centuries. The bishops gained an enhanced status as the old civilian administration broke down. So long as the Germans remained Arians, the Roman population was distinct and vulnerable and they desperately needed protection. The bishops of western towns pleaded for the protection of inhabitants, directed defense and led men into battles. They had to be good administrators as the church was now wealthy, and they had to be courageous, to maintain faith and inspire their followers at a time of uncertainty.

Very often these churchmen were drawn from the old landed aristocracy of the empire. They had learning, administrative experience acquired on their great estates, and the tradition of local leadership. Sidonius Apollinaris became a bishop in 471. His knowledge of theology was limited but he had local prestige and was shrewd and experienced. It was what the church needed to survive.

Supreme among the bishoprics of the west was that of Rome. The early bishops of Rome, or popes as they became known, rested their claims for primacy on the tradition that the Christian church in Rome had been founded by Peter himself who, with Paul, had been martyred there. The influence of the popes in the west increased as other authority figures withdrew. When Attila invaded Italy in 452, it was Pope Leo (440–461) who persuaded him to withdraw. Again, during the sack of Rome by Gaiseric in 455, Leo managed to save many of the city's churches. It was Leo too who argued, for the first time at the Council of Chalcedon in 451, that doctrine for the church ought to be laid down by Rome itself, and not by councils of bishops. Such a claim could never be accepted so long as other strong centers of Christianity remained. It was not until the 7th century, when Antioch and Alexandria were overrun by Islam, that Rome's position was secure.

In the late 5th century the Catholic Church scored its first great success among the Germanic peoples. The Franks were a German people unconverted to any form of Christianity. During the middle of the 5th century they had expanded slowly across the broken frontiers of the northern empire, but now under their king, Clovis, they began to gain control over all the old provinces of Gaul, settling alongside the old Gallic Roman landowners. They soon established friendly relations with their leaders, the local bishops. Finally, from the 490s, the Franks moved toward orthodox Christianity, to the triumph of church officials. With the backing of the church Clovis defeated the Arian Visigoths and Burgundians and established his state as the most powerful in

LEFT **Barbarian warrior on horseback from a 7th-century Saxon gravestone. The barbarian warrior cult was deeply embedded in northern martial cultures and stirred to rampancy by Roman empire-building.**

ABOVE **Many people were afraid of being looted by invaders, and their insecurity led them to hide away their more precious and valuable objects. Silver plates and dishes such as these would have formed part of a family's hoard.**

western Europe. "Your faith is our victory," one jubilant bishop proclaimed, seeing the conversion of immense significance for Christian Europe.

It was in the early 5th century that, for the first time, the western church produced men of an intellectual brilliance which could rival that found in the east. The most influential was Augustine of Hippo, who had enormous influence on the future development of Christian civilization.

Augustine was an African, born in the province of Numidia. In Milan, when he was 32, he was finally converted to Christianity, probably under the influence of Bishop Ambrose, and by 395 he had been appointed Bishop of Hippo in his native north Africa. Like most other Romans, Augustine was horrified by the sack of Rome in 410. He, too, believed that the Roman empire had been created by God as an instrument to allow the spread of Christianity; how then could God let it collapse? This was the question that Augustine set out to answer in his work *The City of God*.

Augustine argued that history moved forward with a purpose, but that of God, not man. God's instrument was not a city or an empire, but the community of those, on earth and in heaven, who believed: unbelievers, however pure their motives, would always be excluded from the city of God. The fall of Rome did not, in the long run, matter.

As the west declined, Constantinople gained grandeur and prestige. The emperors were resident in the Great Palace with affairs of state conducted in its massive Hall of Silence. Under the emperor Theodosius II imposing walls were built around the city. At the Council of Chalcedon in 451 the Bishop of Constantinople was declared to be second only to Rome, a claim resting on the imperial power of the city.

The eastern empire achieves a stability which lasts for many centuries

The stability of the eastern empire was impressive: there were relatively few emperors and they stayed in power for long periods of time. Arcadius died in 408 and was succeeded by his infant son Theodosius II who lived until 450. Between 457 and 518 there were only three emperors: Leo I, Zeno and Anastasius.

There was no lack of intrigue or corruption at the court of Constantinople, particularly when the emperors were young. However, power remained in the hands of civilians rather than generals and the civil service attracted many talented people. The rich could not escape their responsibilities to society. When Attila threatened the east and had to be paid off, the senators of Constantinople sold their wives' jewelry to raise the money.

One emperor – Anastasius (491–518) – showed the virtues of the new state. He was a talented administrator, aiming to rule fairly, and deeply loved by his peoples. Under his control the budget was balanced and he even cut taxes. At his death the state treasury was filled with 15,000 kilograms of gold. All this was achieved at a time when the east was almost continually at war.

Even after the fall of the west the eastern empire saw itself as Roman. The language of court life was Latin and under Justinian there was a major, partially successful, campaign to regain the western provinces. Yet, despite the grandeur of its ceremonies, imperial and religious alike, it was a fragile state, surviving through diplomacy rather than military power and the integration of invaders into the empire as baptized Christians. In this new form the Roman empire became the Byzantine empire and it was to survive until 1453.

LEFT **Augustine believed that human beings needed to control their natural, sensuous selves. Austere morality, not wanton pleasure, was the proper goal.**

BELOW **Augustine was often haunted by his boyhood delight in a senseless crime. In company with other boys, he stole large numbers of pears "to throw at pigs".**

RIGHT **Aspects of St Augustine's *City of God* from the cupola of the baptistery of Bishop Neon (also known as the Baptistery of the Orthodox) at Ravenna. The baptistery contained mosaics symbolizing baptism. In the center of this one, the Holy Spirit descends on Jesus at his baptism. The 12 disciples stand in the outer circle.**

THE BIBLE IN LATIN

The original text of the Old Testament is in Hebrew, but even before the Christian era it had been translated into Greek. Translations multiplied and, by the 3rd century AD, the great church scholar, Origen, was able to produce a text in which four different Greek versions were set alongside the Hebrew original. The New Testament, on the other hand, was originally written in Greek. It was inevitable that in the western part of the empire there would also be Latin translations made of both Testaments, and by the late 2nd century several were circulating in the empire.

Lives or accounts of the sayings of Jesus had also multiplied by the 2nd century, and at least 14 are known to have existed. By the end of the century, in an attempt to consolidate its teaching, the church had given special status to only four, those attributed to Matthew, Mark, Luke and John. These Gospels eventually became sanctified as the only versions of Jesus' life accepted by the church. Other lives, such as the Gospels of Thomas and the Hebrews, were gradually eliminated and survive today only in fragments.

In 382 Pope Damasus was dedicated to establishing Rome

ABOVE **Folio from St Luke's gospel in the 5th-century Codex Alexandrinus, one of the earliest complete Bibles in one volume. These codices replaced the earlier, more cumbersome biblical scrolls.**

RIGHT **St Jerome, in a painting by Carlo Crivelli, with a model of the monastery at Bethlehem and a copy of the Bible. His translation, though seen to be flawed, made him a hero for Renaissance scholars.**

as the center of the Church and standardizing the Bible. He introduced Latin as the language of the Mass and called on Jerome, the greatest biblical scholar of the day, to produce a definitive Latin translation of the Bible.

Jerome was ideally suited to the task. From the age of 12, he was educated in Rome, and studied grammar, rhetoric and philosophy. He also had a mastery of Hebrew, Greek and Latin, acquired through many years of learning. Jerome translated the New Testament first, using the best Greek manuscripts he could find. However, when he dared correct errors from earlier translations, he aroused such criticism that he left Rome in bitter dismay for the

Holy Land. He settled in Jerusalem and continued his work on the Bible. It was not until 405 that he completed the Old Testament, working largely from the original Hebrew texts. This was received no better than his New Testament translation: people used to the Greek and older Latin translations were deeply suspicious of a new version.

In the long run, however, the superiority of Jerome's version was so obvious that its triumph was assured. By the 8th century it was fully accepted as the Vulgate, the text for "the common people". In the 13th century the University of Paris produced an edition which was to be used as a standard for theological teaching and debate, but other translations continued to exist and were used. In 1546 the Vulgate was sanctified by an ecumenical council in which many questions on doctrine were resolved. This Clementine Vulgate, named after Pope Clement VIII, was accepted as the exclusive Latin version with the requirement that it be printed with as few faults as possible. The Vulgate Bible retained this position of authority well into the 19th century and remains one of the supreme intellectual achievements of the early church.

BELOW **A 5th-century mosaic in Galla Placidia's tomb at Ravenna depicting the Gospels of Matthew, Mark, Luke and John. The earliest surviving fragment of a Gospel is from that of St John.**

ABOVE **Illustrated 7th-century Bible, owned by a Lombard queen. Its cover is encrusted with gems and cameos set in gold.**

LEFT **One of the Dead Sea Scrolls, found in 1947. They are non-Biblical religious texts – dating from the 4th century BC – written in Hebrew and Aramaic.**

THE NEW ROMANS

Roman civilization inspired mixed feelings in the barbarians: hatred for many people, but awe for others who were eager to adopt Roman ways. Most barbarian rulers remained proud of their heritage but sought the support of their Roman subjects. Although in part this was enlightened self-interest – barbarians lacked the expertise to administer their kingdoms – there was also a genuine desire to preserve the civilization they had conquered. Most successful in this respect was the Ostrogothic king Theodoric. "My kingdom is an imitation of yours," he told the eastern emperor Anastasius.

Theodoric maintained the fabric of Roman Italy, but there was no real assimilation. Intermarriage between Roman and Goth was forbidden, and law was also a barrier to assimilation. Laws to Romans were universal rules, but barbarians viewed them as a crucial element of their own national identity. Barbarians lived by their traditional laws, while their subjects lived by Roman law. In most kingdoms, barbarians and Romans belonged to separate churches, and religion was the greatest obstacle of all to assimiliation. Although assimilation took centuries to complete, the culture that finally resulted was a blend of both Roman and barbarian.

Christians and barbarians

Although most of the barbarian invaders of the 5th century were Christian, they were followers of the teachings of Arius. When Vandals, Sueves, Lombards and Burgundians established their kingdoms in the west, their beliefs were met with hostility by their Catholic subjects. Barbarians, a minority among native Romans, clung ever closer to Arianism and even persecuted orthodox believers. Arianism was a major source of internal weakness in barbarian kingdoms and of constant friction with the eastern emperors, who saw themselves as champions of orthodox Catholicism.

Only Franks and Anglo-Saxons, still pagan at the time of their settlement in the west, escaped the taint of heresy: both these peoples coverted to orthodox Catholicism. The Franks, in particular, benefited

from this. When king Clovis – later made a consul – was baptized in 496, he was hailed as a "second Constantine" and received the support of the Gallo-Roman church in his wars against the Arian Burgundians and Visigoths.

German cremation urn and part of the grave slab of a barbarian converted to Christianity.

The Vandals in Africa

Vandals were the first to establish an independent kingdom on Roman soil. North Africa was the main granary for the western empire and the Vandal king Gaiseric was easily able to force Roman recognition of his conquests simply by threatening to end shipments of corn. The Vandals were hostile to the empire and made no effort to conciliate their Roman subjects. Gaiseric treated the kingdom as his personal property. Native landowners were given the choice of slavery or exile

and their lands were expropriated and distributed by the king among his followers. Gaiseric showed little interest in preserving the Roman administration.

The Vandals were fiercely Arian and the Catholic Church was actively persecuted: its lands were confiscated, its bishops expelled and its priests ordered to surrender their sacred books and vessels.

A Vandal, owner of a typical Roman villa.

The mantle of power

Barbarian kings enthusiastically adopted the trappings of imperial rule, both to legitimize their rule in the eyes of Romans and to increase their prestige in the eyes of their fellow barbarians. Barbarian kingship was personal in nature, based on success in war, and not on public authority enjoyed by the imperial rulers. Particularly important was the image of triumphant rulership, illustrated by this helmet of the Lombard king Agilulf. He is shown enthroned, holding his sword and flanked by his warriors and winged Victories carrying banners. He is greeted as deliverer by the people of his cities while other barbarians offer tribute.

Barbarian metalwork

Fine jewelry was an important symbol of prestige in barbarian society and was worn by both sexes. Most jewelry also served a practical purpose, such as belt buckles or the popular bow-brooches used to fasten a cloak in place. Even the simplest items were covered with intricate interlace patterns.

Most jewelry was made of bronze. The pattern was engraved on the surface, then fine wires of silver, copper or gilt were hammered into the grooves to make the design stand out. The finest jewelry was made of gold or silver and decorated with delicate filigree or glowing garnets.

LEFT AND BELOW **Various fan-headed and birds-head brooches.**

ABOVE **5th-century Saxon brooch.**

LEFT AND FAR LEFT **Germanic and Vandal buckles.**

FAR LEFT **6th-century Ostrogothic earrings.**

LEFT **Gold and garnet Gothic pendant.**

Queen Amalasuntha (502–531).

The limits of assimilation

Many barbarians, keen to assimilate Roman ways, met opposition and suspicion from Romans and fellow barbarians. The Vandal Stilicho married Serena, the niece of Theodosius; was appointed guardian to the emperor's son Honorius; and his own daughter Maria married Honorius. He was still distrusted by the Roman aristocracy: in 408 he was unjustly accused of conspiring to overthrow Honorius, and was executed.

A century later, the Ostrogothic queen Amalasuntha met with the oppposition of the Gothic nobility when she tried to give her son, Athalaric, a Roman education. Her father Theodoric, she was told, "would never permit his Goths to send their sons to the grammarian-school, for he used to say: 'If they fear their teacher's strap now they will never look on sword or javelin without a shudder'." A Gothic prince was a warrior before all else.

MONASTIC TRADITIONS

After Constantine's Edict of Toleration, Christianity was the favored religion. Clergy were exempt from taxation and military service; churchmen such as Eusebius, bishop of Caesarea from 314, complained of the thousands who had now crept into the church in hope of personal gain. Many Christians, men and women, reacted against the new opulence and worldliness of the church. They sought a way of life which involved the rejection of wealth and comfort and concentrated on holiness. Alternative ways of living were pioneered: some enthusiasts went to live on their own in deserts, others tried to create self-supporting communities of prayer and simple living. From these first beginnings in the 4th century the tradition of monasticism, such an important feature of the later church, developed.

Beliefs and practices

Central to holiness was the renunciation of sex: physical desires pulled believers toward a temporary pleasure which would disturb the relationship with God. A vow of virginity protected women from childbirth and many early monastic foundations were founded by and for women. Along with the renunciation of sex was a disdain for all comforts. At the extreme the body was punished by severe fasting or even mutilation.

Coptic stone relief of a monk in prayer.

The spread of monasticism

Egypt provided two founders of the monastic movement, each of whom established a different tradition. One path to holiness was that of the solitary, exemplified by Antony the Hermit who lived for 70 years in the wildest regions along the Red Sea, dying in 365 aged, it was said, 105. His contemporary, Pachomius believed that monastic life needed to be in communities whose members would collaborate in their spiritual development and in sustaining the community. By the end of the 4th century, there were over 7,000 monks living in the monasteries founded by Pachomius.

A Greek theologian, St Basil the Great (330–79), laid down the first rule of behavior for all monks. This required a measured life of prayer and both mental and manual work. In the west the most successful rule was that of St Benedict, and all over Europe monastic communities adopted the Benedictine rule. From Ireland came another tradition of monasticism. Columban, an Irish missionary, founded monasteries in both Italy and Gaul which became important centers for learning.

Map labels

- Iona
- *North Sea*
- Candida Casa
- Clonard
- Canterbury
- *Rhine*
- *Seine*
- *ATLANTIC OCEAN*
- *Loire*
- Maius Monasterium
- Mediolanum
- *Rhône*
- Vercellae
- *Po*
- Caesaraugusta
- *Corsica*
- **Rome**
- Casinense
- *Balearic Is*
- *Sardinia*
- Hippo Regius
- Thagaste
- *Sicily*
- Vivarium
- *Malta*
- *Mediterranean Sea*
- *Crete*
- *Danube*
- *Black Sea*
- Constantinople
- Caesarea
- Simeon Stylites
- *Nisibis*
- *Tigris*
- *Euphrates*
- Salamis
- *Cyprus*
- Bethlehem
- Mons Nitria
- Scetis
- Mt Sinai
- *Nile*

Legend

✝ monastic community

— boundary of Roman empire, 4th century

area of monasticism c600
- Egyptian
- Celtic
- Benedictine
- other

| 0 | | 600 km |
| 0 | | 400 mi |

Cults of saints and holy men

ABOVE **Ampullae, terracotta flasks for pilgrims, filled with oil or water.**

LEFT **Church in Syria built, in his honor, around St Simeon's pillar.**

Rejection of the world by holy men and women gave them a special aura for their followers as individuals who had broken through the constraints of society. The solitary, who went off into the desert or sat on a pillar for years, had achieved liberation from a troubled world and gained power. St Simeon Stylites took to a pillar to escape the throngs who followed him, but even at 15 meters up they still flocked to catch a glimpse of him.

In the west profound veneration was reserved for saints who had died a martyr's death. Sites of a martyr's death or burial had been marked with shrines from early times but later the veneration turned to their bones. By the 4th century long-standing traditions that corpses should never be buried inside a city wall or disturbed after burial were overthrown in a rush to dig up martyrs' bones. The bishop Ambrose gathered relics of the apostles to sanctify one of the great churches he was building in the center of the city. The more famous of the relics encouraged the faithful to go on pilgrimage.

The church and the state

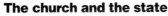

Eusebius, Bishop of Caesarea, believed the empire was designed by God for the spread of Christianity. Church and state could not be divided. By the end of the 4th century, the emperor's powers were dissolving, and Augustine argued that the kingdom of the emperors was insignificant. The western church used this reasoning to justify its withdrawal from state control. As state authority in the west collapsed, bishops took on the duties of local administration and the popes declared themselves heirs of the empire.

Mosaic with ecclesiastical men of the 6th century.

WHY DID ROME FALL?

Contemporary pagans and Christians each blamed the other; the cause of the decline and fall of the western empire has been the subject of speculation ever since. In the Middle Ages historians believed that the empire had been raised by God to spread Christianity around the world; however, it was a sinful state and, when it had served its purpose, God destroyed it.

In the atmosphere of sceptical rationalism of the 18th-century Enlightenment it was Christian-inspired pacifism and superstition that was blamed for sapping the Romans' will to resist. The pseudo-Darwinian racial theories of the late 19th century led some historians to seek the causes of Rome's fall in racial mixing: the vigor of the Roman race was supposed to have been diminished by intermarriage with "inferior" subject races. To Marxist historians, class conflict is a factor; more recently, environmental causes have been proposed.

No single factor adequately explains the fall of the western empire; it was due to a complex interaction of external pressure by the barbarians and internal economic and political weakness exacerbated by the high cost of defending the empire.

They lost their strength

Edward Gibbon (1737–97).

Edward Gibbon, historian and author of *Decline and Fall of the Roman Empire*, believed that Christianity was a major factor. As he put it: "The clergy successfully preached the doctrines of patience and pusillanimity; the active virtues of society were discouraged; and the last remains of the military spirit were buried in the cloister." Later followers of Gibbon blamed not just Christianity but all types of mystery religion and oriental cults, such as the cults of Isis and Mithras.

However, Christianity was not uniformly established in all parts of the 5th-century empire. The east was already strongly Christian and, as Gibbon complained, the church was rich and the clergy were

They lost their morals

Contemporary writers blamed immorality for the fall of the empire. Ammianus Marcellinus, a 4th-century historian, believed that Rome had survived through austerity and the Roman contempt of death. But, he complained, this had been lost through greed and the love of luxury. Citizens of Trier, claimed the 5th-century writer Salvian, hurried to the amphitheater even as barbarians were attacking their city. He compared the immorality of all Romans unfavorably with the virtues of the invading barbarians.

The complaints of these late Roman moralists were not new. In the 1st century AD Tacitus had drawn an unfavorable comparison between Roman decadence and barbarian virtue. In the 2nd century BC, Cato had bewailed the decay of the traditional austere values of Rome under the corrupting influence of Hellenism. It is hard to find a time when the Romans did not think their morals were in dangerous decline.

A 19th-century view of Roman morals: Thomas Couture, *Les Romains de la Décadence*.

They lost their land

numerous. Much of the west, on the other hand, was Christian only superficially. Yet it was the west that had fallen by 476; the eastern empire outlived it by nearly one thousand years. If Christianity and other religions had really sapped the Romans' martial vigor the eastern empire, not the western, would have fallen first.

A rattle, or *sistrum*, used by the priests of Isis.

One theory is the spread of the desert caused by ecological damage. The Mediterranean area has been degraded by farming and deforestation, but this began long before the rise of the Roman empire. The Asian provinces of Caria and Phrygia were deforested by the 1st century AD; in the next century Hadrian legislated to save the trees in Syria, while Italy suffered from the demand for firewood to heat Rome's baths. In all these areas soil erosion resulted, with adverse effects on agriculture.

In Africa there is evidence of deforestation and soil erosion but, in the 5th century, the agriculture of this region was flourishing. Here, the main degradation occured after the fall of the empire when Berber herdsmen moved in with their flocks, denuding the vegetation. Some areas became depopulated in the late empire, but this was not due to environmental factors only. Many farmers in Egypt abandoned their Nile-irrigated land when they could not afford to pay excessive taxation.

Once-fertile regions of North Africa.

They lost their minds

Another theory is that water, supplied via lead pipes, played a role in the fall of Rome: lead poisoning causes a wide range of health problems including brain damage and impaired intelligence.

Most Romans, however, did not get their water from lead pipes. Although these were widely used where flexibility and resistance to pressure were considered an advantage, Romans were aware of lead's toxicity and preferred to used earthenware pipes where possible.

These were cheaper to make and easier to maintain – and delivered more wholesome water than lead pipes.

There is no evidence that later Romans were less gifted than their forebears: the period was one of high achievement in administration, theology and the arts. In any case, lead in drinking water is not the most dangerous form of lead pollution; in the atmosphere it is up to 10 times more toxic.

Roman lead pipe for delivering fresh water to city houses.

LEGACIES OF ROME

The profound impact of the empire on its subjects did not cease completely. As late as the 6th century the aqueducts still brought water into Rome. Latin survived as the language of the church and as the forerunner of Romance languages (including French, Spanish and Italian). New German kingdoms often adopted the Roman system of law and some of the empire-wide trade routes remained.

There was no denying the decay, however. The empire was fragmented between rival kingdoms, forcing people to focus on smaller and more restricted worlds. Town life in the west became stagnant. The cities became strongholds and centers of administration rather than centers of economic activity. Rome's population – 800,000 in the late 4th century – may have been only 25,000 by 550. The church was the one structure that remained intact in the middle of the migrations and shifting political boundaries. In the monasteries, monks were broadminded enough to gather together pagan and religious texts and to copy them. Many classical texts survived until the 9th century when the court of Charlemagne was able to gather them and provide the copies which have lasted until today.

The Holy Roman Empire

Pope Gregory the Great laid the foundations for the church to become a power transcending national boundaries and cultures and providing a universal law to which all were equally subject. What was needed was the alliance of the church with a Catholic king so that religious and secular power could be united. This came in 800 when Charlemagne, king of the Franks and a profoundly religious man, was proclaimed emperor by Pope Leo III. The king's seal bore the words *Renovatio Romani Imperii* – the renewal of the Roman empire. The church now passed into the institutional and cultural life of western Europe. Although Charlemagne's empire survived only one generation, the title of Holy Roman Emperor passed to dynasties of German kings and lasted until 1806.

Charlemagne (Charles the Great) portrayed in this detail from a diptych in Milan.

Christian controversies

In the 4th century the church adopted the Julian calendar and made several changes to avoid the wild celebrations that traditional pagan festivals encouraged. Finally Theodosius abolished them all, introducing a calendar based only on the Christian year.

The bitterest controversy was over the date of Easter, fixed partly by the full moon immediately following the spring equinox. East and west each came up with a different solution. Eastern churches were prepared to celebrate Easter on a weekday but western churches would accept only a Sunday. In Rome it was then decided that if the required full moon fell on one Sunday, Easter would be celebrated on the next. This ruling never reached the Celtic churches who every few years would end up out of step with the rest of the western world.

The tradition of scholarship

As the empire fragmented the old traditions of classical learning disappeared. There was no longer an educated audience for literature or a demand for books. Literacy, needed to understand the scriptures and administer the church, became the preserve of clergymen.

Perhaps the single most influential scholar was Cassiodorus (490–585) who founded his own monastery at Vivarium in Italy. He took his collection of classical manuscripts and encouraged the monks to collect more. It was through his inspiration that so many manuscripts were saved.

Some of Cassiodorus's library was taken to northern England in the late 7th century and from there was carried by Irish and English missionaries to the Netherlands and Germany. One great center of classical scholarship and learning

was Ireland. The brilliance of the Irish achievement lay in its transmission of biblical texts in finely illuminated editions. The art is seen at its finest in the *Book of Kells* (c 700), and in the *Lindisfarne Gospels* (698), which also combined pagan Celtic motifs with patterns from Anglo-Saxon metalwork. The most celebrated feature of both is the richly drawn initial at the beginning of each part of a text.

ABOVE **Early Christian monastery at Skelling Michael in Ireland.**

LEFT **The opening of St Matthew in the *Lindisfarne Gospels*.**

From Ireland and Saxon England this art form spread to the continent. Charlemagne's scholars hunted down every classical text they could find, pagan and Christian. The original of St. Benedict's rule was brought from his monastery at Casinense (Monte Cassino) and the Vatican was searched for early copies of papal decrees. Even St Jerome's Latin version of the Bible was checked against the Greek originals. About 6,700 manuscripts of copied texts survive from these years, compared with only 1,865 from the period before 800 AD. The existing text of nearly every Latin author is drawn from Carolingian manuscripts.

CONCLUSION

The Romans won their empire by force and often exercised appalling brutality over those who opposed them, whether Greeks, Spaniards, Jews or Britons. Many conquered communities, particularly those of the east, had older and more sophisticated cultures than that of Rome, but none could resist the ruthless efficiency of the legions and their determined commanders.

What was truly extraordinary was this vast empire, rather than collapsing through internal revolt as many others had done, survived and flourished over several centuries. It was finally extinguished in the east only when the Byzantine Empire, still ruled from the great city founded by Constantine in 330, fell to the Turks in 1453. The Romans' greatest achievement had been in creating a political entity which could resist the inevitable strains brought about by the passing of time.

The secret lay in citizenship. By allowing those who had shown loyalty to become citizens – and thus equal members of the empire in law, whether they were Greeks, Africans, Celts or Asians – the Romans deflected potential opposition. Outside the heat of battle the Romans were a pragmatic people and were never concerned with racial exclusiveness. A Spaniard, such as Trajan, or an African, such as Septimius Severus, could reach the post of emperor. As a result of this openness to provincial talent the empire inspired loyalty even among a people as skeptical as the Greeks. When the empire eventually came under crushing pressures from its enemies to the north and the east, men, such as Diocletian, from a humble background in the Balkans, were always ready to defend it.

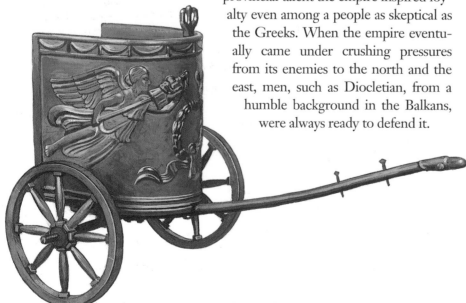

The length of Roman rule in the west was bound to have an enduring effect, but the church ensured the survival of classical Latin as an integral part of Western culture. Most of the 35,000 books printed before 1500 were in Latin and it remained the preferred language of international scholarship for centuries. At a provincial level Latin continued in a variety of dialects which later developed into the Romance languages: Portuguese, Romanian, Italian, French and Spanish. In the 16th and 17th centuries English derived between 10,000 and 12,000 new words from Latin and the process has never stopped.

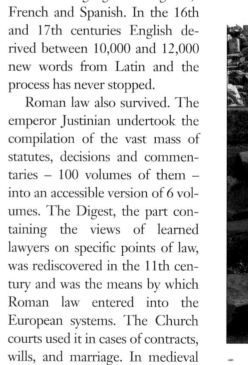

Roman law also survived. The emperor Justinian undertook the compilation of the vast mass of statutes, decisions and commentaries – 100 volumes of them – into an accessible version of 6 volumes. The Digest, the part containing the views of learned lawyers on specific points of law, was rediscovered in the 11th century and was the means by which Roman law entered into the European systems. The Church courts used it in cases of contracts, wills, and marriage. In medieval Germany, where there was no central government, Roman law was often cited as precedent in difficult cases. In the Dutch republic, Roman law pervaded customary local law and from there passed to the Dutch settlements in southern Africa and into the modern legal system of South Africa. In France the Code Napoleon (1804) was based on concepts borrowed from Roman law, as was the German Civil Code of 1900.

Memories of Rome and its achievements persisted at many levels through medieval times, but the Renaissance saw the rebirth of an intense interest in the classical world, revived with sheer excitement after centuries of

remain to inspire later generations. The meticulously planned gradations of the aqueducts, the dome of the Pantheon, the vast halls of the great imperial baths, all remain as a testament to Roman engineering skills. The triumphal arch was chosen as an appropriate monument to victory by Napoleon; the Prussian, Frederick the Great; and the English general, the Duke of Marlborough. Thomas Jefferson used Roman models, including the Pantheon, to create buildings worthy of the new American republic in Washington.

In literature Virgil is still seen as the supreme Roman poet. The *Aeneid* defined the nobility of the Roman mission without underestimating its cost: a model of the burden of empire adopted by later imperialists. Among the Roman historians, Tacitus also stands out for his ability to assess the benefits and costs of the empire. He had the vision to see that Roman rule was not always attractive to those absorbed by it and that there was value even in the culture of the "barbarian" Germans. The legacy of Latin literature was deeply enriched by the additional talents of Horace, Ovid, Catullus, Livy and Cicero.

The Roman empire of the west attracts because of the monumentality of its achievement. It was a civilization which was able to run its full course from birth and youth, through the turmoil of a troubled adolescence in the late republic to the middle age of the empire, and finally to decline and death. To later generations the Romans appeared to have been supermen and their example continued to inspire. It was not only the architecture which was copied. The United States has its Senate. Napoleon created the consulship for himself and when the consul became emperor he was crowned with golden laurel leaves. In the 20th century Mussolini's 1935 conquest of Ethiopia was an unworthy attempt to recreate the empire of his ancestors. The Czars of Russia and Kaisers of Germany perpetuated the name of Caesar. The legacy of Rome continues to be deeply embedded in Western civilization.

neglect. The founder of classical humanism, the Florentine scholar Petrarch (1304–1374) personally rediscovered many ancient manuscripts and enthusiastically proclaimed the importance of classical Rome for an understanding of the culture of Europe. By the 15th century patriotic Florentines were modeling their embattled republic on the Roman republic. Florentine architects such as Brunelleschi hurried off to Rome to gain inspiration from the ruins of the city. The essays of Montaigne (late 16th century), the first in European literature, are infused with quotations from Roman authors.

Much of the architecture and literature of Rome still

ACKNOWLEDGMENTS

1t Wedding rings: BM **1c** Portrait of 4th-c Christian family: S/Museo Civico dell'Eta' Cristiana, Brescia **1r** Medicinal herbs and surgical instruments: BM
2t, 3b Coins: BM **2b** Amorous scene, mosaic: S/Villa romana del Casale Piazza Armerina **2–3** Golden eagle: Stephen Dalton/NHPA **4** Tiberius's scabbard: BM
5t Loaves and fishes: Mark Mason/AA
5b Carved amber: BM **6** Greek temple, Segesta, Sicily: EL/M **6–7** The Capitoline wolf: S/Musei Capitolini, Rome
8 Rural idyll painting, Pompeii: S/MN,N
10-11 Roman forum – Temple of Saturn and the three marble columns of the Dioscuri Temple, 5th c BC: EL/M
13 Wounded horseman, sculpture: RMN
14–15 The defile at Douzère: Peter Connolly, FSA **15** Detail of a plate showing a war elephant from Capena, 3rd c BC: S/Museo di Villa Giulia, Rome
17 The ruins of Corinth: Dave Longley/Mick Sharp **18–19** Aerial view of Emilia: Air Ministry, Rome **20** Terracotta gladiator: S/Museo Archaeologico, Taranto **21b** Villa marittina: S/MN, N
21t Marble statue of a consul of the republic: MH/BM **22t** The dying Gaul: S/Musei Capitolini, Rome **22bl** The Julian Calendar: Ashmolean Museum, Oxford **22br** Votive plaque of Cleopatra as a goddess: Schindler Collection/WFA
23 Bust of Julius Caesar: RHPL
24b Temple of Vesta, the Forum, Rome, 3rd c AD: WFA **24t** Bronze statues of Minerva and Jupiter: BM **25tl** Terracotta figure of Juno: BM **25tr** Bronze coin with the head of Janus: MH/BM Detail of the Canopus, statue of the Tiber deity, Hadrian's villa: WFA **25br** The Pons Amilius, Rome: WFA **26b** Bust of Lucius Brutus: S/Musei Capitolini, Rome
26t Relief with goats: S/Casa Buonarroti, Florence **27** Wall painting of court scene: WFA **28–29t** Wall painting of galleys, Pompeii: S **29tr** Sculpture of a ship on rough seas, marble relief from a sarcophagus (detail), 2nd c AD: EL/M/Ny – Carlsberg Glyptothek, Copenhagen, Denmark **30t** Bronze helmet: BM
30bl Bronze standard bearer, decorative element from a horse's harness: EL/M/ Kunsthistorisches Museum, Vienna
30br Bronze Etruscan style horn: BM
31t Testudo formation, detail from cast of Trajan's column: CMD **31b** Missiles: BM
32–33 Education of Dionysius, wall painting, Villa dei Misteri, Pompeii: S
35l Memorial relief: WFA/Museo Nazionale Romano **35r** Stone jar, Isola Sacra cemetery: WFA **36t** Walnuts: Michael Dudley/AA **36b** Marriage ceremony relief: BM **37l** Wedding rings: BM **37r** Mosaic of amorous scene from Villa Romana del Casale: S **39l** Jug and brush: BM **39c** Boy Slave in kitchen, mosaic from Pompeii: CMD/Hermitage Museum, St Petersburg **39r** Slave identity tag which reads 'Hold me lest I flee and return me to my master Viventius on the estate of Callistus' 4th c AD: MH/BM
40cl & tr Honey bees: Jane Burton/BCL
40bl Statuettes of sacrificial animals and sacrificial knife, 1st–2nd c AD: BM
40cr Household shrine, Casa dei Vettii, Pompeii: S **41** Head of Jupiter: S/Museo Pio Clementino, Vatican **42l** Apollo, fresco fragment: WFA **42r** Bronze flutes and cymbals, 1st–3rd c AD: BM
43 Mosaic depicting Platonic school, Naples: S/MN, N **44l** Statue of Anubis, from Hadrian's Villa, Tivoli: CMD/ Vatican Museums **44r** Coin: BM **45tl** Palimpset of Cicero's *De Republica*, 5th c, overlain by Augustine's commentary on the Psalms, 8th c: M. Pucciarelli/Vatican Library **45bl** Peaches, painting detail: S **45r** "The Orator": Art Resource
46–47 Bone and glass needles, silver distaff, bronze thimbles, glass spindle wheel, onyx perfume bottle and ivory comb: BM **46t** The Poetess of Pompeii: S/MN, N **47** Dressing scene, fresco fragment, Herculaneum: S/MN, N
48t Swaddled baby from the funeral stele of a newborn child: EL/M/Kunst-historisches Museum, Vienna **48b** Wax tablets, reed and bronze pens, ink pots: BM **49l** Sarcophagus of a child with a group of children playing games, marble high relief, 2nd c AD: EL/M/Kunst-historisches Museum, Vienna
49r Ceramic, glass and stone marbles, onyx knucklebones, Egyptian rag doll: BM **50** Bronze clamps: BM **50–51** Bacchanalian revel, wall painting from a columbarium, Villa Pamphili, Rome, 1st c AD: MH/BM **51t** Cave of the Sibyl at Cumae, Pozzuoli: WFA **51b** Peony: Norbert Rosing/BCL **52t** Statue of Marcellus, 1st c AD: Giraudon, Paris/ Louvre **52b** Statue of a marine centaur with a nereid: S/Museo Pio Clementino, sala degli animali **53** Mosaic of actors rehearsing: S/MN, N **54–55** Detail from the Ara Pacis Augustae, Rome: S
56 Serpent bracelet: S **57** Gemma Augustea, carved sardonyx cameo, 1st c AD: EL/M/Kunsthistorisches Museum, Vienna **58** Augustus, marital statue: John G. Ross/RHPL **58–59** Acorns: M.I.Gatwood/NHPA **59** Black onyx seal of emperor Augustus, relief of sphinx: EL/M/Wurzburg Residence, Wurzburg, Germany **60l** Bust of Tiberius Claudius Nero, blue gem (cameo) of glass paste, 1st c AD: Kunsthistorisches Museum, Vienna
60r Marble bust of Caligula: EL/M/ Louvre **61l** Bust of Claudius: BM
61r Bust of Nero: S/Museo Nazionale, Ancona **60–61** Silver medallion of the emperor Hadrian, AD119: BM **63** Detail from Trajan's column: S **64l** Part of the Aurelian Wall: S **64r** Painting of the family of Septimius Severus: BPK
68l Ivory triptych: BM **68r** Coin portraying Postumus as Hercules: BM
68–69 Relief of praetorian guards, 2nd c AD: RMN, Louvre **69l** Golden eagle: Stephen Dalton/NHPA **69r** Murex shells: James H.Carmichael Jr/NHPA
70tl Agaricus lanipes: G.A. MacLean/OSF
70bl Philip I 'Philip the Arab': S/Museo Pio Clementino, Vatican **70tr** Bust of Agrippina:S/Musei Capitolini, Rome
70–71 Sword and scabbard of Tiberius; BM **71l** Coin depicting Caligula's sisters: BM **71r** Bronze equestrian statue of Marcus Aurelius, 2nd c AD: RS/AAAC
72t Sestertius commemorating the Colosseum, AD69: BM **72b** Wall painting of chariot races from Pompeii: RHPL **72–73** Colosseum interior: Didier Barrault/RHPL **73t** Mosaic of gladiator: S/Borghese **73b** Gladiator's bronze helmet showing scenes from the sacking of Troy: S/MN, N **74** Arch of Tiberius, Orange, France: MH **75t** Lake at Hadrian's Villa: CMD **75b** Bust of Caracalla: S/Museo Pio Clementino, Vatican **76-77** Wall painting of a garden with fountains from Pompeii: S/Casa del Bracciale d'Oro, Pompeii **79** Statue of Atlas supporting the earth on his shoulders: S/MN, N **80l** Papyrus fragment of Virgil's *Aeneid*: UCL/BM
80r Sculpture of teacher and pupils, copy of original from Neumagen: L & R Atkins
81 Illustration from Virgil's *Georgics*: Biblioteca Apostolica Vaticana
82l Ptolemaic (geocentric) representation of the universe, from Andreas Cellarius *Harmonia Macrocosmica* Amsterdam, 1708: Ann Ronan Picture Library **82r** Votive offering of injured person: BM
82–83 Island on the Tiber: Mauro Pucciarelli **84** Marcus Aurelius performing a sacrifice, marble relief: S/Musei Capitolini, Rome
84–85 Hannukah candles: Gary Faber, Image Bank **85t** "Judea mourning" coin: Estate of Leonard von Matt
85b Mithraeum beneath the church of St Clemente, 3rd c: WFA **86l** Loaves and fishes: Mark Mason/AA **86r** Fisherman casting his nets, Sea of Galilee: Sonia Halliday Photographs **88b** Dome of the Pantheon, 1st c BC: EL/M **88t** Front of the Pantheon: RS/AAAC **90bl** Bronze mask of Juno Lucina: CMD/National Museum, Budapest **90–91** Herbs and surgical instruments: BM **90tr** Pharmacy and pharmacist, relief: CMD **91** Aeneas, his son and a physician, painting, 1st c AD: S/MN,N **92b** Head of a woman, 1st c AD: Archivi Alinari **92t** Roman noble with his ancestors: S/Museo Capitolini
93t Baker and his wife, fresco: S/MN, N
94b Mithras slaying the bull, sculpture: MH/BM **94t** Bronze magical hand with religious symbols to avert evil eye: CMD/BM **95bl** Aegis of Isis: MH/BM
95tr Isis water purification ceremony, painting: S/MN, N **95br** Palm frond: Charlotte Ward-Perkins **96t** Bronze couch end: S/Musei Capitolini, Rome
96b Selection of fine craft objects: BM
97t "Room of the masks", Palace of Augustus, Rome: **97cl** Mosaic of food leftovers: S/Uffizi Gallery, Florence
97br Stone relief detail: S/Museo Gregoriano Profano, Vatican
98–99 Theater at Leptis Magna, Libya: RHPL **101** Nile scene, mosaic, 1st c: S/Museo Archeologico Palestrina
104 Roman road, Backstone Edge, Greater Manchester, England: Mick Sharp
104 inset Milestone, Leptis Magna: L. & R. Atkins **105t** Aerial view, Timgad: Elsevier Archive **105b** Detail of Trajan's column: EL/M **106l** The Porta Nigra, Trier, 1st c: EL/M **106r** Bronze sestertius, 2nd c: BM **107** Stone relief of barbarian and legionary fighting, 2nd c AD: EL/M/Louvre **108t** Wild boar: Manfred Danneger/NHPA **108b** Soldiers preparing for war, relief of Antonius Pius: S/Cortile delle Corozze, Vatican
109 Masada, the Rock: Zefa
110–111 Hadrian's Wall, Housesteads, England: RHPL **112bl** Oil flask, sponge and strigils: BM **112br** Baths at Aquae Sulis (Bath, England): CMD **112tr** Male and female theatrical comedy masks, marble mask frieze from the 3rd storey of the Ephesus Theater: EL/M/ Kunsthistorisches Museum, Vienna
113t Temple complex, forum Sbeitla, Tunisia: Christine Osborne Pictures
113b Diana of Ephesus: S/MN, N
114l Ornamental pool and mosaic, Pompeii: K.D.Frohlich/Zefa **114r** Four seasons, mosaic: S/Tripoli museum
115t Villa near Augusta Treverorum, painting of workers outside house: Rheinisches Landesmuseum, Trier
115c Lock, key and oil lamp: BM
115b Communal latrines, Dougga, Tunisia: CMD **116t** Head of Eutropios, road constructor: EL/M/Kunsthistorisches Museum, Vienna **116bl** Bricklayers, painting: AA **116br** Folding rule, dividers and plumb bob: BM **116–117** Pont du Gard aqueduct, Nîmes France: MH
118r Bronze citizenship plaques: BM
119l Dice: M **119r** Soldier's bronze mask: Claus Hansmann **120–121** Detail from the Peutinger Map: Ostereichische Nationalbibliothek, Vienna **123** Trajan's market, Rome: RHPL **124** Harbor scene, painting from Stabiae: EL/M/Museo Archeologico Nazionale, Naples
125l Stele with market place scene relief: EL/M/Museo Ostiense, Ostia **125r** Jute sack and wheat berries: Michael Dudley/AA **127** Rome, detail from the Peutinger Map: Osterreichische Nationalbibliothek, Vienna **128l** Grapes: Henry Ansloos/NHPA **128b** Bronze figure of a crouching boy: EL/M/Louvre
128–129 Tabarka mosaic, Tunisia: Musee National du Bardo, Tunis **129t** Grapes: Henry Ansloos/NHPA **130l** Slaves on a treadmill from monument to the Artesi family: Mansell Collection, London
130r Banqueting scene, painting: S/MN, N **131l** Wax portrait of a young woman, from Hawara, Egypt, 2nd c AD: MH/BM
131r Glass jugs and bowls: BM
132t Pompeii street scene: CMD
132b Petrified dog, Pompeii: Mansell Collection London **134l** Carved amber: BM **134r** Amphorae underwater in a Roman shipwreck: Christian Petron/ Planet Earth Pictures **134–135** Animal trade mosaic, Ambulatory of Villa Imperiale, Romano del Casale, Piazza Armeria: EL/M **135** Bronze statuette of an African slave: MH **136b** Farmer and ox, marble relief: Studio Koppermann, Gauting bei München **136–137** Tuscan countryside: Bruno Barbey/M **137b** Bronze statuette of a shepherd: AA **137t** Picking apples, mosaic, 1st half of 3rd c: EL/M/Musee des Antiquities Nationales, St Germain-en-Laye, France **138tl** Abacus: S/Museo delle Terme, Rome
138bl Mostra Augustea, poultry shop, marble relief, 3rd c: Mansell Collection/ Museo Torlonia, Rome **138–139** Bronze, silver and gold coins: BM **139t** Shoe-maker and cordmaker, relief from sarcophagus: CMD/National Archeological Museum, Rome
139b Shoes: Museum of London
140t Baker's stall, wall painting from the House of the Baker, Pompeii: EL/M/ Museo Archeologico Nazionale, Naples
140c Loaf preserved in ash, Pompeii: EL/M/Museo Archaeologico Nazionale, Naples **140b** Pestle, mortar, herbs and spices: BM **141l** Fish mosaic, pavement fragment from a house near the Quacba of Sousse, late 2nd early 3rd c: EL/M/ Archeological Museum, Sousse, Tunisia
141r Edible dormouse, (*glis glis*): E.A. Janes/NHPA **142–143** Mosaic of Christ as a warrior: S/Museo del Arcivescovado, Ravenna **144** Interior of the Senate House of Diocletian: CMD **145** Gold medallion showing Diocletian and Jupiter: BM **146l** Apse of the Aula Palatina, Trier: L. and R. Adkins **146r** Remains of vestibule of Diocletian's palace, Split, Croatia: Hed Wiesner/Zefa **148l** Head of Constantine: EL/M/Palazzo dei Conservatori, Rome **148r** Arch of Constantine, Rome: S **149t** Cross of Constantine: S/Macedonian Museum, Skopje **149b** Triumphal procession of consul, mosaic from basilica of Junius Bassus, 4th c: S/Palazzo Vecchio, Rome
150t Christian votive plaques: BM
150bl Portrait of a 4th-c Christian family: S/ **150br** Gilded silver casket: BM
151l Christian votive plaques: BM
152 The Corbridge Lanx: By permision of the Duke of Northumberland/BM
153l Cameo of Julian and his empress: CMD **153r** Byzantine calendar:

Biblioteca Apostolica Vaticana
154-155 Sunset over the Bosporus, Istanbul: Robert Francis/The Hutchison Library **155tr** Golden Gate and Seven Towers Castle, Istanbul: WFA
155tr Personification of Constantinople, silver gilt statuette: BM
155br Constantinople, frontispiece of the *Notitia* of Constantinople: Bodleian Library, Oxford **156l** Tax collection, sculpture, Neumagen: L and R Adkins
156r Olives: Mark Mason/AA
157tl Magister Peditum, *Notitia Dignitatum* 1436, Ms Canon Misc. 378: Bodleian Library, Oxford **157bl** The provinces of Apulia and Calabria, *Notitia Dignitatum*, Ms Canon Misc. 378, Bodleian Library, Oxford
157tr Quaestor's duties, *Notitia Dignitatum*, Ms. Canon Misc 378, Bodleian Libary, Oxford **157br** Consul's Ivory Diptych: S/Museo del Bargello, Florence **158** Mosaic from Hinton St Mary: Royal Commission on the Historical Monuments of England
158–159t Porchester fort: RS/AAAC
158–159b Fragments of silver: BM
159 Belt buckles, German 4th–5th c: BM
160t Jonah and the whale, Gallo-Roman gold glass painting: RS/AAAC
160b Scene from Christ's Passion, ivory panel: BM **161t** Christ as a young shepherd: S/Museo Pio Cristiano, Vaticano **161bl** Christ in majesty, mid 4th c, painting from the ceiling of the Commodile catacomb: Andre Held/Sonia Halliday Photographs **161br** Bellerophon killing the Chimera, relief: BM
163l Woman with a jewel box, painted ceiling: Lesley and Roy Adkins/ Bischofliches Museum, Trier
163tr Christian catacomb, with Christus Pantokrator, Rome, 3rd c: EL/Archiv fur Kunst und Geschichte, Berlin
163br Bread stamps: BM
164–165 Carved lid of Frankish casket, 8th c: BM **167** Missorium di Teodosio: S/Archivo di Storia, Madrid **168** Flavius Stilicho, detail from an ivory diptych: Mansell Collection London
168–169 Silver spurs, brooch and arrow heads, bow brooch and belt buckles: BM
169 Classis harbor, Ravenna, mosaic: S/S Apollinare Nuovo **170t** Theodoric's mausoleum, Ravenna: S
170b Theodosius's palace, mosaic from the Church of S Apollinare Nuovo: S
171 Deformed Hunnish skull: RS/AAAC
172 Iron spearheads, 4th–7th c: BM
173l Barbarian warrior on horseback, 7th-c stone relief: Archiv fur Kunst und Geschichte, Berlin **173r** Silver dishes: BM **174t** St Augustine, Pacino di Bounaguida, 14th c, Accademia Florence: RS/AAAC **174b** Pears: Mark Mason/AA
175 Baptistery ceiling, Jesus and his disciples, mosaic, Ravenna: S/Battistero degli Ariani **176l** Codex Alexandrinus, folio from St Luke's Gospel: Bridgeman Art Library **176b** St Jerome by Carlo Crivelli: Bridgeman Art Library/National Gallery, London **177cr** Theodolinda's gold bible, 7th c: S/Monza, Tesoro del Duomo **177cl** Codicei: S/Mausoleo di Gallia Placidia Lunetta, Ravenna
177br The Temple scroll, 4th c: Zev Radovan **178b** German cremation urn and grave slab of Gundebibius, 4-5th c: BM **178t** A Vandal leaving his villa, mosaic fragment from Carthage, 6th c: MH/BM **178–179** Helmet piece of Agilulf: S/Museo del Bargello, Florence **179l** Barbarian jewellry, 3rd–7th c, Gothic, Visigothic, Ostrogothic, Vandal,

German and Saxon: BM **179r** Queen Amalasuntha, relief: S/Museo del Bargello, Florence **181tl** Syria, Qalaat Seman – the monastery: Sonia Halliday Photographs **181bl** Plaque of St Simeon Stylite: RMN, Paris **181tr** Ampullae: BM
181br Ecclesiastical men, 6th c mosaic: Andre Held **182** Portrait of Edward Gibbon by Reynolds: Mary Evans Picture Library **182–183** Les Romains de la Decadence, Thomas Couture, 1847: Bridgeman Art Library/Giraudon/Musee d'Orsay Paris **183r** Sahara desert scene: D. Hecker/Zefa **183b** Lead water pipe, inscribed 'Aureli Caesaris': CMD/Museo Nazionale, Rome **184l** Charlemagne, detail of diptych: S/Castello Sforzesco, Milan **184tr** Early Christian calendar: S/Museo Arcivescovile, Ravenna
184br 'Court' Manuscript, 8th c: Mike Dudley/AA/Bibliotheque Royale de Belgique, Brussels **185t** Monastery, Skellig Michael, Co. Kerry: Michael Jenner/RHPL **185b** St Matthew's gospel, Ch.1.v.18, christi Anteni, c. 698 AD, Lindisfarne Gospels: Bridgeman Art Library/British Library **186** Marble copy of a gold votive buckler offered to Augustus by the Senate in 27 BC: EL/M/ Musée Lapidaire d'Art Paien, Arles, France
187l Street of the Kuretes, statue of C. Memmius, Ephesus: EL/M **187r** Bird mosaic from Pompeii: EL/M/Museo Archeologico Nazionale, Naples.

Abbreviations: l = left, r = right, b = bottom,
c = center, t = top
AA Andromeda Archives, Abingdon, England
BCL Bruce Coleman Ltd, Uxbridge, Middlesex, England
BM British Museum, London
BPK Bildarchiv Preussischer Kulturbesitz, Berlin
CMD C M Dixon, Canterbury, England
EL/M Erich Lessing, Magnum Photos, London
KM Kuntshistorisches Museum, Vienna
MH Michael Holford, Loughton, England
MN, N Museo Nationale, Naples
NHPA Natural History Photographic Agency, Ardingly, England
RHPL Robert Harding Picture Library, London
RMN Réunion de Musées Nationaux, Paris
RS/AAAC Ronald Sheridan, Ancient Art and Architure Collection, Harrow on the Hill, England
S Scala Photographic Agency, Florence, Italy
WFA Werner Forman Archive, London

Artists
Stephen Conlin, John Fuller, Nick Harris, Charles Raymond, Colin Salmon, Tony Smith, Roger Stewart

Indexer
Ann Barrett

FURTHER READING

General
Boardman, J, Griffin J and Murray, O (eds): *The Oxford History of the Classical World* (Oxford University Press, 1986)
Bowder, D (ed): *Who was Who in the Roman World* (Phaidon, 1980)
Brown, P: *The World of Late Antiquity* (Thames and Hudson, 1971)
Cornell, T & Matthews, J: *Atlas of the Roman World* (Phaidon, 1982)
Crawford, M: *The Roman Republic* (London, 1978)
Cunliffe, B: *Rome and Her Empire* (The Bodley Head, 1978)
Drinkwater, J: *Roman Gaul* (London, 1983)
Garnsey, P and Saller, R: *The Roman Empire* (Duckworth, 1987)
Jenkyns, R (ed): *The legacy of Rome: A New Appraisal* (OUP, 1992)
Jones, A H M: *The Decline of the Ancient World* (London, 1966)
Millar, F: *The Roman World and its Neighbours*, 2nd edition (London, 1981)
Salway, P: *Roman Britain* (Oxford, 1981)
Scullard, H H: *A History of the Roman World, 753-146 BC*, 4th edition (Routledge, 1980)
Scullard, H H: *From the Gracchi to Nero. A History of Rome from 133 BC to AD 68*, 5th edition (Routledge, 1982)
Starr, C: *The Roman Empire: A Study in Survival* (OUP, 1982)
Vickers, Michael: *Ancient Rome* (Phaidon, 1977)

Daily Life
Aries, P and Duby, G: *A History of Private Life. Volume One. From Pagan Rome to Byzantium* (Harvard University Press)
Carcopino, J: *Daily Life in Ancient Rome* (Penguin, 1941)
Dixon, S: *The Roman Mother* (Croom Helm, 1988)
McKay, A: *Houses ,Villas and Palaces in the Roman World* (Thames and Hudson, 1975)
Paoli, U E: *Rome: Its People, Life and Customs* (Bristol Classical Press, 1963)
Rawson, B (ed): *The Family in Ancient Rome* (Croom Helm, 1986)
Veyne, P: *Bread and Circuses* (Penguin 1992)
Ward-Perkins, J: *Pompeii 79 AD* (New York, 1978)

Art and Architecture
Chevallier, R: *Roman Roads* (Batsford, 1989)
Henig, M (ed): *A Handbook of Roman Art* (Oxford, 1983)
Krautheimer, R: *Early Christian and Byzantine Architecture* (Pelican, 1965)
Lawrence, A: *Greek and Roman Sculpture* (London, 1972)
Percival, J: *The Roman Villa* (Batsford, 1976)

Army
Campbell, J: *The Emperor and the Roman Army* (Oxford, 1984)
Watson, G R: *The Roman Soldier* (London, 1969)
Webster , G: *The Roman Imperial Army* (Black, London, 1969)

Literature
Howatson, M: *The Oxford Companion to Classical Literature* (OUP, 1989)
Griffin, J: *Virgil*. Past Masters series (Oxford, 1986)
Lyne, R: *The Latin Love Poets from Catullus to Horace* (Oxford, 1980)
also Penguin Classics and the Loeb Classical Library

People
Balsdon, J: *Julius Caesar and Rome* (Harmondsworth, 1967)
Gelzer, M: *Caesar, Politician and Statesman* (Oxford 1968)
Miller, F and Segal, E (eds): *Caesar Augustus* (Oxford 1984)
Rawson, E D: *Cicero, A Portrait* (Bristol,1983)
Williams, S: *Diocletian and the Roman Recovery* (London, 1985)

Religion
Chadwick, H: *The Early Church* (Harmondsworth, 1967)
Ferguson, J: *The Religions of the Roman Empire* (London,1970)
Godwin, J: *Mystery Religions in the Ancient World* (Thames and Hudson,1981)
McManners, J (ed): *The Oxford Illustrated History of Christianity* (Oxford,1990)
Scullard, H: *Festivals and Ceremonies of the Roman Republic* (Thames and Hudson, 1981)

Outsiders
Cunliffe, B: *Greeks, Romans and Barbarians* (Batsford)
Sitwell, N: *Outside the Empire:The World the Romans Knew* (Paladin Books, 1986)
Todd, M: *The Early Germans* (Blackwell, 1992)

Sourcebooks
Lewis, N and Reinhold, M: *Roman Civilization: Volume I The Republic* (Harper Torchbooks, New York, 1966)
Lewis, N and Reinhold, M: *Roman Civilization: Volume II ,The Empire* (Harper Torchbooks, New York, 1966)
Nichols, R and McLeish, K: *Through Roman Eyes* (CUP, 1976)
Shelton, J: *As the Romans Did* (OUP, 1988)

INDEX